INDIAN CHRISTIANS

INDIAN CHRISTIANS

Issues and Perspectives

VIJU WILSON

MANOHAR
2025

First published 2025
First eBook edition 2025

ISBN 978-93-6080-473-2 (hardbond)
ISBN 978-93-6080-955-3 (eBook)

Published by

Ajay Kumar Jain *for*
Manohar Publishers & Distributors
4753/23 Ansari Road, Daryaganj
New Delhi 110 002

Typeset by Kohli Print, Delhi 110 051

Cover design by Manoj Kumar

Printed and bound in India

Contents

Preface

India's religious landscape is pluralistic in nature, though not polemical. It has been enriched by the traditions and spiritualities of various religions. Both Indic and non-Indic religious traditions have contributed extensively to the vibrant and inclusive religious life of India. Except for certain occasional aberrations, religious communities strive to protect the pluralistic heritage of this nation. The large majority of Indians are religious, but their religiosity does not succumb to communalism. However, there are common and specific issues religious communities face in India today. They respond to the issues within the theological and ethical framework of respective religious traditions. This book attempts to engage with Indian Christianity, particularly some of the issues that they should respond to in the present socio-political-religious context.

The first chapter addresses the question of the Indic identity of Christianity, and the negative portrayal of Christianity in the religious nationalist discourses. Christianity is generally portrayed as foreign religion in India though it has been part of this land for more than two millennia. This chapter argues that Christianity is Indian because its adherents are Indians who are entitled to practice any religion in the republic. The national identity of Christians corresponds to the Indic identity of Christianity.

In the second chapter, the issue of caste in Christianity is discussed. Christianity is not immune to the reality of caste in society. This chapter explains how Christianity responded to the practice of caste and critically looks at caste from a Christian perspective. The practice of caste is not Christian because it perpetuates discrimination, exclusion, and unequal social relations.

Chapter three describes the Christian theological and social view of the freedom of religion and conversion. It rebuts the narrative that Christians involve in 'forced' conversions. In the Christian view, freedom of religion is a divinely ordained human right. Conversion should be a conscious act based on personal conviction.

Any targeted restriction to the freedom of religion questions the idea of freedom guaranteed by the Constitution.

The Constitution of India guarantees some specific rights to religious and linguistic minorities. Some interpret them as means of appeasement and contradiction to secularism. In the context of communalizing minority rights, the fourth chapter deliberates on minority rights from a Christian perspective. Minority rights should not be construed as 'communal' rights. For Christians, minority rights are rights to serve the nation. The fifth chapter discusses on the relationship between Church (Religion) and state in a secular democracy. In the Christian view, State is a divine gift. Church and State are equally mandated to serve humanity. The State should not be prejudiced against a particular religion. It should protect the rights of people, religious freedom in particular. The Church (Religion) has a prophetic role to correct the State if it fails to protect the interests of citizens.

Today, we witness the rapid spread of religious communalism in the society. The communal forces continue to polarize the citizenry on religious grounds. They communalize politics for wielding power and to marginalize the minorities. In this context, the sixth chapter provides a Christian response to religious communalism. It argues that 'othering' is not religious, but communal. Therefore, communalism is anti-religious. Every religious community should cultivate an inclusive-prophetic approach to combat communalism.

When the majoritarian religious nationalism attempts to profile minorities as disloyal to the nation or a threat to the nation, chapter seven talks about the inclusive nationalism. It argues that the Christians cannot endorse any nationalist thinking that excludes fellow citizens in the name of his/her religion or ethnicity. Any nationalist ideology that speaks the language of exclusivism is 'anti-national', because it does not help nation-building. In the eighth chapter, the issue of reservation, particularly the reservation of Dalit Christians, is discussed. The interplay of religion and caste contributes to the disempowerment of Dalit Christians. The exclusion of Dalit Christians from the Scheduled Caste reservation because of their religious identity is a denial of social justice.

Irrespective of religious communities, women are victims of patriarchal caste even today. They experience devaluation and exclusion at the intersection of caste, gender, class and religion. This oppressive intersectionality restricts her agency and space in 'his' society. Christian faith affirms that she is also the image of God, and deserves equal privilege and status with him. She has the agency to assert her space against 'patriarchally controlled social and religious space'. Therefore, the final chapter defines gender justice as equalizing the space. To equalize the space, she should be courageous to claim her space and he should identify with her in her efforts to come out of patriarchal 'spacing'.

I am thankful to Manohar Publishers for their editorial guidance, and for publishing this book on time. This is my second book from this renowned publishing house. I also thank my wife Mrs. Sonia Wilson, and my children, Sia V. Wilson, and Vihaan V. Wilson, for their encouragement and assistance in completing this work. Above all, I am grateful to God for enabling me to write a book that, I hope, may give a comprehensive view of the issues and perspectives of Indian Christians in the contemporary context.

VIJU WILSON

Pune
Union Biblical Seminary

Abbreviations

AICU	All India Catholic Union
AICIC	All-India Conference of Indian Christians
ATC	Asian Trading Corporation
BJP	Bharatiya Janata Party
BTESSC	Board of Theological Education, Senate of Serampore College
BUILD	Bombay Urban Industrial League for Development
CAA	Citizenship Amendment Act
CBCI	Catholic Bishops' Conference of India
CDS	Centre for Dalit Studies
CFCC	Centre for Contemporary Christianity
CISS	Centre for Indian and Inter-Religious Studies
CISRS	Christian Institute for the Study of Religion and Society
CLS	Christian Literature Society
CMS	Church Missionary Society
CMS/UBS	Centre for Mission Studies, Union Biblical Seminary
CSI	Church of South India
CSS	Christava Sahitya Samiti
CWI	Christian World Imprints
DJVP	Dharma Jyoti Vidya Peeth
DP	Dharmaram Publications
EFI	Evangelical Fellowship of India
ETC	Eastern Theological College
EWS	Economically Weaker Sections
HSS	Hindu Swayamsevak Sangh
ICHR	Indian Church History Review
INC	Indian National Congress
ISPCK	Indian Society for Promoting Christian Knowledge
ITA	Indian Theological Association

IVP	InterVarsity Press
IWIT	Indian Women in Theology
KUTS	Kerala United Theological Seminary
LMS	London Missionary Society
MANF	Maulana Azad National Fellowship
NCCI	National Council of Churches in India
NCDC	National Council of Dalit Christians
NCM	National Commission for Minorities
NCCR	National Council of Churches Review
NMDFC	National Minorities Development and Finance Corporation
NSCN	National Socialist Council of Nagaland
OBC	Other Backward Classes
RSS	Rashtriya Swayamsevak Sangh
RZIM	Ravi Zacharias International Ministries
SATHRI	South Asia Theological Research Institute
SC	Scheduled Castes
SCM	Student Christian Movement
SPCK	Society for Promoting Christian Knowledge
ST	Scheduled Tribes
TLC	Theological Literature Committee
UCA	Union of Catholic Asian
VHP	Vishwa Hindu Parishad
VJTR	Vidyajyoti Journal of Theological Reflection
WCC	World Council of Churches
WME	World Missionary Evangelism

CHAPTER 1

Christianity in India: Question of Identity

India is known for its pluralistic nature which is reflected in all aspects of national life. It endorses plurality in thinking, beliefs, ideologies, outlook, and lifestyles. It also asserts that India is not a homogenous but a heterogeneous society. This pluralistic nature upholds the values of tolerance, mutual respect and communal harmony. Every stream of thought or religious orientation is respected as long as it does not promote conflict and disorder in society. Though the nation is heterogeneous, it has developed a common identity for everyone irrespective of caste, creed, culture and colour. All (citizenry) are called 'Indian' even though the historical roots of their religious traditions are located outside the nation's geography. However, the narrative of an 'outsider' attached to particular religion not only questions the identity of its citizens but also challenges the pluralistic ethos preserved throughout the centuries. Some religions are identified as non-Indic, and therefore the followers of those religions are not really 'nationalistic'. There have been many attempts to present Christianity as 'Indian' but they are viewed as tools for propagating the faith. Is it necessary to prove that Christianity is Indian? If the 'Indianizing' of Christianity is negatively portrayed in the majoritarian religious and nationalistic discourses, what are the alternative foundations for the Indianness of Christianity? This chapter attempts to bring out some reflections on the space of Christianity in the Indian religio-cultural landscape.

'YOU ARE HINDU, MUSLIM, CHRISTIAN, SIKH . . . NOT INDIAN'

We live in a society where 'religious profiling' gets speedy momentum. S/he is identified more as a religious being than a citizen of this country: you are a Hindu, Muslim, Christian, Sikh and Jain . . . not Indian! The primary victims of 'religious profiling' are religious minorities, particularly Muslims and Christians. While Muslims are framed largely by 'cow politics' and nationalistic disloyalty, Christians the narratives of 'forced' conversion. In a country where freedom of religion is a fundamental right, minorities experience different forms of violence for exercising their right to profess, practise and propagate what they believe. For instance, according to the Religious Liberty Commission Yearly Report 2021 of Evangelical Fellowship of India (EFI), there were '505 individual incidents of violence' against Christians in India in 2021.[1]

Today, the social atmosphere is conditioned by majoritarian religious sentiments. Everything is looked at through the eyes of religion. If a voice is raised against injustice or corruption, 'who raises it' (religious 'who') matters a lot in our society. The fringe Hindutva dogmatists continue to question the nationalistic credentials of minorities. They are subject to mob violence (mob lynching) and forced to publicly chant 'Jai Shri Ram' and 'Jai Bajrang Bali'.[2] Unfortunately, 'religious slogans (Jai Shri Ram) became political slogans'.[3] On many occasions, religious identity (in the case of minorities) determines his/her fate in the hands of the mob. Many Dalits and Minorities (mainly Muslims), have lost their precious lives because of mob violence.[4] Communal/mob violence and religious conditioning of the social mind are part of the religio-cultural homogenization process that aims to achieve the goal of 'One Nation, One Language, One Culture, One Religion and One Thinking'. It is the 'reduction of ethnic heterogeneity'.[5] The claim of making a 'vegetarian' state,[6] the appearance of 'religious housing', exclusive housing complexes or apartments based on religions,[7] and the Citizenship Amendment Act (CAA) 2019 need to be read as signs of the majoritarian religious conditioning of the land known for its plural thinking and tolerant attitude.

Contemporary Christianity is located in this religio-cultural landscape. Any deliberate attempt to 'Indianize' Christianity would invite criticism of appropriating the rituals, symbols and ideas of Indian religious traditions for conversion.[8] Is it necessary that

Christianity should be baptized in Indian religious and cultural traditions so that it has validity on Indian soil? While not downplaying the importance of Indianizing Christianity in terms of culture and native religious traditions, one would argue that the 'Indianness' of Christianity comes from the identity of people who practise it and their participation in the life of the nation. This discussion should begin with what the present condition of Christianity is.

INDIAN CHRISTIANITY TODAY

Though it is contested, the history of Christianity in India begins with the arrival of St. Thomas in AD 52. It has a rich heritage of 'Christianities'[9]—Catholic, Protestant, Evangelical, Pentecostal and Indigenous. Irrespective of social backgrounds, the new faith (non-Indian origin) attracted people of different social backgrounds throughout the centuries. The pluralistic nature of the society provided space for the new religion to exist and grow with other religious traditions. It also experienced cultural and religious encounters with native faith traditions. The missionaries who propagated the faith used different methods and strategies to communicate the Gospel in a new religio-cultural context. Today, Christianity is one of the minority (numerically) religious traditions in India. The 2011 census informs one that Christians constitute only 2.3 per cent (2.78 crores) of the total population of India.[10] Though it has many centuries of existence in the land of religions and has contributed to nation building, it has been branded as a 'foreign' religion. To locate Christianity in the current cultural and religious landscape, one also needs to look at the condition of Indian Christianity in India through a critical lens.

First, available census records prove that 'the story of Christianity in India is a story of dismal failure, demographically speaking'.[11] Though it may be incompatible with the claims of Christian organizations, one of the main reasons for the 'official' decline is dual-religious membership. For example, many Dalit-Christians keep their 'Hindu identity' in official documents for getting benefits meant for those belonging to the Scheduled Castes.[12] However, the quantitative decline and the imbalanced geographical presence (more in southern and north-eastern states) of Christianity shows the demographic space it occupies in the cultural and religious landscape of India. Christianity has not grown as projected in the public domain by its enthusiastic exponents and anxious opponents. The exaggerated growth is not proportionate to Christian representation in the legislative, executive and judicial spheres of the nation.

Second, there is a decline in the quality of community life in society. The sacrificial lives of early missionaries-native and overseas, upheld the quality of Christian faith in word and action. Today qualitative Christian life, with few exceptions, is questioned within and outside the faith community. For instance, Christians continue to live in a divided house! B.R. Ambedkar described Indian Christians 'disjointed-it is a better word than the word disunited-community'.[13] In the service sector, elite Hindus and Christians rather than their poor co-religionists enjoy the benefits of the majority of Christian institutions. Many denominations and churches function as 'caste' or 'ethnic' entities. Gender prejudices continue to prevail in community life and the ministerial space. With some exceptions, Indian Christian leadership-clergy and laity, are not free from corruption, nepotism and immorality.

Third, most Indian Christians, if not the majority, are more conscious of their caste/ethnic identity rather than faith identity. Therefore, they are divided and known by their caste/ethnic titles: Reddy Christians, Nadar Christians, Syrian Christians, Dalit Christians and Tribal Christians. Some may argue that identity assertions make respective faith communities culturally contextual. But, as Amartya Sen noted, '. . . within-group solidarity can help to feed between-group discord'.[14] This happens among Christians though it may not become a law and order problem. The caste identity within the faith community and the inability to affirm faith identity beyond caste/ethnic barriers, place the Christian communities in a predicament in terms of their identity, spirituality and unity. It has become one of the 'religious' communities (distinction in the content of faith) than 'faith' communities which stand for the 'faith-praxis' than 'rite-praxis'.

CHRISTIANITY: OUTSIDE THE INDIAN LANDSCAPE

Christianity, according to Hindutva ideology, falls outside of India's cultural and religious landscape. V.D. Savarkar, who articulated the Hindutva ideology, categorically stated that this land belongs to the people who consider it as their fatherland and holy land. For him, Christians may fulfil the first clause (fatherland), but they do not think that India is their holy land. For them, Palestine is the 'holy land'. Therefore, their love and loyalty are divided. However, the 'choice of love' invites them into the Hindu fold.[15] While Savarkar placed Christians outside of Hindustan ideologically and gave 'choice of love' to the Hindu fold, M.S. Golwalkar demanded them to be 'wholly subordinated to the Hindu claiming nation nothing, deserving no privileges, far less any preferential treatment not even citizens' rights'.[16] For him, Christians are disloyal and with the change of religion, their love and devotion for this nation has disappeared.[17] He does not consider Christianity equal to Indic religions. For him, religious identity alone determines the status of a person in this country. It shows the space of Christianity in the Hindutva-defined religio-cultural landscape of India. Though he represented a minority view in the past, it has already conditioned the mind of a large majority and created anxiety, fear and pain among religious minorities today.

Anti-conversion discourses also underline the ideological dislike of Christianity in the Hindutva mind. They do not question conversion to Indic religions but frown at conversion to Semitic religions, particularly Islam and Christianity. 'Freedom of Religion Acts' is strategically designed to stop conversion to these religions. The dominant narratives portray a convert as an enemy in the community. For Swami Vivekananda, 'Every man going out of the Hindu pale is not only a man less but an enemy the more.'[18] Though current anti-conversion discourses come out of the fear of the numerical decline of a particular religion and the loss of political power,[19] the essence of Hindutva ideology (driving force behind anti-conversion narratives) is that Christianity is not equally preferred because it is not 'Indian' in origin and outlook.[20] This position contradicts the divine creative plan that affirms plurality. However, the Hindu inclusive outlook locates Christianity in the Indian landscape.

RELIGIOUS MINORITIES: DIVINE CREATIVE PLAN

Religious minorities are a common phenomenon throughout the world. The majority cannot simply reject or eliminate them from their respective countries or regions. They face problems when they fail to respond to the majoritarian imagination that minorities will gradually be absorbed into the majority religious, cultural and social system. If minorities live on this earth, it is because of God who created them to survive. They have lived since ancient times. Diversity/plurality (a blend of minorities and majorities) is a divine creative agenda. The Biblical story of enslaved Jews in Egypt is one example of the existence of minorities. Though they had gone through painful experiences their existence contributed to the diversity of Egyptian society. The story of Babel Tower in the Bible (Genesis 11: 1-9) speaks about the importance of diverse cultures, ethos, values and languages in society. According to the story, when people attempted to build up one world order against the divine order that recognizes differences, God destroyed that plan by confusing the language of the people. The Babel Tower project aimed at mono-language, mono-culture and possibly mono-religion in the later stage. A context becomes diverse when a minority culture or faith becomes visible. In the story of Babel Tower, one sees a God who wants society to be heterogeneous rather than homogenous.[21] The 'Indianness' of Christianity can be questioned but not its existence because it contributes to the diversity of the land. Its existence with distinctive content of faith, value system and outlook is the choice of God though not 'Truly Indian' in the eyes of the communal ideologues.

IMPEDIMENTS TO BE 'TRULY INDIAN'

Apart from naming Christianity as non-Indic religion, certain impediments place Christianity 'outside' of India's religio-cultural landscape. According to Swami Vivekananda, though 'the Indian mind is first religious . . .'[22] it is inclusive in outlook. Indic religions, particularly Hinduism, do not prohibit their adherents strictly from observing the beliefs and practices of other religious traditions.[23] A moderate/liberal Hindu may not have a problem keeping Jesus' photo or Christian symbols along with Hindu gods/goddesses in his/her *pooja* room or vehicle. This 'embrace-cum-rejection'[24] attitude is visible throughout the country. Non-objection to other religious symbols and beliefs is the result of the influence of the belief that all religions are salvific. Hindus have no theological restriction to go and pray in a church/mosque/synagogue. Theologically they are inclusive, and can worship any animate or inanimate beings/things.[25] Though Christians are socially and politically inclusive, majority of them remain exclusive in terms of worship and faith. They may not have a problem being part of the 'other' religious crowd but restrict themselves from direct participation in the worship and ceremonies of other religious traditions. This 'inclusive-but-exclusive' behaviour may be one of the impediments for Christianity to present itself as 'Indian' sharing an inclusive religious outlook.

Christianity is a missionary religion. Historically, as a 'missionary religion', Christianity has been challenged by negative and positive evaluations in India. But aggressive evangelistic activities, particularly with a condemnatory approach, have dissuaded many Indians from liking Christianity.[26] They believe disrespecting a religion for promoting another is not an Indian approach. Though Indic religions also do their missionary activities, they are not as judgemental as some of the Christians who are involved in propagating their faith. Also, conversion is less appreciated in a religio-cultural setting where, as Monier Williams said, 'people are proud of their religion and traditions'.[27] Another side of the conversion story is that high castes will not be receptive to the Christian faith because it teaches brotherhood/sisterhood of believers which leads to social equality.[28] However, the Christian understanding of mission/evangelism and its aggressive expressions remain an impediment to the claim that Christianity is 'Indian'.

LOCAL (INDIAN) BY PRESENCE

Though some of the religio-cultural ethos and practices (today claimed to be Hindu) are shared in our daily lives, Christian attempts of 'Indianizing' the faith through majoritarian religio-cultural traditions have been interpreted as the process of 'Christianizing' Hindu religious heritage. Indian lifestyle and religiosity are conditioned by this religio-cultural heritage. Indian Christians have been practising the faith (despite its Western garb) within the framework of 'what is Indian'. Inculturation/indigenization might have contributed to presenting the faith in Indian categories. However, it cannot rule out the possibility that because of their inherent 'Indianness', the natives have already lived out their faith in the Indian way. In the context of the Hindutva assertion of Christianity as a foreign religion and the inability of the Christian faith to align with the inclusive theological outlook of Indic religions, one would like to look at the possibilities of locating Christianity in the religio-cultural landscape through the proposition that Christianity is 'Indian' because of its adherents whose constitutional and nationalistic identity is Indian. It does not negate the importance of 'inculturating' the faith in the respective cultural settings. However, in one's search for 'how Indian Christianity is Indian', the content of faith and outlook is more contentious than baptizing the faith in the waters of Indian cultures. As long as the content of faith (dogmatic) and outlook do not align with native religious traditions, Christianity remains outside the religious landscape of India. This is not the end of the story for the claim of the 'Indianness' of Christianity. There is space for naming Christianity 'Indian'. Following are some of the attempts to locate the space.

National Identity of Christians

The national identity of Christians automatically locates Christianity in the Indian religious landscape. Contrary to the existing societal trends, the secular state prioritizes autonomy and constitutional freedom of the individual, not religion. Therefore the 'Indianness' of a religion depends on the national identity of its adherents. If India is a religious republic, the argument for presenting the faith in the religious framework of the official religion would have been valid and unquestionable. The religious profiling of the national identity of Christians is not new. Abbe J.A. Dubois, a Catholic missionary (late eighteenth and early nineteenth centuries) informs one that the caste Hindus had a negative attitude to Christianity because of its non-Indic status (which may be one of the reasons). Therefore, new converts were not 'Indians'.[29]

However, the history of the freedom movement and the post-Independent discourses on nationalism show that religious identity does not define the identity of the citizens who have the freedom to follow any religion. M.K. Gandhi discouraged religion from being 'mixed with national affairs'.[30] Sardar Vallabhbhai Patel affirmed that religion does not define an Indian. S/he is a citizen who shares the heritage of this nation.[31] Jawaharlal Nehru, who clearly articulated the national identity of religious minorities, said,

> Indian converts to some of these religions (Christianity, Islam, and Judaism) never ceased to be Indians on account of a change of their faith. They were looked upon in other countries as Indians and foreigners, even though there might have been a community of faith between them. . . . An Indian Christian is looked upon as an Indian wherever he (she) may go.[32]

S/he must be conscious of this fact. The 'consciousness of being Indian' (Romila Thapar)[33] is the essence of national identity that does not need any religious endorsement. As far as Christians are concerned, the national loyalty/identity does not contradict their faith because they believe God is the sovereign of the universe and its history.[34] They experience God in the geographical location where they dwell and affirm their identity. Therefore, the love of country and love of religion can go together.[35] Affirming a national identity that gives space to religious freedom is the point of departure for the status of Christianity in India.

Christianity is 'Indian' because Christians in this land are Indians. A majority of them are descendants of dalits and tribals who were the original inhabitants of this land.[36] They belong to this land. Their conversion does not uproot them from the soil. Whether they sing like others or translate their faith in the light of native faith traditions or not, the bottom line is that their existence as Indians embraces what they also believe. Though

Christianity is not inherently Indian-origin, practices, content, and theological outlook—the land conditioned by the plurality of thinking and arguments, gives space to people having different faith orientation. The existence and identity of religion in a particular location is determined primarily by its followers (citizens). 'Indianness' is the natural ingredient of 'Indian' Christianity because of adherents who live, think and present themselves as 'Indians'. They preserve national and ethnic identity and some of the social and cultural practices (marriage and birth ceremonies, use of surnames, etc.) even though they have stopped believing the tenets of a particular Indic religious tradition.[37] Practically, an Indian Christian remains 'Indian' with his or her ethnic identity intact even after conversion.

Freedom of Religion

The Constitution of India protects the citizens from religious discrimination (Articles 15 and 16)[38] and guarantees freedom of religion: to profess, practise and propagate religion. Article 25 (1) of the Constitution says, 'Subject to public order, morality and health and to the other provisions of this Part, all persons are equally entitled to freedom of conscience and the right freely to profess, practice, and propagate religion'.[39] The word 'propagate' was inserted in the clause mainly because of Christians in India. It is evident in the debate on this provision in the Constituent Assembly. K.M. Munshi, one of the leading members of the Drafting Committee said,

> I know, it was on this word that the Indian Christian community laid the greatest emphasis, not because they wanted to convert people aggressively, but because the word 'propagate' was a fundamental part of their tenet. Even if the word was not there, I am sure, under the freedom of speech which Constitution guarantees, it will be open to any religious community to persuade other people to join their faith. So long as religion is religion, conversion by the free exercise of the conscience has to be recognized.

But in the case of Rev. Stanislaus *vs.* State of Madhya Pradesh (1977 1 SCC 677), Chief Justice A.N. Ray, ruled that 'what Article 25 (1) grants is not the right to convert another person to one's religion, but to transmit or spread one's religion by an exposition of its tenets'. H.M. Seevai, a constitutional lawyer, criticized this ruling and said, '. . . Successful propagation of religion would result in conversion. . . .'[40] Whether a particular religion promotes conversion or not, the freedom of religion is indispensable because '. . . a person's religious convictions are the result of his/her inner convictions', and 'it (freedom of religion) is essential to experience the other forms of freedom'.[41] In fact, the freedom of religion gives space to Christianity in the Indian context.

The freedom of religion in the Constitution affirms the right of a citizen to live in this land with religious conviction. No religion is constitutionally non-Indic. When the Constitution prohibits discrimination based on religion, it recognizes the validity of any religion embraced by citizens. A religion becomes 'Indic' through the citizens' exercise of the fundamental right to religion. A particular religion need not have the characteristics of Indic religions. The Constituent Assembly's discussions on Article 25 (1), particularly propagation and conversion, also lead to the point that a particular religion cannot be kept outside the ideological or religious landscape of the nation just because it affirms freedom of choice and maintains an exclusivist theological outlook. Though the Presidential Order of 1950 and Freedom of Religion Acts question the spirit of constitutional freedom, the personal choice of religion is strongly embedded in the Constitution. When a citizen affirms that 'my religion is my freedom', s/he cannot be framed as a follower of a 'foreign religion'. Through his/her freedom, a particular religion breaks geographical and cultural boundaries and occupies a legitimate space in the nation's life. It begins to serve the nation with the exercise of the freedom of religion. Constitutional validity for Christianity and its acceptance by the people make it 'Indian' and break new grounds for contributing to the cultural and religious life of the nation.

Participation in Nation Building

Throughout centuries Christians in India have faced an allegation of non-participation in national life despite their active involvement in the freedom movement and post-independent nation building process. Though they practise a faith that did not originate on the Indian soil, they have contributed immensely to building up the nation through their services at personal and community levels: education, health care, social empowerment, and political participation. As citizens of this nation, they have also sacrificed their lives for the protection and development of their motherland. Their religion was never an impediment to their participation in nation building. It always encouraged them to initiate any effort that would contribute to the nation through empowering its citizens, particularly the marginalized among them. Their faith taught them 'state as a good gift of God', and their participation in the life of the state is an expression of their love and commitment to Jesus Christ.[42] Whether they are the majority or not, they are religiously mandated to represent (witness) the Lord who endorses any life-affirming actions. Indeed, the loyalty and obedience to God and the love for neighbour (commandments) theologically validate their participation in the nation building process.[43] The life and work of Christian communities in the past contributed to the conscientization of the larger society, which led to the emergence of many social reform movements and the assertion of subaltern communities.

The religion that contributed to the development of a nation cannot be called 'foreign' or 'outsider'. It is practically 'Indian' in terms of its life and works in society. In the case of Christianity, it has shared its resources (both material and spiritual) through educational institutions, NGOs, health care facilities and media to empower people, particularly those deprived of the benefits of nation building. It shows the praxis of the faith. The missionaries journeyed with the people who did not get the attention of the ruling class. By bringing them into the mainstream of social life, Christianity participated in nation building. The relevance of Christianity in India depends on how it shapes the outlook of Christians and encourages them to engage with different spheres of national life. Often Christians withdraw from public life because of the influence of the otherworldly outlook of Christianity. Active social and political participation should be spontaneous because of their faith and identity. It will destroy the Hindutva myth that Hindus alone constitute this nation, and nation building is primarily their calling. The level of participation in nation building defines the space of Christianity in the religious landscape of India. It also helps to counter the narrative of the 'non-Indic' identity of Christianity. What makes Christianity Indian is its historical existence and contributions. Any religion plays a positive role in the public life of its followers.

Minority Rights

Christians are one of the religious minority communities in India. The Constitution acknowledges religious minorities and guarantees them certain rights to protect their interests. While Article 29 empowers them to preserve their language or culture, Article 30 gives them the 'right to establish and administer educational institutions of their choice'. Though they experience various forms of violation of these constitutional provisions, minority rights imply two things regarding the 'Indianness' of Christianity. Firstly, the Constitution does not restrict the status of minority to citizens who practise specific religions.[44] Second, it pledges to protect any religion embraced by the citizens. In that sense, Christianity carries the Indian identity granted by Constitution. However, Christians live with 'minority psychology',[45] a negative impact of a positive clause. They face allegations of undue privilege because of their minority status. It has to note how minority rights contribute to build the nation and this determines the space of a minority religion in the Indian context. While criticizing Church's over emphasis on minority rights to safeguard its interests, Paulose Mar Paulose argues that Christians should combine minority rights and human rights. The logic behind this approach is that Jesus was born in a minority situation in his context. He never stood for minority privileges but worked for human rights. In this way, Indian Christians should consider minority rights as part of each citizen's fundamental human rights.[46]

Mar Paulose identified two dangers in the minority consciousness of the Indian Christians. First, it often restricts the involvement of the Church and the Christians in the common issues of society. They are afraid even to participate in the socio-political and economic struggles for social justice. Secondly, the Church is too concerned about its rights and privileges and not about the human communities outside the Church.[47] Indian Christians have responded positively to the criticisms and continue to rectify their approach to minority rights. When they use their constitutional privileges for the holistic development of disempowered communities other than Christians, they serve the nation also. It explains the approach of a religion born outside of India's religio-cultural landscape. Constitutional legitimization should be accompanied by the commitment of a particular faith to the nation. It requires bold steps to break the shell of excess minority consciousness that alienates Christians from the mainstream of society. It will eventually break the myth of Christianity as an alien religion.

Universality of Faith

Christianity claims the universality of its basic tenets. They are believed to be applicable in any cultural/religious context. The doctrine of salvation that portrays a Saviour who alone can save the entire humanity, lays the foundation for the universality of the Christian faith. This is the starting point of the missional/evangelistic activities of the Church. The exclusivist theological outlook of Christians also derives from this understanding of salvation. Every faith tradition is contextual in origin but claims its global relevance. Some religions may not make an exclusive claim but attempt to place their beliefs equal to or more acceptable to other faith traditions and prove the validity of their existence. As a missionary religion, Christianity has attempted to propagate its beliefs outside the land of its origin. In its missionary endeavours, it has given importance to the content of its faith rather than the place of origin. If the place of origin is the criterion for recognition, then no religion can cross the boundaries and appeal to the world. What matters is how a particular religion contributes to human life in a particular context more than where it originated. What matters is how it shapes the mindset of people and establishes harmonious life, how it enables people to celebrate their lives with fullness of joy and peace and how it counters life-negating forces and systems all of which are crucial for the existence and acceptance of religion. Every religion has some elements of universalism. This universal nature is achieved through dialogue with different contexts. Though a dialogue may take different forms (social, cultural, religious and theological engagements), it facilitates a religion to become local. While Christianity is a universal religion because of its content of faith, it also carries an 'Indian' identity by the virtue of its existence and transforming engagement with the people of this land for many centuries. It might have modified its 'appearance' with local cultural/religious garb, but not the content of faith. This is the point of contention for the advocates of Hindutva ideology. I doubt if any religion maintains its uniqueness if it compromises its content of faith for the sake of getting accepted in a particular context. For Christians, their faith tradition is universal but its adherents make it contextually present.

The presence of Christianity on Indian soil for many centuries, has contributed to nation building through its constituency, qualifies it to be called 'Indian'. Though its space is often questioned or downplayed under the pretext of 'Indic' origin, Christianity cannot locate outside of the cultural and religious landscape of the nation. Its constitutional validity, national identity through its adherents, theological outlook on the nation, and participation in nation building affirmatively answer how Indian Christianity is. It is not the place of origin but its acceptance by the natives that make a religion 'local' in a particular cultural milieu. The contextual appropriation of a religion has relevance to its existence and praxis. However, the content of faith often remains contentious for the ideologues of majoritarian religious and cultural hegemony. In such a scenario, the Indianness of Christianity depends on the level of participation of Christians in national life. The involvement of Christian faith communities in public space, particularly extending support to the welfare initiatives of the governments and reminding the state of its role when it fails to protect the interests of the citizenry, should be critically assessed. Theo-'graphy' embraces any topography. The transformative presence of Christianity and Indian topography are not contradictory but complementary.

NOTES

1. 'Religious Liberty Commission Yearly Report 2021', https://efionline.org/2022/02/15/religious-liberty-commission-yearly-report-2021/, accessed on 10 August 2022.
2. Vincent Rajkumar, 'Editorial', *Religion and Society*, vol. 64/no. 3 (July 2019): III-VI at III.
3. Probir Pramanik, 'Bugles Before Round Two', *Outlook* (17 June 2019), 20.
4. Ashutosh Sharma, 'Spectre of Mob Lynchings Continues. . .', *Outlook*, 28 April 2022, https://www.outlookindia.com/national/spectre-of-mob-lynchings-continues-to-haunt-india-amid-lacklustre-laws-news-193743, accessed 10 August 2022.
5. Chad M. Bauman, 'The Interreligious Riot as a Cultural System', in *Constructing Indian Christianities*, ed. Chad M. Bauman and Richard Fox Young (New Delhi: Routledge, 2014), 207.
6. http://www.dnaindia.com/india/report-want-to-make-gujarat-a-vegetarian-state-cm-rupani-after-making-cow-slaughter-a-life-term-offence-2377704, accessed on 20 April 2019.
7. Siddharth Varadarajan, 'Why can't Mr. Zaveri live where he wants?' *Sunday Times of India* (12 April 2015, New Delhi), 12.
8. Rowena Robinson, 'Afterword', in *Constructing Indian Christianities*, ed. Chad M. Bauman and Richard Fox Young (New Delhi: Routledge, 2014), 250.
9. It includes 'hybrid' groups such as Christ-Bhaktas in Chennai, Krist-Bhakti Movements, Yeshu Satsangs in Punjab and North West India. They stand outside traditional Christianity but affirm their faith in Jesus Christ within the cultural and religious framework of Hinduism, Islam etc. Roger E. Hedlund and Lisa R. Roberts, 'Tracing Indigenous Christianity in South Asia', *ICHR*, vol. 52, no. 1 (January, 2018): 8-26 at 17-19.
10. *Indian Currents*, vol. XXVII, no. 36 (7-13 September 2015): 26. http://www.censusindia.gov.in/2011census/c-01.html (accessed on 24 November 2020).

11. Tony Joseph, 'A Religion That Lost The Race', *Outlook* (13 April 2015), 30.
12. James Massey, 'Christianity to be Renewed? Rethink Theology', in *Rethinking Theology in India,* ed. by James Massey and T.K. John (New Delhi: Manohar and Centre for Dalit/Subaltern Studies, 2013), 29-30.
13. Vasant Moon, Comp. *Dr. Babasaheb Ambedkar: Writings and Speeches,* vol. 5 (Bombay: Education Department, Government of Maharashtra, 1989), 476.
14. Amartya Sen, *Identity and Violence* (New Delhi: Penguin Books, 2006), 1-2.
15. V.D. Savarkar, *Hindutva* (Bombay: Veer Savarkar Prakashan, 5th edn., 1969), 113-16.
16. M.S. Golwalkar, *We or Our Nationhood Defined* (Nagpur: Bharat Prakashan, 1947), 55-6. Today many Sangh Parivar organizations disown this particular position and the book. But their outlook is already shaped by it. It is very much evident in their approach towards religious minorities.
17. Shashi Tharoor, *Why I am a Hindu* (New Delhi: Aleph Book Company, 2018), 152.
18. Arun Shourie, *Harvesting Our Souls* (New Delhi: Association for Social Advancement Publications, 2000), 1-2.
19. E.V. Mathew, 'Secular State in India', in *Secularism: Collection of Articles,* compiled by Vincent Rajkumar (Bangalore: Christian Institute for the Study of Religion and Society, 2018), 95.
20. 'Can Christians and Muslims say all religions are one?' 'A Hindu can say that', Anuradha Raman, Interview with Yellapragada Sudershan Rao, Chairman, Indian Council of Historical Research, *Outlook* (21 July 2014), 15.
21. James Massey, *Minorities and Religious Freedom in a Democracy* (New Delhi: Manohar & CDS, 2003), 139-40; James Massey, 'Minority Rights', *NCC Review* cxxi/2 (February-March 2001): 119-44 at 137.
22. Swami Vivekananda, 'The Future of India', in *My India, Arise,* Calcutta: Ramakrishna Math and Ramakrishna Mission, 1993, 74-5, cited by V. Sebastian, 'Cultural Constructions of Indian Christian Theology', in *Indian Theologies: In Search of Methods and Models for Theologizing,* ed. Mathew Jayanth (New Delhi: CWI and Pune: JDV, 2017), 51.
23. Arun Shourie, *Missionaries in India Continuities, Changes, Dilemmas,* (New Delhi: ASA Publications, 1994), 187.
24. Tony Joseph, 'A Religion That Lost The Race', *Outlook* (13 April 2015), 30.

25. Devdutt Pattanaik, 'Hinduism isn't a Country Club one can Waltz in and out of', *Sunday Times* (4 January 2015, New Delhi), 12 & Shashi Tharoor, op. cit., *Why I am a Hindu*, 33.
26. M.K. Gandhi, *An Autobiography or The Story of My Experiments with Truth* (Ahmedabad: Navajivan Publishing House, 1927, rpt. 1996), 28-9.
27. Arun Shourie, *Missionaries in India Continuities, Changes, Dilemmas*, 152-3. This point applies to other religious traditions also.
28. Moon, *Dr. Babasaheb Ambedkar: Writings and Speeches*, vol. 5, 444.
29. Abbe JA Dubois, *Hindu Manners, Customs and Ceremonies* (New Delhi: Rupa (rpt.) 15th Impression 2018), 338.
30. Bipin Chandra, *Essays on Contemporary India*, revd. edn. (Delhi: Har-Anand Publications, 1999), 127.
31. Bipin Chandra, *Essays on Contemporary India*, 182.
32. Jawaharlal Nehru, *The Discovery of India* (London: Meridian Books Limited, 3rd edn., 1951), 46.
33. Ziya us Salam, 'Unfazed by Attack, *Frontline*, vol. 33, no. 18 (16 September 2016): 123-5 at 123.
34. M.M. Thomas, Comp., *Christian Participation in Nation-Building* (Bangalore: National Council on Compensation Insurance and Construction Industry Scaffolders Record Scheme, 1960), 295.
35. Poulose Mangai, 'Editorial: Stand for Stan', *VJTR*, vol. 84, no. 11 (November, 2020): 3-6 at 5.
36. T.K. Oommen, 'Religious Nationalisms and Democratic Polity in India: Impossibility of Reconciliation', in *Nationalism and Hindutva: A Christian Response*, ed. Mark T.B. Laing (Pune, Delhi: Centre for Mission Studies/ Union Biblical Seminary/Indian Society for Promoting Christian Knowledge, 2005), 38.
37. Joseph Marianus Kujur, 'Christian and Tribal: The Dynamics of Scheduled Tribe Status in the Field', in *Minority Studies*, ed. by Rowena Robinson (New Delhi: Oxford University Press, 2013), 169.
38. *The Constitution of India* (New Delhi: Ministry of Law and Justice, Government of India, 2011), 6-7.
39. *The Constitution of India* (Delhi: Ministry of Law and Justice, Government of India, 1989), 12.
40. A.G. Noorani, 'Conversion to Hindu Raj', *Frontline* (9 January 2015), 123.
41. S. Robertson, *Freedom of Religion: A Human Rights Issue* (Bangalore: Board of Theological Education of Senate of Serampore College/South Asia Theological Research Institute, 2007), 244 & 245.

42. P.D. Devanandan, Korula Jacob and M.M. Thomas, 'Preface', in M.M. Thomas, comp., *Christian Participation in Nation-Building* (Bangalore: NCCI and CISRS, 1960), III & 16.
43. Herbert Jaya Singh, 'The Christian Community in a Secular State', in Vincent Rajkumar, comp., *Secularism: Collection of Articles*, 99.
44. According to the National Commission of Minorities Act, Section 2, Clause (c), there are six minority religious communities: Muslims, Christians, Sikhs, Buddhists, Jains and Zoroastrians.
45. M.M. Thomas, comp., *Christian Participation in Nation-Building* (Bangalore: National Council of Churches in India and Christian Institute for the Study of Religion and Society, 1960), 51.
46. Paulose Mar Paulose, *Nisabdharayirikkan Ningalkkenthadhikaram?* (Malayalam) (Noorannad: Fabian Books, 1998), 86-7.
47. Paulose Mar Paulose, *Spirituality for Struggle* (Thiruvalla: CSS, 1999), 24-6. He does not negate the importance of minority rights and the role played by Christian communities to serve the country.

CHAPTER 2

Caste in Christianity: A Historical and Contemporary Look

Every society has socio-religious institutions. Caste is one of the social institutions sanctioned by Hinduism in India. Historically, it has gone through modifications from time to time and encountered different religious traditions and communities. This encounter had elements of resistance and assimilation. Both Indic and Semitic religions have had a history of assimilation and resistance to caste. There is no religious community in India directly or indirectly untouched by the institution of caste. Christianity is a case in point. While many Christians practised caste, there were attempts to oppose it within the community. However, Christianity in India has not entirely come out of the influence of caste. The historical vestige of caste continues with contemporary Christianity. The practice of caste among Christians contradicts the message of Christianity. Christianity in India has become 'caste' Christianity in social life. This chapter examines caste in Christianity from historical and biblical point of view.

HISTORICAL REALITY

The story of creation, narrated in the *Purushasukta* of *Rigveda,* is considered the source of the institution of caste. It spells out four orders, namely Brahmin, Rajanya (Kshatriya), Vaisya, and Shudra, respectively originating from the four parts of the *Purusha,* the embodied spirit: the mouth, the arms, the thighs, and the feet. Occupationally, they represented the priest, the king, the tradesman and the labouring man correspondingly. Later these four orders evolved into numerous castes.[1] Hindu literature like *Manusmriti* strengthened the institution of caste by prescribing regulations for social and religious life. Though the caste system developed and functioned as a Hindu religious-social institution, it has touched all religious communities, including Christianity, throughout the centuries. Caste has been a historical reality among Indian christians, particularly in multi-caste congregational (church) contexts. On the one hand, they have practised caste and on the other they have also become victims of caste and all that it involves.

The story of caste among Christians begins with the story of the conversion of Namboothiri Brahmins in Kerala. According to the narrative,[2] St. Thomas, one of the apostles of Jesus, came to India in AD 52, propagated the faith and converted Brahmins to Christianity in Malabar in the present Kerala state. It is also believed that St. Thomas assigned the priestly duty to the high caste converts. This story laid the foundation for the claim of the upper caste identity of Syrian Christians[3] who later migrated from Jerusalem and Persia to Malabar in the fourth and nineth centuries[4] and the practice of caste among Christians. The migration of Syrian Christians[5] has not only contributed to the pluralistic heritage of India but also enlarged the hierarchy of caste. The local kings welcomed them by granting land and certain privileges enjoyed by the upper castes. Thus, from the very beginning, Syrian Christians functioned as a caste due to the 72 privileges (using umbrellas, riding on elephants, observing caste rules of purity-pollution, etc.) granted to them. They considered themselves equal to the Nairs (one of the upper castes). In all areas of social life, they were influenced by Hindu caste practices and customs. They were happy with their social position and never bothered to put their faith into practice in the caste ridden society. They lived within the framework of caste through centuries. The caste outlook reflected in their social relationship with lower caste converts also.[6] It continues even today with a few exceptions. Though Syrian Christians spread across different sects (denominations) of Christianity, they prefer to remain as endogamous communities.

The influence of caste manifested itself in the Roman Catholic mission also. Francis Xavier had to limit his work among Paravas on the south-east coast and Mukkuvars. He could not attract high castes to Christianity.[7] However, Robert de Nobili, an Italian Jesuit, who came to Madurai in 1606 realized the impact of the caste system in Indian society and the importance of attracting higher castes, particularly Brahmins, to expand the Roman Catholic mission. He never questioned caste but allowed upper castes to follow their social heritage. He accommodated caste practices under the pretext of indigenizing Christianity. He allowed Brahmin converts to follow their dress code, food style and social ethos. They maintained their social identity by not associating with other Christians like Paravas.[8] Though he faced opposition against his method, Nobili convinced the Catholic church to allow Brahmins to continue with 'their caste symbols like the tuft of hair, use of a cord, etc., that indicate their nobility and caste'.[9] However, the increase of lower caste converts put the missionaries in a predicament. Instead of challenging the caste, they gave tacit support to it by performing their priestly duties among the upper caste Christians in the daytime and the lower caste Christians at night. When this arrangement became difficult to continue, missionaries were appointed exclusively to work among the lower castes.[10] The story of caste that began with Syrian Christians continued through early Roman Catholic missions. It is observed that the Catholic missionaries had no problem working within the framework of the caste system because they considered caste a social institution rather than a religious institution.[11]

The Protestant missions also gave silent support to caste among Christians in India. For instance, the Tranquebar mission, established in 1706, under the leadership of Bartholomew Ziegenbalg and Henry Pluetschau accommodated caste distinctions among the converts. The cruciform structure of the New Jerusalem Church built by Ziegenbalg proves it. The upper caste men and women sat on one side of the Church while others were on the other. The upper castes received eucharistic elements first and others later in the Holy Communion service.[12] The church could not resist the entry of caste into its worship service, particularly during the Holy Communion that remembers Jesus' death on the cross for humanity.

The caste Christians could not tolerate the presence of low caste Christians in the congregations. For example, the Synod of Syrian

Christians (January 1836) decided to disassociate themselves from Church Missionary Society (CMS) missionaries who encouraged them to share social and religious life with low caste converts.[13] The Syrian Christians thought that they would lose their social standing among upper castes if they associated with their lower caste co-religionists. Rev. Henry Baker, a missionary, narrates the story of caste reality among Kerala Christians in the nineteenth century, '. . . on a few out-caste converts entering the door of the Church at the insistence of the missionary, the Syrians left by the windows'.[14] There were instances in which Syrian Christians supported upper castes who opposed the admission of Dalit children into schools.[15] There were separate churches for Dalit Christians in the Church of South India, Mar Thoma, Roman Catholic and Orthodox traditions in Kerala. According to Ninan Koshy, Mar Thoma or Jacobite churches did not recruit priests from Dalits converts till the 1960s.[16] There is not much change even today.

The European Christians also maintained racial superiority in their relationship with native Christians. They limited their social and religious relationship among themselves. They did not consider native Christians equal to them even though both followed the same faith.[17] European racial superiority must have found a partner in the caste system which had already crept into the church.

The caste system has not left even Pentecostal Christianity untouched. Despite their emphasis on egalitarian spiritual life informed by the otherworldly life, caste controlled the mindset of many Pentecostals. Just before his first foreign trip, one Pentecostal leader said 'I hope to carry the message of the Gospel to Europe in four levels: first as a Pentecostal; then as a Syrian (caste identity) and thirdly as an Asian Christian and finally as an Indian'.[18] A few decades after the establishment of Pentecostal Christianity in India, particularly in Kerala, differentiation on the basis of caste developed among Pentecostals. Many Syrian Pentecostals were reluctant to have social and spiritual fellowship with Dalit Pentecostals. This approach led to the formation of Dalit congregations and churches like the World Missionary Evangelism (WME) Church. Caste divided even the Church of God (Full Gospel) in India, one of the Pentecostal denominations, into two: the Church of God in India

(Kerala State) and the Church of God in India (Kerala Region) in 1972. While Syrian Pentecostals constituted the former, Dalit Pentecostals made up the latter.[19]

Indian Christians practised caste, irrespective of different sects throughout centuries. Christianity survived, according to Duncan B. Forrester, in some regions like Kerala because it accommodated the caste system at different levels. Though Christianity did not sanction caste scripturally, or historically it failed to root out caste from the church.[20] However, voices were raised against caste in the Christian community.

RESPONSE

There were strong reactions against the practice of caste in Christianity, particularly in Protestant traditions. The Protestant missionaries had a different outlook regarding caste. Unlike the Catholic missionaries, they understood caste as a religious institution having the scriptural sanction of Hinduism.[21] Many of them opposed the practice of differentiation on the basis of caste among Christians and faced opposition from upper caste converts. Benjamin Schultze, a missionary in Tranquebar in the 1720s, attempted to stop caste distinctions in the Church through an order. But he had to leave the mission because of the opposition of converts who wanted to maintain their 'caste' identity.[22] C.F. Schwartz, another missionary, who worked in Tranquebar and Tanjore and witnessed how Christians of different caste origins were seated separately in the congregations, 'carefully avoided all unnecessary (caste) restraint', in the churches.[23]

Bishops like Reginald Heber and Daniel Wilson had strong views against the practice of caste among Christians and supported the efforts of missionaries to stop it. Bishop Reginald Heber appreciated young missionaries in his letter dated 26 May 1826, 'the old school missionaries tolerated all this as a merely civil question of pedigree and worldly distinction . . . but on the other hand, some of the younger missionaries, both German and English, have not only warmly preached against caste, but in the management of their schools, and the arrangement of their congregations, have thwarted it as much as possible'.[24] But he had to transfer a missionary, who encouraged Adi-Dravida children and Shudra children to sit together in a church in Chennai, due to the strong opposition of the congregation against his anti-caste experiment. After observing caste among Christians in south India, Bishop Daniel Wilson wrote strongly to the missionaries, pastors and believers that 'The distinction of caste then must be abandoned decidedly, immediately, finally. . . .'[25] Once he conducted a service of Confirmation and Holy Communion in a Mission Church at Chennai without following existent caste distinctions among the believers in the order of receiving Eucharist elements.[26]

Missionary Conferences denounced caste and asked Christians to discontinue it. The first South India Regional Missionary conference (19 April to 5 May 1858) held at Ootacamund, called caste the 'monster evil of India' and condemned it. The Missionary Conference for South India and Ceylon (Bangalore, 1879) resolved that 'it (caste) is diametrically opposed to the Christian doctrine of the oneness of human nature'. The South India Missionary Conference (Madras, 2 to 5 January 1900) decided to 'convince mission agents and the members of our mission churches of the folly and wickedness of the caste prejudice'.[27]

In the nineteenth century William Carey and his associates (Serampore missionaries) also opposed the practice of casteism. The college and schools established by the missionaries were open to all irrespective of caste and creed.[28] Irrespective of caste identity every student was allowed to study Hindu Scriptures even though it was opposed by the pundits.[29] It was a sign of breaking the barrier of caste in education. The missionaries' stand against caste was reflected in the faith community as well. They discouraged the new converts vehemently to maintain their caste identity and mindset. They taught that caste stood against the values of the Christian faith. For them, Christianity was one 'caste'. It does not imply that they attempted to strengthen the caste system by introducing one more 'caste' into the cluster of castes in India. But they wanted to build up a Christian community beyond 'caste' lines, a community of equals. In their attempt to counter the caste system, they promoted and conducted inter caste marriages in their congregation. The marriage of a Brahmin convert with the daughter of a carpenter[30] is a case in point. For Carey and his associates, it was a victory over the powers of caste.[31] Though the process of the annihilation of caste started with education, it touched every aspect of their mission. The native Christian community also followed Carey and his associates in their approach toward caste. A public display of the negation of caste occurred when a converted Brahmin and a converted Muslim along with Marshman and Felix Carey carried the dead body of a Shudra Christian. It happened in the social context where a Brahmin would never touch the dead body of a Shudra and vice versa.[32] Whenever a lower caste was baptized, he and his associates used to celebrate the event by arranging fellowship meals which would be attended by the converts from all castes and the Europeans.[33]In their anti caste attitude, Serampore missionaries exhibited social morality and inclusive approach of the Christian faith.

There were attempts to challenge caste consciousness in the Malankara Orthodox Syrian Church. The life and work of Metropolitan Geevarghese Mar Gregorious of Parumala (1848-1902) was exemplified by his anti caste attitude. He encouraged his community to do mission work among the Dalits and use its resources to uplift them socially and spiritually. Despite the objection of his co-workers, he worked among the Dalits and baptized hundreds of them. He tried to integrate them into the Orthodox community but could not overcome the systemic evil of caste in the church. Though he had to build a separate church for the Dalits,[34] Mar Gregorious took the bold step to reach out to the Dalits against the social outlook of Orthodox Christians in the nineteenth century. Metropolitan Petros Mar Osthathios (1886-1968) followed the path of Mar Gregorious and worked among the Dalits. He opposed separate churches and cemeteries for Dalit converts. He condemned the practice of addressing Dalit Christians as *puthu Christiani* (newly converted Christians). He also started *Sleeba Dasa Samooham* (the Servants of the Cross Society) to work among the oppressed communities.[35] In their mission approach, both Mar Gregorious and Mar Osthathios raised a different voice for social inclusion in the Church.

Not only missionaries and leaders but believers and priests also protested against caste among Christians. Though Syrian Christians maintained a casteist outlook in their social relationships, individually many of them supported anti caste movements in church and society. The work of CMS missionaries motivated them to sympathize with lower caste converts.[36] Many Dalit Christians left traditional churches and established their denomination as a mark of protest against caste. For example, Rev. V.J. Stephen and Dalit Christians quit the Madhya Kerala Diocese of the Church South India (CSI) and formed the Travancore Cochin Anglican (CMS) Church in 1964. Dalit Christians also organized conferences to expose caste in Christianity and to conscientize fellow Christians. For a case in point, Dalit Christians organized Anti-untouchability Conference in 1925 against caste practices like caste based seating arrangements and refusal to membership in the churches. Adi-Dravida Catholic Conference condemned caste distinctions in Roman Catholic Church in Tamil Nadu. Many lower caste converts left Christianity and went back to their previous religious communities because of caste discrimination in churches.[37] Reconversion is also one of the responses to caste in Christianity. The responses prove that caste was not left unchallenged in Christianity.

CHRISTIANS: VICTIMS OF CASTE

The Christian identity did not guarantee protection from caste victimization. Both upper caste and low caste converts and Europeans faced caste discrimination in society. A typical example is the condition of Christians in Travancore society in the nineteenth century. The Syrian Christians, who enjoyed caste privileges since their arrival in the fourth and fifth centuries, had faced a lot of social and religious discrimination such as *ūḻiaṁ* (gratuitous services), supplying provisions to *ūttupura* (free inn for Brahmins), being treated as equal with low caste converts, considering their approach to temples as pollution, exclusion from government services, denying admission to all schools, all streets or public wells, ill treatment by government officials, discrimination in schools, etc.[38] The law of purity pollution did not allow a Syrian Christian to touch a Nair. A Nair would not eat with a Syrian Christian. The Pulayas and Pariahs could approach other castes within a stipulated distance only but were never allowed to touch them.[39]

In Travancore, Europeans were prohibited from travelling on the main roads. The capital of Travancore, where the Brahmins were more in number, was out of bounds for the Europeans for many years. The high castes Hindus would sit and talk with the Europeans, but never dined with them.[40] Europeans were considered polluted because of their lifestyle; particularly their association with low castes and slaves, etc.[41] The King or Queen met European officials like the Resident and others outside the capital, for many years, to avoid the danger of pollution.[42] The rulers did not permit the construction of churches near the public roads used for religious processions.[43] This religious discrimination had the underpinning of caste because Christians were polluted in the eyes of religious and political authorities of that time.

Christians, both men and women had to pay various taxes and were forced to do the work for the temples. They were compelled to carry lights in the Hindu religious processions. They were whipped if they disobeyed. False charges were imposed on them and they were thrown into prison without proper judicial trials. On several occasions, Sunday services were disturbed with the support of government officials. Many churches, schools, and houses were burned down during the tension between upper caste and lower caste converts. The government officers systematically obstructed the construction of churches by negating the required permission. In 1827, a royal proclamation was issued to control the erection of worship places. The accessibility of Christians to government offices, schools, streets, and public wells was restricted. They were fined even for walking nearby the temple premises. The conversion of high caste people was dealt with unkindly by the respective caste people and the government.[44] Low castes had to give gifts to high caste landlords on special occasions such as marriage. All low caste converts had to perform *ūḻiaṁ* duties except on Sundays. They were not permitted to reside in tiled houses.[45] The low caste woman converts were not allowed to dress like upper caste women. They were forbidden to cover their bosoms with the upper cloth. They were not allowed to wear anything above the waist till 1812. Because of the intervention of missionaries and Col. John Munro, Dewan of Travancore, they were allowed to wear a form of jacket called *ravakkay.*[46] The converts, particularly those from the low caste among them, faced different kinds of victimization because of their caste identity throughout the country. The upper castes primarily treated low caste converts within the framework of caste. Their post-conversion experience had caste imprints. It continues even today. Dalit Christians are a case in point.

DALIT CHRISTIANS: LIFE OF EXCLUSION IN CHURCH AND SOCIETY

Though the exact numerical strength of the Dalit Christians is uncertain due to the lack of systematic study, most scholars place their proportion between 50 and 75 per cent of the total Christian population in India.[47] They constitute the majority of Indian Christians.[48] They come mainly from the communities previously called 'untouchables'.[49] Even now they feel that conversion has not changed their social status in the eyes of non-Dalits, particularly, the upper castes in Church and society. They carry the stigma of low caste origin even today.[50] Often, others address Dalit Christians with their caste names in a pejorative sense.[51] The co-religionists regard them as 'socially inferior'. They are treated first as Dalits and then as Christians within and outside the faith community.[52] While they are defined and treated within the framework of caste in the church and society, they are excluded by fellow Dalits and the government due to their faith affiliation. They experience discrimination and exclusion: in society, within the Church, among the Dalits and by the government.[53] This leads them to an identity crisis: they don't know whether their identity is determined by faith or caste. The ill treatment within the multi-caste Church is more painful for them than in society. The Dalit Christian housing is segregated from that of the high castes in many of the multi-racial Christian villages or locations. There are separate church buildings and cemeteries for Dalit Christians.[54] The discriminated life realities of Dalit Christians show that they live a life of exclusion as they lived before changing their faith. With conversion, they got a new 'religious' identity along with other identities, but not equality, dignity and recognition as promised by the new faith.

According to a study, Dalit Christians face discrimination in educational institutions: the negation of admissions, ill treatment, separate seating arrangements, refusal to be given drinking water, refusal to serve lunch/midday meals, etc. Though the literacy rate is reasonable, a majority of them are either dropouts or discontinue before they reach high school. The number of graduates among them is very low and still fewer people have taken up technical education.[55] This situation is mainly due to the lack of economic resources, limited access to higher education facilities, and an unaffordable education system.[56] Church and government are equally responsible for the backward condition of Dalit Christians. Instead of providing quality education to Dalit Christians, the church institutions serve upper-caste Hindus and Christians who can afford the expenses. Though the church manages the best schools, Dalit Christians do not get quality education to improve their lives in society.[57] With a few exceptions, Dalit Christians are educationally backward as compared to non-Dalit co-religionists.[58]

The economic deprivation of their forebears has directly or indirectly influenced the present situation of Dalit Christians.[59] A majority of them are landless agricultural labourers or casual labourers.[60] Though a small number of them are employed in government and private sectors, the majority of such employees are working in low-grade positions in Municipal Corporations, hospitals and banks.[61] The living conditions of Dalit Christians in rural areas are the same as fellow Dalits of other religious traditions. They do not have proper housing and access to civic amenities.[62] Also, caste prejudices compel them to take up traditional jobs.[63]

The 'casteist mentality' is deeply rooted in the psyche of the majority of Indian Christians.[64] Therefore, Dalit Christians experience discrimination at various levels in the multi caste churches. Their social status is the same inside and outside the church. Dalit priests are preferably not appointed in non-Dalit dominated churches. Talented Dalit leaders and priests get less significant responsibilities in the churches/dioceses. Dalit Christians do not get job opportunities in many Church run institutions in proportion to their membership. They get recognition only in Dalit dominated churches/dioceses. They are consciously excluded from the decision-making bodies and prominent positions in the churches where they are in a minority or equal in proportion.[65] Dalit Christians allege that the Church needs them only for conversion, not for leadership. They are also aware that their brothers and sisters in other religious traditions, especially Dalit Hindus, have improved their economic and social status thanks to the reservation policy and other welfare programmes of the government.[66] Based on their experiences of caste victimhood in the Church, they feel that they are the 'wounded' sheep and Church is the 'uncaring shepherd'. They endure the stigma of caste in both public and ecclesial spaces. Christianity has given them hope but caste prejudices among their co-religionists douses it.

CHRISTIANITY AND CASTE TODAY

Technological and educational advancement has not changed the attitude of the Indian mind engrossed in caste consciousness.[67] The prevalence of caste in today's society proves the observation of the Mandal Commission Report that 'In India caste system has endured for over 3,000 years and even today there appears no symptoms of its early demise.'[68] Christianity cannot claim immunity in this regard. The casteization of Christianity continues in newer forms today. The body of Christianity has 'symptoms' of caste contrary to its claim of the church as the 'Body of Christ'. The analysis of B.R. Ambedkar remains true for contemporary casteized Christianity as well. His analysis had a prophetic element. He observed that:

> Indian Christians like all other Indians are divided . . . by caste. Their religion has not been a sufficiently strong unifying force as to make difference of language, race and caste as though they were mere distinctions. The result is that the Indian Christians are too disjointed to have a common aim, to have common mind and to put a common endeavor. . . . In short, the term Indian

Christian is just a statistical phrase. There is no community feeling behind this phrase. Indian Christians are not bound together by what is consciousness of kind, which is the test of the existence of a community.[69]

Another scenario of present Christianity, particularly related to caste, was predicted by Nirad C. Chaudhuri. He was prophetic when he said that,

> The wealthy and well-placed among them will become merged in the Anglicized Hindu upper middle class, with only a difference of faith, which nobody, including themselves, will take very seriously. On the other hand, the majority of Indian Christians, that is those who are poor and already depressed socially, will become something like inferior castes in Hindu society.[70]

Christianity could not shake off caste throughout the centuries. Indian Christianity has become 'hyphenated' Christianity and its followers 'hyphenated' Christians. Hyphenated Christians form hyphenated churches.[71] There are Syrian Christians, Dalit Christians, Tribal Christians, Nadar Christians, Reddy Christians, etc., today. Churches/Denominations are known by the caste identity of the majority of members. For example, Mar Thoma Church, Syro-Malabar Church and Syrian Orthodox church etc. are 'socially' known as Syrian churches even though non-Syrians also have membership in those churches. Some dioceses of the Church of South India are 'socially' known as Nadar/Dalit/Tribal dioceses. Many dioceses of the Roman Catholic Church in India are formed on the basis of the caste identity of believers. The churches/dioceses in north India also witness power struggles between Dalit/Tribal communities. Though they also promote caste identity, many Dalit majority congregations are reactions to non-Dalit demographic Christian consolidation through churches and denominations because of the influence of caste. People identify local congregations by caste. While caste defines the identity of churches and Christians, in some places as Nirad C. Chaudhuri said, 'The power of the caste system is such that the Hindus from the low castes who embraced Christianity did not raise themselves to a higher level, but on the contrary brought down the religion to their level.'[72]

The Indian Christians (a majority of them) prefer to take membership in the Church/denomination where they are in majority or the leadership/pastor belongs to their community. They may not have a problem bypassing a nearby Church belonging to another 'caste' or 'tribe' of the same denomination and walk an extra mile to reach the church of their community.[73] Casteist Christians, prefer to marry those belonging to their own 'caste'. Christians, irrespective of caste, observe marital exclusion though they belong to the same denomination/Church. A Syrian or Nadar or Reddy or Dalit Christian is comfortable choosing a partner from his/her own community. Some argue that inter caste marriages cause tensions in family and community life.[74] A D'Souza, Mascarenhas, Pinto or Lobo from Mangalore may not prefer a Christian from another community for marriage because they consider themselves superior to other Christians including their Catholic co-religionists. A Bengali Christian with Banerji, Chatterji, Mukherji, Bose or Dutt as surname may not marry a Biswas.[75] Some Goanese Christians claim Brahmin ancestry and promote endogamy. Maharashtrian Christians of Brahmin origin also uphold their racial superiority to other Christians. It is observed that upper caste Christians including Syrian Christians, assert their caste identity to overcome the lower caste 'identity' of Indian Christianity.[76] Social and ecclesial exclusion exists among Mahar and Mang Christians in Maharashtra, Biswas, Mondal and Das Christians in West Bengal, Mala and Madiga Christians in Andhra Pradesh and Telangana, etc.[77]

It is common among Christians that if a community is numerically dominant in a Church/denomination, it occupies important positions of power and ignores other communities that are numerically less. Often, the dominance of a particular community in the 'committees of power' is justified as the 'sign' of 'democracy' in the church. Sadly, wilful exclusion happens between Christians in the areas of power sharing. Dalits get elected or selected only to the reserved seats in non-Dalit-dominated churches. At the same time, non-Dalits are completely ignored in some Dalit-dominated denominations.

Christians, who once resisted caste tyranny, practise caste today. The caste system placed Nadars in low social status and deprived them of their dignity and freedom in Travancore society. They endured many social disabilities in the eighteenth-nineteenth centuries. But they fought against caste practices and advanced in social and economic life in all aspects of social life. Christianity provided resources such as education for their present empowerment. Today, they consider themselves superior to certain communities. They discourage inter caste marriage, which B.R. Ambedkar considered the real remedy for annihilating the caste system.[78] Unfortunately, in many places, social relations among Christians also have the imprint of caste. They maintain close relationships mainly with their fellow caste persons/families rather than their co-religionists. Family socials often display caste identity and create group consciousness.

Another phenomenon in Indian Christianity is that Christians are 'infected with denominational differences'.[79] It also has 'caste' characteristics. Denominationalism demands marriage within the denomination. Often Christians strive to meet two requirements in marriage alliance: caste and denomination. If casteism requires physical (body) and ancestral (blood) purity, then denominationalism calls for 'doctrinal purity'. Casteism and denominationalism promote hierarchical and exclusive outlook. Both restrict social intercourse among the group members. Like caste, a denomination prioritizes denominational identity. As a particular caste builds up its social and political capital, so a denomination attempts to increase its space of influence in society. Both casteism and denominationalism facilitate competition with others. In short, while caste has already shaped the social psyche of Indian Christians; functionally denominations and churches have typical characteristics of 'caste'.

PERSPECTIVE

Caste is a reality among Indian Christians. But Christianity teaches that the practice of caste is not biblical. The Bible provides plenty of anti-caste narratives and teachings. The Biblical story of creation informs that God created human beings in God's image (Genesis 1: 27). It means every human being reflects the image of God. His/her dignity and status are derived from the image of God. The 'Image of God' defines his/her identity, not the caste. Christians cannot perpetuate caste distinctions among them because all are equal in Jesus Christ (Galatians 3: 28). The Bible also teaches that a Christian is a new creation (2 Corinthians 5: 17) after his/her confession in Jesus. S/he should put off 'caste identity' and assume a new identity. S/he is in the process of restoring his/her original status—the image of God.

The Church is not a caste institution, but a communion of God's people. It is primarily a communion of equals. This is the location where Christians experience their identity as God's people. In this communion, all are equal, irrespective of their origin, language, ethnicity, etc. There is no space for caste based separation and discrimination in the Church.[80] Denouncing the evil and announcing the good news is the core of its life.[81] Casteism is 'contrary to the Christian faith, and inimical to the Christian fellowship (Church).'[82] The practice of caste is an unchristian behaviour because Christian faith demands an ethical life shaped by the values of justice, equality, and love.

Caste is a sign of the crisis of faith among Christians. The practice of caste makes Christian faith irrelevant in caste ridden society. Caste questions the identity of the Church and Christians as the 'agent of the Kingdom of God' on earth. It restricts the missional space of the Church and makes the Church redundant.[83] Hyphenated Christians are a betrayal of the brotherhood and sisterhood taught by Christianity. Gandhi aptly reminds Christians that "Christian Harijans" is a contradiction in terms'.[84]

Dalit theology explains the anti caste perspective of Christianity. Dalit theology emerged out of the past and present experiences of Dalits which were full of discrimination, their struggles against casteism and their aspirations for social justice in the church and society.[85] It questions the practice of caste theologically and stands for the liberation of Dalits from the bondage of caste. It declares that 'casteism within the Christian fellowship is a theological contradiction and a spiritual problem'.[86] Caste system is a sinful and demonic structure. The practice of it is idolatry.[87] Practitioners and victims of caste need liberation. The former should be liberated from the 'caste psyche', and the latter the 'caste oppression'.[88] Dalit Christians allege that the oppressive mentality of upper caste people in the Church and society is the root cause of their stigmatization.

Jesus' life and work give a framework for countering caste. He rejected the existing socio-religious structures of his time and introduced an alternative form of community. He denounced social and religious exclusion and attempted to build up a new community based on the values of love, justice, equality and freedom. He embraced the people who were considered socially inferior and laid the foundation for a new community that transcends class (caste), gender, and cultural distinctions. He affirmed the equal and inherent value of every human being in his teachings. His view of equality challenged the dominant binary of 'superior' or 'inferior' in community life. He taught that unequal relationship is not the will of God. Jesus invited people to become part of the new community where mutual empowerment taken place. The Church is the sign of a new community on earth.[89] It should exist as a community that accomplishes the divine vision of a new community, an alternative community of hope, acceptance, love, equality, justice, social healing and empowerment.

The sacrament of baptism changes the identity of every baptized person. This is why St. Paul stated that a baptized person is clothed with Jesus Christ (Galatians 3: 27). The vow s/he takes at the time of baptism requires him/her to express the identity of Jesus in society. When a person dies with Jesus in the baptismal experience (Rom 6: 3), s/he dies with his/her old identity. In the Indian context, a person primarily buries his/her caste identity in baptism. S/he will no longer be known by his/her caste identity, but rather by his/her faith identity derived from the life of Jesus Christ. Since baptism destroys all walls of separation created by caste, all baptized persons are equal in status and privilege in the faith community (Galatians 3: 28).[90] Thus, baptism builds up a community of Jesus, a sign of the kingdom of God. In this community, caste consciousness is replaced by the consciousness of right relationships, equality, and justice. Baptism becomes meaningful in the Indian context if it leads to the death of caste consciousness in the life of baptized believers. It is a ritual that proclaims not only salvation in Jesus Christ but also announces the annihilation of caste in his/her life.

In the sacrament of Eucharist, the Christians remember the sufferings and death of Jesus Christ. It is a memorial of what Jesus has done for the salvation of humanity. It has both spiritual and social value. As a sacrament, Eucharist facilitates the unity of believers in Christ. But in the context of caste, the Eucharist demands the unity of believers beyond caste identities.[91] Eucharistic unity invalidates overt and covert forms of caste solidarity. As a symbol of faith, Eucharist points to the social responsibility of the believers. It teaches that unity achieved through faith should be reflected in social relations. Jesus' table fellowship, the primal form of the Eucharist, was a table of empowerment and inclusion. It invited everyone who experienced discrimination and exclusion in society and empowered them to start a new journey in life. It was a symbol of reaching out to the outcasts of His time.[92] Thus, all are equal shareholders in the Eucharistic community. The social praxis of Eucharistic equality leads to the creation of a new community. It demolishes all walls of separation and brings forth a community of equals. 'Sharing the bread and one cup implies the breaking of all social divisions based upon racial, ethnic or caste system'.[93]

Christian spirituality also informs that Spirit of God is against the spirit of caste. Therefore, a Christian cannot live with caste. In Christian spiritual life, s/he allows the Spirit to kill caste consciousness in his/her life. S/he cannot support any system which supports social inequality because the Spirit nurtures freedom, justice, love and equality. The Spirit encourages right (equal) human relations against 'right-caste relations'[94] which maintains social inequality. The spiritual equality in Jesus Christ should manifest itself in social equality. In sum, Christianity affirms an anti-caste perspective.

Caste is a historical reality among Christians. Christianity could not overcome the power of caste in society. Christians irrespective of churches came under the shadow of caste. Either they consciously observed caste or became victims of caste in the larger society. Many missionaries, leaders, and commoners challenged the practice of caste among Christians. Though they constituted a minority, they raised strong voices against the unchristian social structure. They reminded Christians that the practice of caste was contraction of the existence of Christianity. Dalit Christians are primary victims of caste in Christianity. They endured discrimination from co-religionists and caste people outside the church. They experienced the same with new forms. The practice of caste has also provoked them to assert their 'caste' identities. Contemporary Christianity disproves the claim that caste has lost its ground among Christians. For many Christians, caste is a lifeline or capital for upward mobility. Caste is silently or openly present in the life of many Christian institutions, organizations, and Churches. It 'rules' in social relations, selection of marital partners, selection/election of leaders, etc. It does not mean that there is no hope for the redemption of Christianity from the bondage of caste. Christianity is inherently anti-casteist because its faith and ethical values denounce hierarchical and oppressive structures like the caste system. Its social perspective is egalitarian and inclusive. Christianity and caste do not go together even though many Christians walk with caste.

NOTES

1. Ralph T.H. Griffith (tr. & cr.), *The Hymns of the Rigveda*, new revd. edn., rpt. (Delhi: Motilal Banarsidass, 1986), 603.
2. Some call it a 'myth' while others a 'historical event'.
3. They were also called St. Thomas Christians. If the story of the conversion of Brahmins is historically true, then the assimilation of early converts of St. Thomas and Syrian Christians would have happened.
4. Cyril Bruce Firth, *An Introduction to Indian Church History* (Madras: Christian Literature Society, 1983 rpt.), 30; M.P. Joseph, *Legitimately Divided: Towards a Counter Narrative of the Ethnographic History of Kerala Christianity* (Tiruvalla: Christava Sahitya Samithi, 2004), 13.
5. The 'Syrian' identity of Syrian Christians comes from the use of the Syriac language in their liturgy in the past. Liturgical language identity became upper caste social identity. Cf. M.P. Joseph, *Legitimately Divided*, op. cit., 19.

6. Duncan B. Forrester, *Caste and Christianity* (London and Dublin: Curzon Press Ltd & NJ: Humanities Press Inc, 1979), 97 & 99; L.W. Brown, *The Indian Christians of St. Thomas* (Cambridge, Cambridge University Press, 1956), 173; F.E. Keay (1938), *A History of the Syrian Church in India* (Madras: Society for Promoting Christian Knowledge, 1951), 22-4; Shalva Weil, 'Symmetry between Christian and Jews in India: The Cnanite Christians and the Cochin Jews of Kerala', *Contributions to Indian Sociology*, vol. 16, no. 2 (1982): 175-96 at 185; Samuel Mateer, *Native Life in Travancore* (London: W.H. Allen & Co. 1883), 158-68, 296; James Massey, *Dalits in India* (New Delhi: Manohar, 1995), 46.
7. Cyril Bruce Firth, *An Introduction to Indian Church History*, op. cit., 58-62.
8. Firth, *An Introduction to Indian Church History*, op. cit., 111-13.
9. M.K. Kuriakose, *History of Christianity in India: Source Materials* (Madras: CLS, 1982), 52.
10. Firth, *An Introduction to Indian Church History*, op. cit., 117.
11. John C.B. Webster, *The Dalit Christians: A History* (New Delhi: ISPCK, revd. & enlgd. edn., 2009), 43.
12. Firth, *An Introduction to Indian Church History*, op. cit., 137.
13. M.P. Joseph, *Legitimately Divided: Towards a Counter Narrative of the Ethnographic History of Kerala Christianity*, 54.
14. Ibid., 24.
15. C.P. Mathew and M.M. Thomas, *The Indian Churches of Saint Thomas* (Delhi: DJVP/ISPCK, 2005), 159.
16. Ninan Koshy, *Caste in the Kerala Churches* (Bangalore: Christian Institute for the Study of Religion and Society, 1968).
17. Nirad C. Chaudhuri, *The Continent of Circe* (London: Chatto & Windus, 1967), 275.
18. V.V. Thomas, *Dalit Pentecostalism: Spirituality of the Empowered Poor* (Bangalore: Asian Trading Corporation, 2008), 215.
19. Ibid., 229 & 314.
20. Forrester, *Caste and Christianity*, op. cit., 100.
21. Webster, *The Dalit Christians: A History*, op. cit., 45.
22. Firth, *An Introduction to Indian Church History*, op. cit., 138.
23. Kuriakose, *History of Christianity in India: Source Materials*, op. cit., 69.
24. Ibid., 109.
25. Firth, *An Introduction to Indian Church History*, op. cit., 162.
26. Kuriakose, *History of Christianity in India: Source Materials*), op. cit., 121.
27. Ibid.,174, 228 & 273.
28. Woba James, *Revisiting Ecumenical Theological Education in India* (New Delhi: Christian World Imprints, 2016), 255.

29. John Clark Marshman, *The Life and Times of Carey, Marshman and Ward: Embracing the History of the Serampore Mission*, vol. 2 (London: Longmans & Roberts, 1859), 486.
30. Krishna Pal, the first convert of the Serampore Mission, whose social rank in the caste hierarchy was low.
31. John William Kaye, *Christianity in India: A Historical Narrative* (London: Smith, Elder and Co., 1859), 235-8; F. Deaville Walker, *William Carey: Missionary Pioneer and Statesman* (London: Student Christian Movement, 1926), 226.
32. F. Deaville Walker, *William Carey: Missionary Pioneer and Statesman*, 226; John Clark Marshman, *The Life and Times of Carey, Marshman and Ward: Embracing the History of the Serampore Mission*, vol. 1 (London: Longmans & Roberts, 1859), 186.
33. Vishal and Ruth Mangalwadi, *The Legacy of William Carey* (Illinois: Crossway Books, 1999 rpt.), 123.
34. George Varughese, 'The Caste Identity of the Indian Orthodox Church: An Appraisal from Christian Ministry Perspective', *UBS Journal*, vol. 12, no. 2 (September 2018): 91-110 at 94-5.
35. George Varughese, 'The Caste Identity of the Indian Orthodox Church: An Appraisal from Christian Ministry Perspective', ibid., 98-100.
36. Mathew and Thomas, *The Indian Churches of Saint Thomas*, op. cit., 159.
37. Webster, *The Dalit Christians: A History*, op. cit., 107, 140, 229 & 231.
38. C.M. Agur, *Church History of Travancore* (Madras: S.P.S. Press, 1903; New Delhi: Asian Educational Service, 1990), 18, 53, 60 & li- lii; Susan Bayly, *Saints, Goddesses and Kings: Muslims and Christians in South Indian Society, 1700-1900* (Cambridge: Cambridge University Press, 1989), 293, cited by V.V. Thomas, *Dalit Pentecostalism*, 111; Mateer, *Native Life in Travancore*, op. cit., 346.
39. G.S. Ghurye, *Caste and Race in India* (rpt. of 5th edn., Bombay: Popular Prakashan, 1994), 9-10; A.H., *Day Dawn in Travancore: A Brief Account of the Manners and Customs of the People and the Efforts that are being Made for their Improvement* (Kottayam: C.M.S Press, 1860), 8-9; Samuel Mateer, *Land of Charity* (London: John Snow & Co, 1871), 28 & 31.
40. Samuel Mateer, *Land of Charity*, op. cit., 32 & 64.
41. Mateer, *Native Life in Travancore*, op. cit., 332.
42. P. Shungoonny Menon, *A History of Travancore from the Earliest Times* (Madras: Higginbotham and Co, 1878), 380-2.
43. Mateer, *Native Life in Travancore*, op. cit., 333-4.
44. Agur, *Church History of Travancore*, op. cit., 52-6.

45. *Selected Proclamations by the Sovereign from 1811-1939 AD* (Trivandrum: Government Press, 1937), Archives Directorate, Trivandrum, 18-20, 64-5, 136-7 & 227.
46. Letter from Rev. E. Lewis to the Resident, 21 January 1859, Bundle No. 29, Cover File No. 2115 of 1858, *Shanar Disturbances in South Travancore*, Archives Directorate, Trivandrum; Samuel Mateer, *Land of Charity*, 41, 61-2 & 305. Though they appeared with jackets Nadar Hindu women were given the privilege of wearing jackets legally only in 1859.
47. Satish Deshpande and Geetika Bapna, *Dalits in Muslim and Christian Communities* (New Delhi: Centre for Dalit Studies, Catholic Bishops' Conference of India and National Council of Churches in India, 2010), 60 & 108 (reference no. 5.)
48. K.E. Rajpramukh, *Dalit Christians of Andhra* (New Delhi: Serials Publications, 2008), 80.
49. Chuhras, Chamars, Vankars, Mahars, Paraiyars, Bhangis, Mangs, Malas, Madigas, Pulayas, etc.
50. Camil Parkhe, *Dalit Christians: Right to Reservations* (Delhi: Indian Society for Promoting Christian Knowledge, 2007), 1-3; James Massey and T.K. John, eds., *Christians of Scheduled Caste Origin in India* (New Delhi: Centre for Dalit /Subaltern Studies, 2013), 14; Rajpramukh, *Dalit Christians of Andhra*, op. cit., 80-1.
51. S. Lourduswamy, 'Catholic Church and Dalit-Tribal Movements in India', in *Rethinking Theology in India*, ed. James Massey and T.K. John (New Delhi: Manohar and Centre for Dalit/Subaltern Studies, 2013), 185; S. Lourduswamy, *Towards Empowerment of Dalit Christians, Equal Rights to all Dalits* (New Delhi: Centre for Dalit/Subaltern Studies, 2005), 20-1.
52. Deshpande and Bapna, *Dalits in Muslim and Christian Communities*, op. cit., 128.
53. Felix Wilfred, 'Editorial', *Jeevadhara*, vol. XLI, no. 241 (January 2011): 3-5 at 3.
54. Massey and John, eds., *Christians of Scheduled Caste Origin in India*, op. cit., 16; Indukuri John Mohan Razu, 'Towards a Critical Theology of Risk Taking: The Changing Landscape and Discourse', in *Rethinking Theology in India*, op. cit., 362.
55. Massey and John, eds., *Christians of Scheduled Caste Origin in India*, op. cit., 75-82.
56. Lourduswamy, 'Catholic Church and Dalit-Tribal Movements in India', op. cit., 186.

57. S. Lourduswamy, 'Dalit Christians: Has Anything Changed?', *Jeevadhara*, vol. XLI, no. 241 (January 2011): 7-13 at 12-13; Lourduswamy, *Towards Empowerment of Dalit Christians, Equal Rights to all Dalits*, op. cit., 26-7.
58. Deshpande and Bapna, *Dalits in Muslim and Christian Communities*, op. cit., 133.
59. Camil Parkhe, *Dalit Christians: Right to Reservations*, 4.
60. Deshpande and Bapna, *Dalits in Muslim and Christian Communities*, op. cit., 131-2.
61. Massey and John, eds., *Christians of Scheduled Caste Origin in India*, op. cit., 83-6.
62. Rajpramukh, *Dalit Christians of Andhra*, op. cit., 81.
63. Deshpande and Bapna, *Dalits in Muslim and Christian Communities*, op. cit., 129.
64. Pauline Chakkalakal, *Discipleship, A Space for Women's Leadership* (Mumbai: Pauline Publications, 2004), 28.
65. K.E. Rajpramukh, *Dalit Christians of Andhra*, 80; Indukuri John Mohan Razu, 'Towards a Critical Theology of Risk Taking: The Changing Landscape and Discourse', op. cit., 348.
66. Massey and John, eds., *Christians of Scheduled Caste Origin in India*, op. cit., 155f.
67. Felix Wilfred, *Asian Public Theology* (New Delhi: Indian Society for Promoting Christian Knowledge, 2010), 30.
68. *Reservations for Backward Classes, Mandal Commission Report of the Backward Classes Commission, 1980* (Delhi: Akalank Publications, 1990), 19.
69. *Dr. Babasaheb Ambedkar: Writings and Speeches*, vol. 5, compiled by Vasant Moon (Bombay: Education Department, Government of Maharashtra, 1989), 476.
70. Chaudhuri, *The Continent of Circe*, op. cit., 277.
71. Joseph, *Legitimately Divided: Towards a Counter Narrative of the Ethnographic History of Kerala Christianity*, op. cit., 12.
72. Chaudhuri, *The Continent of Circe*, op. cit., 274.
73. K.C. Alexander, *Social Mobility in Kerala* (Poona: Deccan College, 1968), 49 referred in Y. Antony Raj, *Social Impact of Conversion* (Delhi: Indian Society for Promoting Christian Knowledge, 2001), 4.
74. P.G. Abraham, *Caste and Christianity: A Pentecostal Perspective* (Kumbazha: Crown Books, 2003), 103 ff.
75. Chaudhuri, *The Continent of Circe*, op. cit., 257.
76. Nidhin Donald, 'The "Brahmin" in Syrian Christian Family Histories', *Indian Church History Review*, vol. 56, no. 2 (July 2022): 63-81 at 65 & 67.

77. Observations and Interactions with Christians from respective states.
78. *Dr. Babasaheb Ambedkar Writings and Speeches*, vol. 1, Compiled by Vasant Moon (Bombay: Education Department, Government of Maharashtra, 1989), 67.
79. *Dr. Babasaheb Ambedkar: Writings and Speeches*, vol. 5, op. cit., 476.
80. Felix Wilfred, 'What Can "Upper Caste" Christians Learn from Dalit Christians', *Jeevadhara*, vol. XLI, no. 241 (January 2011): 67-76 at 71.
81. Editorial Board, 'Editorial: Christians and Politics', *Vidyajyoti Journal of Theological Reflection*, vol. 77, no. 8 (August 2013): 1-8 at 8.
82. M.M. Thomas, Comp., *Christian Participation in Nation-Building* (Bangalore: NCCI & Christian Institute for the Study of Religion and Society, 1960), 235.
83. Joseph, *Legitimately Divided: Towards a Counter Narrative of the Ethnographic History of Kerala Christianity*, op. cit., 29.
84. C.B. Webster, *The Dalit Christians: A History*, op. cit., 128.
85. M.E. Prabhakar, 'Introduction', in *Towards a Dalit Theology*, ed. M.E. Prabhakar (Delhi: Indian Society for Promoting Christian Knowledge, 1989), 2.
86. M.E. Prabhakar, 'The Search for a Dalit Theology', in *A Reader in Dalit Theology*, ed. Arvind P. Nirmal (Chennai: Gurukul, 2007 rpt.), 43.
87. V. Devasahayam, 'Doing Dalit Theology: Basic Assumptions', *Frontiers of Dalit Theology*, ed. V. Devashayam (Delhi: ISPCK/Gurukul, 1997), 276-7.
88. James Massey, *Introducing Dalit Theology* (New Delhi: Centre for Dalit Studies, 2004), 27.
89. James Massey, 'On Being a New Community and Ecclesia of Justice and Peace', in *On Being a New Community and Ecclesia of Justice and Peace*, ed. James Massey and NOH, Jong Sun (Bangalore: Board of Theological Education of Senate of Serampore College/South Asia Theological Research Institute, 2010), 20-3.
90. Massey, 'On Being a New Community and Ecclesia of Justice and Peace', op. cit., 28-9.
91. Keith Hebden, *Dalit Theology and Christian Anarchism* (Farnham, Surrey, England: Ashgate, 2011), 146-7.
92. Michael Amaladoss, *Life in Freedom: Liberation Theologies from Asia* (Oregon: WIPF and Stock Publishers, 2014), 29.
93. Massey, 'On Being a New Community and Ecclesia of Justice and Peace', op. cit., 23.
94. M.E. Prabhakar, 'Christology in Dalit Perspective', in *Frontiers in Dalit Theology*, ed. V. Devasahayam (Madras: Gurukul, 1997), 430.

CHAPTER 3

Freedom of Religion and Conversion

Religious people always desire the freedom to practise their respective faiths. Secular democratic societies give constitutional or legal protection of religious liberty. Religious communities understand and practise it according to the theological framework of their faith traditions. They don't tolerate any infringement of religious freedom. In pluralistic societies, minorities are more concerned about the issues of religion, particularly any impediment related to the practice of faith. India is home to all major religious traditions. The Constitution of India grants citizens the right to practise any faith freely and ensures equal treatment of religions. But the freedom of religion has not always remained unviolated. It has also opened the issue of religious conversion. In India, majoritarian ideologues accuse minority religious traditions, particularly Islam and Christianity, of promoting religious conversion and creating 'population imbalance'.[1] This chapter discusses freedom of religion and conversion from a Christian perspective.

CONTEXT

Religious pluralism is one of the characteristics of Indian society. It is true that 'Religion runs through India's consciousness like a gene: it orders reality, it shapes social behavior, it moves and it anchors, as much as it estranges and cleaves.'[2] Irrespective of denominations, the majority of Indians are religious. Despite some historical aberrations, they enjoy the freedom of religion as guaranteed in the Constitution. Of course, freedom of religion is a necessary ingredient of a pluralistic society. However, it is a fact that religious minorities particularly Christians come across various forms of the violation of the freedom of religion. The direct violation comes in the form of physical attack: destruction of houses of worship, disruption of religious meetings, physical assaults, vandalism of houses, schools, forceful closedown of churches, arrests of Christian priests and community workers on the grounds of false allegations of inducing conversions etc.[3] It happens irrespective of states and ruling dispensations. For instance, recently, Adivasi Christians endured concerted attacks in Chhattisgarh, a state under the rule of the Congress party.[4] Caste also plays a role in the physical attack on Christians. Dalit Christians are a case in point.[5] Mostly, violence against Christians is perpetuated by mobs, often with the secret connivance of members of the ruling class who then disclaim any involvement. In many places, Christians continue to be the victims of hate campaigns and vigilante violence. The call for a campaign against conversion leads to 'physical targeting of Christian worship services' and activities.[6] Majoritarian religious sentiments aroused by fringe groups lead to the violation of freedom of religion.

According to the Evangelical Fellowship of India (EFI), there were 135 cases of violence against Christians in India from January to June 2020. Persecution Relief, another organization, working for Christians' rights, reported that 293 cases of hate crimes against Christians, including five rapes and sex murders, happened during this period. Even the Covid 19 and national lockdown did not reduce the attacks against them.[7] 'The fresh spate of attacks against churches and Christian organizations,' according to Vijayesh Lal, general secretary of EFI, 'is all part of a systematic strategy to once again centre-forward the term "conversion", and use that bogey to attack Christians both physically and structurally. . . .'[8] Violence has become a major device to restrict the freedom of religion. Indirect violation of the freedom of religion comes in the form of bureaucratic malevolence: endless administrative delays, denial of permission to build places of worship/educational institutions and conduct religious meetings, withdrawal of police protection, etc.

There are attempts to portray Christianity negatively to play down the violent behaviour of communalists. Instead of condemning mob violence, its origin was attributed wrongly to Jesus Christ. Mohan Bhagwat, RSS chief, publicly alleged that 'the word (lynching) comes from an incident in the Bible (referring to the incident of a woman caught in adultery, John 8: 1-11) where Jesus Christ told the people to hit a woman with stones if they had never committed any sin in their past'.[9] Without fully understanding the incident and its context, he accused Jesus erroneously, who protected a woman from a mob (men), for promoting mob lynching. All India Catholic Union (AICU) strongly condemned his remarks about mob lynching and stated that he intended to 'denigrate Christianity and shift the focus from the rash of lynching of Dalits and religious minorities by gangs, who claim to be protectors of the cow'. Jesus' intervention rescued the woman from 'a kangaroo court justice' of the time.[10] Negative profiling hurts the sentiments and choices of believers protected by the freedom of religion.

A negative feeling covertly or overtly prevails against Christian religious activities in different parts of the nation. The centre of opposition is conversion. Some Hindu organizations and fringe groups strongly oppose any Christian activities: religious or humanitarian. They look at every Christian activity with suspicion. Dwarkapeeth Shankaracharya Swaroopanand Saraswati asks, 'Why would people change their religion if the government fulfils their needs?'[11] He interprets every Christian work as means of conversion and misjudges the intention behind conversion. Ashok Singhal, former international working President of Vishwa Hindu Parishad (VHP), said, 'Unless conversions were stopped immediately, the day would not be far off when Hindus would be reduced to a minority in this country'.[12] The purpose of such unrealistic statements is to target Christian religious activities. When they propagate or practise religion in non-Christian locations, Christian religious workers and organizations are charged with promoting religious conversion. Many villages or village councils banned social or religious activities of Christians directly or indirectly. For example, 50 village councils in Bastar district in Chhattisgarh banned the entry of 'non-Hindu missionaries'.[13] The critics view conversion to Christianity as more 'sinful' than conversion to Indic religious traditions. Conversion is the choice intrinsic to the freedom of religion.

Anti-conversion (ideological) discourses also contribute to a violation of freedom of religion. For some, conversion disrupts the family and community. Others find force or inducement in every conversion. They portray conversion to certain religions as fraudulent. A convert is perceived also as an enemy. Swami Vivekananda once said, 'Every man going out of the Hindu pale is not only a man less but an enemy the more'.[14] If people are taught conversion negatively, those who voluntarily embrace another faith and the members of the respective faith equally, face the fury of indoctrinated minds. It happens in the land which once provided shelters to the persecuted and the refugees of all religions. Anti-conversion discourses come from the unwarranted fear of the numerical decline of a particular religion and the loss of political power.[15] The anti-conversion outlook, on the pretext of forcible conversions fundamentally questions the freedom of religion enshrined in the Constitution. The freedom of religion and the issue of conversion need to be discussed in this context.

CONSTITUTION, FREEDOM OF RELIGION AND CONVERSION

The Constitution of India protects the citizens from religious discrimination (Articles 15 and 16)[16] and guarantees freedom of religion: to profess, practise, and propagate religion. Article 25 (1) of the Constitution says, 'Subject to public order, morality and health and to the other provisions of this Part, all persons are equally entitled to freedom of conscience and the right freely to profess, practice, and propagate religion.' Article 26 gives them the 'right to form and manage institutions for religious and charitable intents . . . and to manage its own affairs in the matter of religion. . . .'[17] Article 25 (1) protects the religious freedom of an individual provided it does not disturb 'public order, morality or health'. This article should also be read with Articles 14, 15, 16, and 19 (1) (a) (freedom of speech and expression).[18] 'Freedom of conscience' in Article 25, grants citizens the right to believe or not to believe in any religion or belief system.[19] According to Meera Kumari, freedom of conscience is 'the absolute inner freedom of the citizens'.[20] The 'right to profess' is understood in two senses: 'to belong to' and 'to declare' the faith. The 'right to practice' has tenetary and social dimensions. The former refers to the practice of rituals, the latter the social implications of what religion teaches.[21] The State interferes if they conflict with 'public order, morality or health'. It is observed that the right to practise 'confers on a person the right to practice 'religion' and not a right to practice his (independent) religious convictions'.[22]

The word 'propagate' was inserted in Article 25 (1) based on the recommendation of the Minorities sub-committee headed by M. Ruthnaswamy. The committee observed that certain religions, particularly Christianity, emphasize the 'propagation of faith' as a part of the practice of faith. It is evident in the debate on this provision in the Constituent Assembly. Purushottam Das Tandon (Uttar Pradesh) said, 'We congressmen deem it very improper to convert from one religion to another religion or to take part in such activities and we are not in favor of this. . . . But we have agreed to keep the word 'propagate' out of regard for our Christian friends'.[23] K.M. Munshi observed that '. . . I know, it was on this word that the Indian Christian community laid the greatest emphasis, not because they wanted to convert people aggressively, but because the word 'propagate' was a fundamental part of their tenet. Even if the word was not there, I am sure, under the freedom of speech which Constitution guarantees, it will be open to any religious community to persuade other people to join their faith. So long as religion is religion, conversion by the free exercise of the conscience has to be recognized'.[24] It is also argued that the inclusion of the word, 'propagate' is the outcome of Indian Christians' decision to relinquish special representation for minorities.[25]

Though Article 25 (1) does not restrict conversion, it does not grant the right to convert others by coercion.[26] In the case of Rev. Stanislaus *vs.* State of Madhya Pradesh (1977 1 SCC 677), Chief Justice A.N. Ray, ruled that 'what Article 25 (1) grants is not the right to convert another person to one's religion, but to transmit or spread one's religion by an exposition of its tenets'.[27] According to H.M. Seevai, a constitutional lawyer, '. . . Successful propagation of religion would result in conversion. . . .'[28] But conversion is 'not the right itself'.[29] For Christians (not all), propagation of faith is an important aspect of their religious life. The Constitutional provision of the 'propagation of religion' complements the biblical mandate of proclaiming the Gospel of Jesus Christ. Accordingly, Christians prioritize propagation over conversion which ought to be a conscious act of an individual. For many of them, neither proclamation nor conversion constitutes their religious life. They exercise freedom of religion in terms of practising the rituals associated with the faith. Freedom of religion is the right of every citizen. The protection of this right is the duty of every citizen and the State.

RELIGIOUS RIGHTS AND 'FREEDOM OF RELIGION' LAWS

Irrespective of the state or ruling party, all religious minorities have endured violations of their religious rights at one time or another, in one place or another. Moreover, some of this finds its way into the making of our laws. For example, Article 15 of the Constitution prohibits any kind of discrimination 'on grounds only of religion, race, caste, sex, place of birth, or any of them'.[30] However, the Presidential Order of 1950, as amended in 1990, states 'no person who professes a religion different from the Hindu, the Sikh or the Buddhist religion shall be deemed to be a member of a Scheduled Caste'.[31] It, therefore, bars Christians and Muslims of Scheduled Caste origin from taking advantage of the numerous social welfare programmes targeted at those who share their de facto caste status.[32] We are proud of Article 25 of the Constitution, which guarantees to all Indians 'freedom of conscience and the right freely to profess, practise, and propagate religion'.[33] However, the so-called 'Freedom of Religion' laws (the anti-conversion laws)[34] adopted by various states have curtailed religious freedom[35] and made conversion to another religion a cognizable and non-bailable offense. For instance, the Uttar Pradesh Prohibition of Unlawful Conversion of Religion Act, 2021 stipulates a punishment up to ten years in jail.[36] The Madhya Pradesh Freedom of Religion Act, 2021 required an individual to declare his/her religious conversion to the District Magistrate and obtain prior permission. However, in an interim order, the Madhya Pradesh High Court ruled this provision 'unconstitutional'. It observed that 'Article 25 has it implicit in it the ability to choose a faith'.[37] According to Faizan Mustafa, 'By insisting prior permission of public authorities for conversion, the freedom of religion laws promote the premise that women, SCs and STs are vulnerable, need protection and cannot take vital decisions in their life on their own. Thus, these laws perpetuate social hierarchies of a casteist and patriarchal society'.[38] Although its protection has played an important role in unifying the country, central and state governments are now leaders in the assault on that freedom.[39]

Proponents of these 'Freedom of Religion' laws argue that they are necessary to prevent forced conversions. This argument may sound plausible, but the reality is that such laws target minority religious communities, particularly the Christian community, whose message often proves attractive to members of the lower strata of society. Most criminal cases brought under these laws have been against Christians, though so far none of those charged have been convicted.[40] Often proper investigations are not conducted before charges are filed; instead, they are generally based on false allegations levelled by specific communal organizations. At this juncture, it is significant to note that Christianity is not alone in pursuing the mission and seeking conversions. Most religions, and all monotheistic religions, do the same.[41] The 'Freedom of Religion' laws are rarely, if ever, applied to adherents of any religion except Christianity and Islam.[42] Ironically, the advocates of anti-conversion laws support induced or forced re-conversions, popularly known as *ghar wapsi* (returning home). It refers to the religious homecoming of Christians and Muslims to Hinduism, their original home. For the supporters of *ghar wapsi,* it is not conversion but coming back to their ancestor's religion. On many occasions, force, molestation, and physical attacks happened when *ghar wapsi* was resisted.[43]

Dalits who become Christians lose all privileges associated with Scheduled Caste status. These include so-called 'reservation' benefits—access to government jobs, university positions, etc., set aside for members of Scheduled Castes and Scheduled Tribes[44] as well as the safeguards afforded by the Protection of Civil Rights Act of 1955; the Protection of Civil Rights Rules of 1977;[45] and the Scheduled Castes and Scheduled Tribes (Prevention of Atrocities) Act of 1989.[46] In this frustrating situation, it is important to underscore two fundamental points. First, Dalits are not allowed to change their religion without restriction, even though the Constitution guarantees them this right. Second, Christian and Muslim Dalits are discriminated against because they or their ancestors exercised this right at some point in the past. The bottom line is that Dalit Christians face extreme discrimination in the name of religion—indeed, ironically, in religious freedom. The restriction or abrogation of their fundamental legal rights through the enactment and enforcement of 'Freedom of Religion' laws that have, and are intended to have, precisely the opposite effect, a violation of the freedom of religion.

FREEDOM OF RELIGION AND HUMAN RIGHTS

Humans are born free, but unfortunately, they are bound to tradition, religion, culture, ideologies and class/caste mechanisms. People enjoy freedom at different levels. In the case of religious freedom, some enjoy restricted freedom if they do not follow a majoritarian/official religion in a state. Others in a secular state enjoy equal freedom (theoretically but 'not' fully practically) with co-citizens who belong to different religious traditions. Though it is defined contextually with legal/constitutional restrictions, the freedom of religion is a universally accepted human right. The Universal Declaration of Human Rights (Article 18) affirms that irrespective of state and context, the freedom of religion is an inherent human right. It says that 'Everyone has the right to freedom of thought, conscience, and religion: this right includes freedom to change his religion or belief, and freedom, either alone or in community with others and in public or private, to manifest his religion or belief in teaching, practice, worship, and observance'.[47] According to Article 25 (1) of the Indian Constitution, freedom of religion is a fundamental right of a citizen.[48] The freedom of religion is essential because '. . . a person's religious convictions are the result of his/her inner convictions', and 'it (freedom of religion) is essential to experience the other forms of freedom'.[49] Today, though not fully, our secular society is polarized in the name of religious identities. The religious polarization appears to be more disastrous than any division in India. It spews out the poison of intolerance which results in the discrimination of minorities and the violation of the freedom of religion. Any violation of freedom of religion is a violation of human rights. It questions the spirit of human freedom fundamentally. The State has a moral and legal responsibility to defend human rights.

FREEDOM OF RELIGION: A CHRISTIAN PERSPECTIVE

Like other religious communities, Indian Christians are content with the freedom of religion protected by the Constitution. However, the Christian view of freedom of religion comes from the Bible. For them, the Constitution and the Bible complement each other in the case of religious freedom. For Christians, the freedom of religion lies in the greatest commandment given by God recorded in Deuteronomy 6:5 and reiterated by Jesus in Mathew 22: 37.[50] This mandate requires the freedom of choice or freedom to practise religion according to his/her conviction. It may be interpreted as a 'human/fundamental right' today. According to Tertullian, 'It is only just and a privilege inherent in human nature that every person should be able to worship according to his own convictions; the religious practice of one person neither harms nor helps another. It is not part of religion to coerce religious practice, for it is by choice, not coercion that we should be led to religion'.[51] The Biblical God, who commanded the people of Israel to worship him, also instructed them not to mistreat and oppress a foreigner (probably a religious minority) in their land (Leviticus 19: 33-4, Deuteronomy 23: 7). Though on several times they failed to respect others' freedom of religion on the pretext of obeying the commands of their God (Deuteronomy 7), the Biblical God never ceases to be 'the defender of the vulnerable'[52] including the persecuted.

The Book of Exodus in the Bible portrays how God restored the rights of the people of Israel, who had experienced violation of basic human rights, particularly the right to worship their God. The Egyptian bondage curtailed their freedom of religion.[53] When the Israelites demanded their (religious) liberty, the Pharaoh responded by persecuting them with increased daily work. (Exodus Ch. 5). However, the divine intervention and subsequent liberation of the people of Israel underline that freedom of religion is as imperative as any other form of freedom for meaningful human existence. Jesus' act of cleansing the Temple (Mathew 21: 12-13), his respect for others' faith (e.g. dialogue with Samaritan woman, John 4), and his love commandment, 'Love your neighbor as yourself', also provide a base for the Christian view of the freedom of religion. Jesus' concern for human rights had both spiritual (freedom of religion) and physical components.[54]

The Church, the community of Jesus that derives energy from God, who commanded people to worship and defended the rights of the vulnerable, must strive to protect religious freedom. According to K.C. Abraham, the Church must internalize every human rights assertion as a divine endeavour.[55] It should lead her to take initiatives of awareness on the violations of religious freedom, express solidarity with the persecuted, initiate legal actions against the violators, participate in the activities of human rights movements, join with similar voices of liberty, etc. Though it is risky, the Christian faith demands the community to walk on the perilous path. Though the Christians of one tradition suppressed the freedom of another tradition within Christendom in the past[56] the recognition and protection of religious freedom must be intrinsic to the life of Christian communities (Daniel 3; Matthew 22: 39; 28: 19-20). For John Perkins, 'A separation of Church and rights (freedom of religion) is like the separation of faith and works, words and deeds, theology and sociology, theory and practice. There is no biblical basis for these separations'.[57] Therefore, religious freedom is 'the matter for the Church'.[58] The Biblical God works through human beings because 'God is an ethical God, not a magical God.'[59] It gives a theological framework to Christian participation in the protection of freedom of religion.

Of course, the mandate of worshipping God implies freedom of religion and one needs to resist any attempt at its violation. However, what is the Christian attitude if the offense survives resistance and constitutional and legal remedies? Historically, Christians have experienced violations of the freedom of religion worldwide, mainly where they were a minority. It continues in many countries. Christians define such violations as persecution. In other words, for them, theologically and biblically, persecution accompanies freedom of religion. This position is not to encourage a resistant agency to be silent in the time of the violation of rights but to resist with a realization that persecution is part of their faith affirmation: ritual and social praxis.

Biblical stories teach one that experience of the violation of the freedom of religion is often the inevitable destiny of those who follow the path of God. The prophets endured suffering because they stood for the faith, upheld moral values, and fearlessly proclaimed God's message to the people and the rulers. For instance, Jeremiah was beaten, chained, and imprisoned (Jeremiah 1: 8, 17, 5: 3, 18: 19, 20: 2, 20: 10, 37: 13-16, 38: 6, 40: 1). Amos was asked to be silent (Amos 2: 12, 7: 10, 12-13). Micaiah was slapped and ordered to be imprisoned (I Kings 22: 24). Elijah had to face a death threat from Queen Jezebel (I Kings 19: 1). Zechariah and Uriah were killed (2 Chron 24: 21, Jer 26: 20-3). Jesus endured rejection, mockery, threats, and death on the cross because he did not move away from His mission of proclaiming and practising the message of the Kingdom of God. It gave him a new image, 'suffering servant'.[60] John the Baptist was beheaded because he castigated Herod for his immoral relationship (Matthew. 14: 1-12). James, the brother of John, was killed by King Herod to please the Jews. He imprisoned Peter (Acts 12: 1-4) also. Paul was arrested, faced trial and imprisoned (Acts 24-8). These examples of victimized life prove that persecution happens when s/he lives out his/her faith and boldly participates in the work of God.

Biblically speaking, persecution and Christian life are inseparable. A Christian is called 'not only to believe in him but also to suffer for him' (Phil 1: 29). According to John Chrysostom

> This is our life, that is, the natural consequence of an apostolic way of life is to suffer countless evils. . . . So the apostolic life is purposely designed to suffer abuse, to suffer evils, to never have a respite, to never have a cessation of hostilities. And for however many are vigilant, they are not only not harmed by these events, but instead profit from them.[61]

Dietrich Bonhoeffer narrates the inseparability of discipleship and persecution beautifully, 'Discipleship involves suffering. When Christ calls a man (woman), he bids him (her) come and die'. It involves not only sacrificing personal comforts and aspirations but also experiencing suffering and shame at the hands of those who hate Jesus Christ. There is only one option left for the disciples in such a situation: forgive the sins of others as Jesus did on the cross. The passion of Christ provides the energy to forgive the tormentors. The persecuted share the fellowship of suffering from Christ on the cross (I Peter 4: 13; 2 Corinthians 1: 5).[62] The words of Sr. Meena, a nun raped during anti-Christian violence in Kandhamal, Odisha in 2008,[63] express the feeling of being partaken in the suffering of Jesus (Colossians 1: 24), 'Looking back, I feel that Jesus is not dead on the cross. He is alive on the Cross and is still suffering'. 'I feel happy that I got a chance to undergo the experience of being crucified'.[64] The experience of direct fellowship with Christ overcomes the pain of discrimination.

The Bible also teaches one that earthly persecution is compensated by heavenly reward (Matthew 5: 10-12, Acts 5: 41; 2 Cori 4: 17; I Peter 1: 6-9). According to John Calvin, Christians are persecuted because they live out the Gospel which resists the desires of the 'flesh' and continuously exposes its vices. It is, indeed, their destiny on earth. It does not mean that Christians should always be subjected to or long for persecution, but 'rest on the hope of future reward' if they are persecuted. Christ called his disciples to experience that hope in this world.[65] God suffers (participates in suffering) with His persecuted people (Acts 9: 4). The persecuted are the extended body of Jesus in whom God took human form. Since God participates in the suffering, the persecuted not only exhibit forgiveness but also experience the 'will-to-overcome' pain inflicted upon them. However, divine participation also calls for human solidarity (Christian solidarity) with the persecuted in times of rejection, humiliation, torture and death. For Christians, freedom of religion is a divinely ordained human right. It should be nurtured and protected for everyone. The experience of the violations of this right is also integral to the practice of religion.

PROPAGATION OF RELIGION

The issue of conversion is closely connected to the right to propagate religion. The 'propagation of faith' is one of the tenets of the Christian faith. It is based on the Great Commission of Jesus Christ, 'Go therefore and make disciples of all the nations, baptizing them in the name of the Father and of the Son and of the Holy Spirit, teaching them to observe all things that I have commanded you. . .' (Matthew 28: 19-20). The word used in Christian literature for 'the propagation of faith' is 'evangelism', which means 'to announce or proclaim the Good News or the Gospel of Jesus Christ'.[66] Some call it 'mission' or 'evangelization'. The Lausanne Covenant proclaims that 'To evangelize is to spread the gospel, that Jesus Christ died for our sins and was raised from the dead, according to the Scriptures. . .',[67] According to *Evangelii Nuntiandi*, evangelism means 'proclaiming Christ to those who do not know him, of preaching of catechesis, of conferring Baptism and other Sacraments'.[68] The Nazareth Manifesto (Luke 4: 18-19) gives further direction for the 'propagation of the faith'. It underlines that the proclamation of the Gospel should be accompanied by actions that respond to the broken realities of people. In line with Nazareth Manifesto, Leonardo Boff observes that evangelization should be 'saving the lives of poor'.[69] The ultimate goal of evangelism is to enable a person to live a dignified life with God given rights and privileges. For Christians, this life has an otherworldly import. The 'propagation of faith' is the duty of Christians but not the act of converting people to Christianity. Conversion is a voluntary response to the propagation of the faith.

CONVERSION: A CONSCIOUS ACT

Christianity came to India in AD 52, but it became a missionary religion with the arrival of the Portuguese. It began its missionary work in a religious context primarily conditioned by the Hindus who never encouraged conversion. Though missionaries worked during the British rule, the British 'authorities were never very sympathetic to them, and were never enthusiastic about conversion'.[70] Many natives indeed became Christians because of the work of foreign and indigenous missionaries. The majority of converts came from Dalit, Tribal and Other Backward Class (OBC) Communities. Apart from the religious quest, social reasons brought them closer to Christianity. Irrespective of denominations, missionaries have encountered the allegation of forcible conversion in the past. Christian priests and social workers continue to face it even today. But the testimonies of new converts prove the contention of forced conversion wrong.[71] Some strongly oppose conversion because they perceive that it impacts 'number game' in politics. They also look at the nation's identity through the lens of religion. For them, converts are 'denationalized'. 'Conversion' is a subversive activity of Christian missionaries.[72] But M.K. Gandhi observed that conversion is not denationalization.[73] The critics of conversion allege that Christians allure others by offering educational, medical and spiritual resources.[74] This accusation does not have any basis because converts, particularly Dalits, lose more privileges compared to the so-called 'Christian benefits.' It is a myth to believe that Christians are after conversion. Except for independent evangelists, pastors and organizations, mainline Churches do not directly involve in evangelistic activities. They limit their religious activities to official members.[75] However, Christians have a view on conversion.

The Constitution guarantees the freedom of religion in which voluntary conversion is implicitly allowed though it does not mention it. However, there are legal provisions that directly or indirectly discourage conversion. For example, according to the Hindu Marriage Act, conversion by a spouse to another religion (non-Indic religions) is one of the grounds for divorce. The Hindu

Adoptions and Maintenance Act, the Hindu Succession Act, etc., restrain Hindus from converting to other religions. Some state laws like the Gujrat 'Freedom of Religion Bill' requires citizens to obtain permission from the authorities in the event of conversion. It is not applicable if a Hindu converts to the Indic religion.[76] Dalits, who wish to convert to Christianity, would lose reservation benefits of Scheduled Caste status accorded by the Presidential Order of 1950 and special protection under the Scheduled Castes and Scheduled Tribes (Prevention of Atrocities) Act 1989. On the pretext of protecting Dalits from 'forcible conversion', the State laws have stipulated stringent procedures and penalties[77] to dissuade them from embracing non-Indic religions.

Conversion is not a new phenomenon in India. It happened among Hindu sects (intra-Hindu conversion), and between Indic religions. The Arya Samaj[78] promoted reconversion or *shuddhi karan* (purification). Conversion to Christianity is not always 'from above' as alleged by the Hindutva ideologues. History proves that it is a 'bottom-up' movement too. The converts had 'agency' to decide their faith in a particular social context.[79] For example, many Dalit and backward communities embraced Christianity to come out of their disempowered social condition because of the caste system. According to J.W. Gladstone, the conversion of low castes '. . . cannot be narrowed down as an expression of their desire for social advancement. This was a sign of forsaking a religion which did not offer spiritual satisfaction, and accepting a new religion in which they found a new life, new meaning, and satisfaction.'[80] Even if it is for social advancement, as C.F. Andrews noted about the material motive behind conversion, 'yet this desire had a good and noble side, and was not without spiritual value'.[81] John W. Grant observes that conversion for social advancement is undoubtedly Christian because the New Testament categorically endorses the empowerment of the poor, the downtrodden in society.[82]

'Conversion' is not a biblical term. It has become an ideologically loaded word with multi-dimensional implications. The Bible talks about repentance and confession of faith in Jesus as Lord and Saviour as the initial experience of a Christian. It may lead to what one today calls 'religious' or 'institutional' conversion. The Bible gives the theological meaning of 'conversion' rather than the sociological and political sensing of the term. Therefore, for Christians, conversion is a 'theological' rather than a 'socio-political' category. They cannot look at conversion through the eyes of political equations.[83] Biblically, 'conversion' is a conscious act. The Bible neither encourages forcible conversion nor justifies any allurement for it (Romans 10: 9; Matthew 10: 5-16, 28: 16-20; Luke 10: 1-11). It is purely an individual experience with God through Jesus Christ. Jesus never promoted 'conversion' from one religion to another but repentance and transformation of life. He encouraged people to experience God-consciousness. The proclamation of the Gospel is an open invitation into the consciousness of Jesus Christ.[84] Christians believe that Jesus is the embodiment of God-consciousness. Jesus invited everyone into the Kingdom of God. However, this fact has institutionalized into a religion. Jesus always respected an individual's decision to follow or not follow him (Matthew 19: 16-22; John 1: 43-51, 6: 41-71, 7: 5). Therefore, any 'forcible' or so-called 'fraudulent' conversion is not biblical but sinful.

There is a strong view that Christians understand the practice and propagation of faith (mission) only in terms of conversion. The fact is that they have a holistic understanding of the practice of faith. According to Geevarghese Mar Osthathios, 'mission is the penetration of love, justice, and holiness into the fabric of the individual and the society'.[85] Its scope is not limited to the propagation of the faith. It shares the life of God with others.[86] For him, 'conversion is a matter of religious freedom and not necessarily the primary aim of mission or aid'.[87] The strength of Christianity is not the quantity of the baptized but the number of disciples (quality). A baptized is not necessarily a disciple who follows the footprints of Jesus. Conversion and compulsion are not compatible with the Christian faith. Mar Osthathios is of the view that conversion should happen by sharing the love of Jesus with others. There is no place for compulsion in the love of Jesus. The great commission of Jesus does not insist on numerical strength[88] but on discipleship. Samuel Amirtham points out that the practice and propagation of the Gospel should enable people to live dignified life.[89] In other words, humanization is the ultimate goal of the Christian mission because, as M.M. Thomas observed, 'Humanization is inherent in the message of salvation in Christ'.[90] For many Christians, conversion is not the intention of the proclamation of the Gospel. Paulose Mar Paulose insists that the proclamation of the Gospel should respond to the hopes and aspirations of the people.[91]

Christians believe that the propagation of the faith is integral to their religious life. Practically, many of them do not follow this theological position. The proclamation of the faith may or may not facilitate the so-called conversion. But it is not the criterion to measure the importance of the practice and proclamation of faith. 'Religion' demands conversion; the Gospel of Jesus facilitates liberation and transformation.

This chapter concludes that freedom of religion, according to Christians, is a biblical and constitutional right. The Bible informs that religious freedom survives its violation. Suffering is part of the practice, profession and propagation of the faith. One of the contentious issues in freedom of religion in India is conversion. Christians are at the receiving end of the allegation of converting others by 'force' 'allurement' or 'fraudulent ways'. Their religious and humanitarian activities get the tag of 'conversion' exercises. This negative profiling disturbs the community. Though the freedom of religion is guaranteed by the Constitution, there are legal restrictions that discourage conversion. The freedom of religion cannot nullify conversion. The paradox is that conversion to Indic religions does not become a 'political' or 'religious' issue. Christians believe that conversion is a conscious act of an individual. It is a person's choice to affirm a particular faith. Christians know that they have no constitutional right or biblical mandate to convert another person. However, they emphasize the importance of the propagation of the Gospel but without confrontation. The majority of them do not involve in the act of propagating the faith personally or collectively. For them, religion is personal, and restricted to personal and community ethics and rituals. The Biblical faith does not support forcible conversion. It respects an individual's decision in the case of religious choice. Everyone has religious freedom. While upholding their freedom, Christians should protect others' freedom and stand with the victims of religious discrimination. The State should be neutral in the treatment of religions and proactive in protecting the rights, but should take the side of the victims.

NOTES

1. Ishita Mishra, 'Population Imbalance due to Infiltration and Conversion: RSS', *The Hindu* (New Delhi), 20 October 2022, https://www.thehindu.com/news/national/population-policy-should-be-made-applicable-to-all-in-the-country-rss/article66031659.ece, accessed on 6 November 2022.
2. Anilesh S. Mahajan and Sunil Menon, 'The Pastors of Punjab', *India Today*, vol. 47, no. 46 (14 November 2022): 46-59 at 46.
3. Shibu Thomas, 'Persecution and Relief', *Voice of the Christians,* vol. 1, no. 12 (October, 2018): 7-23; 'UP and Tamil Nadu top attacks on Christians. . .', *National Herald,* 31st October 2019, https://www.nationalheraldindia. com/india/up-and-tamil-nadu-top-attacks-on-christians-247-attacks-reported-up-to-september accessed 29 March 2021; 'Nuns accused of conversion, forced to get off train Jhansi', *The Hindu* (Lucknow), 24 March 2021, https://www.thehindu.com/news/national/other-states/nuns-accused-of-conversion-forced-to-get-off-train-in-jhansi/article34153286. ece accessed 29 March 2021, Ziya us Salam, 'Christians at Receiving End', *Frontline*, vol. 39, no. 1 (1-14 January 2022): 56-8 at 56 & MP: Pastor among seven held for pressuring tribal man to change religion', *The Print,* 25 January 2023, https://theprint.in/india/mp-pastor-among-seven-held-for-pressuring-tribal-man-to-change-religion/1335283/, accessed on 5 February 2023.
4. Brinda Karat, 'Chhattisgarh's area of darkness', *The Indian Express* (Pune, 11 February 2023), 11.
5. Christophe Jaffrelot and Philip Varghese, 'A Continuing Exclusion', *The Indian Express* (Pune, 26 April 2022), 9.
6. Ziya us Salam, 'Christians at Receiving End', op. cit., 57.
7. Ziya us Salam, 'Christians as Target', *Frontline* (28 August 2020): 58-9 at 58.
8. Ziya us Salam, 'Christians at Receiving End', op. cit., 57.
9. 'Term Mob Lynching Comes from Bible, says Mohan Bhagwat', *India Today,* 8 October 2019, https://www.indiatoday.in/india/story/lynchings-

being-used-to-defame-india-hindus-rss-chief-mohan-bhagwat-1607257-2019-10-08 accessed 30 March 2021.

10. Lynching: Christian Body Fumes over RSS Chief's Remark', *Outlook*, 13 October 2019, https://www.outlookindia.com/newsscroll/lynching-christian-body-fumes-over-rss-chiefs-remark/1639492 accessed on 31 March 2021.
11. Yashwant Dhote, 'Streak of Violence', *Outlook* (28 July 2014), 14.
12. *Sunday Times of India* (23 February 2014, New Delhi), 26.
13. Yashwant Dhote, 'Streak of Violence', *Outlook* (28 July 2014), 12.
14. Arun Shourie, *Harvesting Our Souls* (New Delhi: ASA Publications, 2000), 1-2.
15. E.V. Mathew, 'Secular State in India', in *Secularism: Collection of Articles,* compiled by Vincent Rajkumar (Bangalore: CISRS, 2018), 95.
16. *The Constitution of India* (New Delhi: Ministry of Law and Justice, Government of India, 2011), 6-7.
17. *The Constitution of India* (Delhi: Ministry of Law and Justice, Government of India, 1989), 12.
18. M.T. Cherian, *Hindutva Agenda and Minority Rights: A Christian* Response (Bangalore: Centre for Contemporary Christianity, 2007), 146-7.
19. Sunita Gangwal, *Minorities in India: A Study in Communal Process and Individual Rights* (Jaipur: Arihant, 1995), 118.
20. Meera Kumari, *Religious Freedom* (New Delhi: Capital Publishing House, 1990), 33.
21. Gangwal, *Minorities in India,* op. cit., 110-11.
22. Ibid., 120.
23. Ibid., 129.
24. A.G. Noorani, 'Conversion to Hindu Raj', *Frontline* (9 January 2015), 123.
25. Rowena Robinson, 'Introduction', in *Minority Studies,* ed. Rowena Robinson (New Delhi: Oxford University Press, 2013), 10.
26. Gangwal, *Minorities in India,* op. cit., 131.
27. Noorani, 'Conversion to Hindu Raj', op. cit., 123.
28. Ibid.
29. Gangwal, *Minorities in India,* op. cit., 138.
30. *The Constitution of India,* 7.
31. Quoted in Franklin Caesar Thomas, 'Why SC status for Dalit Christians, Muslims should not be linked to religion', *The Federal* (15 August 2020), https://thefederal.com/opinion/why-sc-status-for-dalit-christians-muslims-should-not-be-linked-to-religion/, accessed on 5 April 2021.

32. Iqtidar Karamat Cheema, *Constitutional and Legal Challenges Faced by Religious Minorities in India* (Washington, D.C.: United States Commission on International Religious Freedom, 2017), 9.
33. *The Constitution of India,* 12.
34. The anti-conversion laws existed in princely states such as Raigarh, Bikaner, Kota, Jodhpur, Surguja, Patna, Udaipur and Kalahandi. Faizan Mustafa, 'Who's afraid of conversion?' *The Indian Express* (Pune, 18 November 2022), 11.
35. Tariq Ahmad, 'State anti-Conversion Laws in India', Library of Congress, October 2018, https://www.loc.gov/law/help/anti-conversion-laws/india.php#:~:text=Summary,Pradesh%2C%20Jharkhand%2C%20and%20Uttarakhand. Accessed on 5 April 2021 & Apurva Vishwanath, '3 states, 3 anti-conversion laws: What's similar, what's different', *The Indian Express* (New Delhi), 3 January 2021, https://indianexpress.com/article/explained/religion-conversion-bill-bjp-7129285/, accessed on 6 April 2021.
36. Raksha Kumar, 'Religious Conversion in Punjab: Not All Churchgoers are Christian and That Makes Majority Sikhs Nervous', *article 14.com*, 6 September 2022, https://article-14.com/post/religious-conversion-in-punjab-not-all-churchgoers-are-christian-that-makes-majority-sikhs-nervous-6316b7212f2d7, accessed on 19 November 2022.
37. Iram Siddique, 'HC: MP Law requirement on declaration before conversion is illegal', *The Indian Express* (Pune, 19 November 2022), 3 & 4.
38. Mustafa, 'Who's afraid of conversion?' op. cit., 11.
39. James Massey, *Minorities, and Religious Freedom in a Democracy* (New Delhi: Manohar, 2003), 114.
40. Tariq Ahmad, 'State anti-Conversion Laws in India', op. cit.
41. Rodney Stark, *One True God: Historical Consequences of Monotheism* (Princeton, N.J.: Princeton University Press, 2001).
42. Kashif Kakvi, 'Madhya Pradesh: Is Anti-Conversion Law being used to Target Muslim , Christian Youth?', *News Click,* 20 March 2021, https://www.newsclick.in/madhya-pradesh-anti-conversion-law-being-used-target-muslim-christian-youth, accessed on 6 April 2021.
43. Abhik Bhattacharya, 'Forced Gharwapsi, Molestation and Series of Attacks: Hundreds of Christian Adivasis Leave Their Villages in Chhattisgarh', *Outlook,* 21 December 2022, https://www.outlookindia.com/national/forced-gharwapsi-molestation-and-series-of-attacks-hundreds-of-christian-adivasis-leave-their-villages-in-chhattisgarh-news-246858, accessed on 5 February 2023.

44. Scott Grinsell, 'Caste and the Problem of Social Reform in Indian Equity Law', *Yale Journal of International Law* 35, no. 1 (2010): 199-236; Cynthia Stephen, 'The Theory of Reservations in India from the 1800s to the 1950s', *Integral Liberation* 10, no. 2 (June 2006): 17-25; James Massey, 'Dalits and Human Rights', *Religion and Society* 49, 2-3 (June-September 2004): 4-5; S.R. Maheshwari, 'Reservation Policy in India: Theory and Practice', *Indian Journal of Public Administration* 43, no. 3 (July 1997): 662-79.
45. http://socialjustice.nic.in/writereaddata/UploadFile/arpcr08.pdf, accessed on 6 April 2021.
46. http://socialjustice.nic.in/writereaddata/UploadFile/The%20 Scheduled% 20Castes%20and%20Scheduled%20Tribes.pdf, accessed on 6 April 2021.
47. 'Universal Declaration of Human Rights', in M.A. Thomas, *The Struggle for Human Rights* (Bangalore: Asian Trading Corportion, 1992), 112.
48. *The Constitution of India* (Ministry of Law and Justice, Government of India, 1989), 12.
49. S. Robertson, *Freedom of Religion: A Human Rights Issue* (Bangalore: Board of Theological Education, Senate of Serampore College/South Asia Theological Research Institute, 2007), 244 & 245.
50. 'You shall love the LORD your God with all your heart, with all your soul, and will all your mind' (Deut. 6: 5). It points to a person's faith and obedience to God. Earl S. Kalland, 'Deuteronomy', *The Expositor's Bible Commentary,* vol. 3 (Grand Rapids, Michigan: Zondervan Publishing House, 1992), 64.
51. Robert Louis Wilken, *Liberty in the Things of God: The Christian Origins of Religious Freedom* (New Haven and London: Yale University Press, 2019), 1. https://books.google.co.in/books/about Liberty_in_the_Things_ of_ God.html?id=2ik_vAEACAAJ&redir_esc=y accessed on 5 April 2021.
52. K.C. Abraham, *Transforming Vision* (Tiruvalla: Christava Sahitya Samithi, 2006), 129.
53. M. Stephen, *Human Rights: Concepts and Perspectives* (New Delhi: Concept Publishing Company, 2002), 40.
54. J. Russell Chandran, *Christian Ethics* (Delhi: ISPCK, 2002), 137.
55. K.C. Abraham, *Transforming Vision*, 132.
56. Robert Louis Wilken, *Liberty in the Things of God: The Christian Origins of Religious Freedom* 1-2, 83-9, 101 & 109.
57. Shimreingam Shimray, 'Tribal Theology and Human Rights', in *Tribal Theology: A Reader*, ed. Shimreingam Shimray (Jorhat: Eastern Theological College, 2003), 159.

58. Robert A. Evans and Alice Frazer Evans, *Human Rights: A Dialogue between the First and Third Worlds* (Maryknoll: Orbis Books, 1983), 164.
59. Robert A. Evans and Alice Frazer Evans, *Human Rights: A Dialogue between the First and Third Worlds*, 197.
60. Alan J. Delotavo, 'Images of Christ in Filipino Culture and Atonement Experiences', *Asia Journal of Theology*, vol. 15, no. 1 (April 2001): 143-4.
61. Christopher A. Hall, *John Chrysostom's 'On Providence': A Translation and Theological Interpretation* (Ann Arbor, Mich.: University Microfilms International, 1991), 361, quoted in Christopher A. Hall, *Reading Scripture with the Church Fathers* (Downers Grove, Illinois: Inter-Varsity Press Academic, 1998), 99-100.
62. Dietrich Bonhoeffer, *The Cost of Discipleship* (New York: The Macmillan Company, revd. and enlgd. edn., 1966), 99-101.
63. During the anti-Christian violence in 2007 Christmas and August 2008, according to the Odisha government, 38 Christians lost their lives, while Christian workers compiled a list of over 90 Christians who sacrificed their lives.Cf. Anto Akkara, *Shining Faith in Kandhamal* (Bangalore: Asian Theological Corporations, revd. edn., 2010), 31.
64. Akkara, *Shining Faith in Kandhamal*, op. cit., 67 & 69.
65. John Calvin, *Commentary on a Harmony of the Evangelists-Mathew, Mark and Luke* (Michigan: Baker Book House, 1989 rpt.), 265-6.
66. Prakash Yesudian, *Fishers of Men* (Chennai: Ravi Zacharias International Ministries Life Focus Society, 2001), 16.
67. https://www.lausanne.org/content/covenant/lausanne-covenant accessed on 5 May 2018.
68. http://w2.vatican.va/content/paul-vi/en/apost_exhortations/documents/hf_p-vi_exh_19751208_evangelii-nuntiandi.html accessed on 8 May 2018.
69. Leonardo Boff, *Good News to the Poor* (New York: Orbis books, 1992), 36.
70. Nirad C. Chaudhuri, *The Continent of Circe* (London: Chatto & Windus, 1967), 272.
71. Mahajan and Menon, 'The Pastors of Punjab', op. cit., 46-9.
72. Robinson, 'Introduction', in *Minority Studies*, op. cit., 33 & 40.
73. M.K. Kuriakose, *History of Christianity in India: Source Materials* (Madras: Christian Literature Society, 1982), 332.
74. Chad M. Bauman and Richard F. Young, 'Minorities and the Politics of Conversion with Special Attention to Indian Christianity', in *Minority Studies*, 191.

75. Ibid., 192.
76. Robinson, 'Introduction', op. cit., 11-12.
77. Laura Dudley, 'Scheduled Castes, Christians and Muslims: The Politics of Macro-Majorities and Micro-Minorities', in *Minority Studies,* 111.
78. One of the reform movements in Hinduism attempted to bring Christian converts back into Hinduism. They used to conduct *shuddhi karan,* a ritual for those who returned to their old faith.
79. Bauman and Young, 'Minorities and the Politics of Conversion with Special Attention to Indian Christianity', op. cit., 186.
80. J.W. Gladstone, *Protestant Christianity and People's Movements in Kerala* (Trivandrum: The Seminary Publications, Kerala United Theological Seminary, 1984), 97.
81. C.F. Andrews, *Handbook of English Church Expansion North India* (London: A.R. Mowbray & Co. Ltd., 1908), 38-9.
82. John W. Grant, *God's People in India* (Madras: CLS, 1960), 8.
83. Joseph Marianus Kujur, 'Christian and Tribal: The Dynamics of Scheduled Tribe Status in the Field', in *Minority Studies,* 161.
84. John Martin Sahajananda, *Mission without Conversion* (Delhi: Indian Society for Promoting Christian Knowledge, 2013), 20 & 22.
85. Geevarghese Mar Osthathios, *Theology of Classless Society* (Thiruvalla: CSS, 2004, 2nd Impression), 114.
86. Geevarghese Mar Osthathios, *Sharing God and a Sharing World* (Delhi: ISPCK & Christava Sahitya Samithi, 1995), 52.
87. Geevarghese Mar Osthathios, *Sharing God and a Sharing World,* op. cit., 97.
88. Geevarghese Mar Osthathios, *God of Agape Leads Us to Justice and Peace* (Thiruvalla: CSS, 2013), 29.
89. Israel Selvanayagam, *Samuel Amirtham's Living Theology* (Bangalore: BTESSC/SATHRI, 2007), 443.
90. M.M. Thomas, *Salvation and Humanization* (Madras: The Christian Literature Society, 1971), 10.
91. Paulose Mar Paulose, *Spirituality for Struggle* (Thiruvalla: Christava Sahitya Samithi, 1999), 28.

CHAPTER 4

Christians and Minority Rights

Every society has minorities. The defining factors of minorities vary from context to context. Generally, socio-cultural and religious conditions determine the minority status of a community. In India, minorities are identified and officially notified in terms of religion and language. However, minorities are popularly defined as a religious category. In today's world, the protection of minorities is one of the major concerns of democratic societies. Unlike other countries, minorities in India have been granted special rights by the Constitution. They give much importance to those rights because of the protection and privilege inherent in them. Majority and minority communities perceive minority rights differently. Some have a sympathetic view of minority rights while others find problems with them. Christians understand minority rights within the framework of the Constitution and the Christian faith. This chapter looks at minority rights from a Christian perspective. To put across a perspectival position, the chapter also narrates some of the major concerns of minorities, constitutional provision of minority rights, current welfare schemes for minorities, etc.

MINORITY CONCERNS

The Indian Census of 2011 found that Hindus constituted 79.8 per cent of the total population, Muslims 14.2 per cent, Christians 2.3 per cent and Sikhs 1.7 per cent. Smaller slices of India's demographic pie went to the Jains, the Buddhists, and other religious communities.[1] This underscores the diversity of Indian society. Though Hindus, constituting the vast majority of the population, are socially and politically dominant nationwide, the nation is not homogenous in tradition and culture. Each of its smaller religious communities is socially and politically dominant somewhere.

While acknowledging the beauty of this religious and ethnic diversity, one cannot evade its inherent problems, particularly the communal polarization and consequent violence it makes possible. A degree of conflict is natural and inevitable in such a society; it may arise over issues related to ethnic and religious identity, government policies, perceived inequities in the sharing of resources and opportunities, etc.[2] But harmonious life in a pluralist society depends on the resistance to conflict offered by good governance and an informed, tolerant citizenry. The Constitution has explicit provisions for protecting minorities and their institutions, yet they are often targeted by other communities and prevented from exercising their rights.

For example, members of minority communities, especially Christians, are responsible for the direction of many Indian educational institutions. These provide access to quality education for all, irrespective of religious affiliation.[3] The Constitution grants religious minorities this right explicitly: 'All minorities, whether based on religion or language, shall have the right to establish and administer educational institutions of their choice' (Article 30 [1]).[4] However, members of minority communities involved in education often face a great deal of government interference.[5] This is one of the most prominent problems minorities face today. Instead of helping and encouraging them to develop the education sector, government bureaucrats impose unnecessary employment rules and other regulations that leave minority educators anxious and distracts them from undertaking new initiatives.[6] Moreover, communally minded officials purposely tarnish the reputations of minority led schools.[7] Many institutions are targeted to help private individuals who run educational institutions.

Another problem facing minorities, particularly Christians, is encroachment on their property by local landlords and government officials. In many places where members of minority communities own prime commercial real estate, business people and landlords will try to intimidate them into selling it, perhaps threatening to drag them into court, hoping to get the land at a low price. There are cases of encroachment on Christian graveyards and properties controlled by churches and organizations that hold the right to land donated for religious purposes.[8] Such cases of unlawful expropriation would not be possible without local politicians' indirect and even direct support for the malefactors. This is in spite of the guarantee of religious minorities' right by the constitution 'to own and acquire movable and immovable property; and to administer such property in accordance with law'.[9] It is unfortunate that some minority community leaders, particularly those with responsibility for minority properties, choose to betray their communities and work on behalf of outsiders seeking control of the land. They seek administrative and ecclesiastical positions to amass wealth by selling or leasing the property.

The central and state governments have welfare programmes for the social, economic and educational advancement of various communities. However, minority communities have only limited access to these programmes and the funds they control. On the one hand, specific development and welfare programmes for minorities are fewer; on the other, there always exists confusion regarding the inclusion of minorities in many welfare programmes. The National Minorities Development and Finance Corporation (NMDFC) was established specifically to foster the economic development of minority communities, but often its benefits do not reach them.[10] The non-corporation of state governments makes minorities deprived of the benefits of NMDFC. The procedure involved to get the benefits also keep the minorities, the majority of them are poor, away from such institution.[11] The ideology of the ruling party also plays a major role in implementing welfare programmes for minorities. The communal minded ruling dispensation may not give much attention to the empowerment of religious minorities. Traditional politicians even describe minority welfare programmes as 'minority appeasement'.[12]

In 1992 an Act of Parliament established the National Commission for Minorities (NCM) to 'evaluate the progress of the development of minorities under the Union and States' and 'monitor the working of the safeguards provided in the Constitution and in laws enacted by Parliament and the State Legislatures.'[13] Individual states were mandated to establish their minority commissions. However, most of the latter are moribund and even the NCM has often been reduced to a political tool. There are two main reasons for this situation. Firstly, the majority of the state governments show less interest to form commissions with full membership. The appointment of members is political most of the time. Second, state minority commissions do not get sufficient funds to carry out their responsibilities. Except for NCM, state minority commissions don't have a statutory status. It affects the functioning of state minority commissions. The work of minority commissions should be considered a part of the social justice enforcement mechanism. The success of state minority commissions also depends on the political outlook of the state government. If the state is ruled by a communal party, then the formation of the state minority commission gets deferred indefinitely. The formation of minority commissions can create a sense of protection among minorities. James Massey stresses that NCM 'has to represent the people to the government, not government to the people if it [is] to fulfil the statutory role given to it [by] the Act of 1992'.[14] Above all, it must be a defender of minority rights.

Violent communal conflict is a major problem for all of India's minority communities. Most victims of sectarian violence are members of minority communities.[15] In India, communal violence happened during the regime of the political parties of different ideological persuasions. After any such incident, the government often appoints a judicial commission to examine the situation, propose ways of preventing future conflict, and recommend legal action. However, too often, such recommendations are not implemented.[16] One problem is that the state governments may lack the political will if the culprits identified belong to the majority community. Yet failure to do this encourages the criminal elements in society.[17] Only a state with a strong political will and an equally strong commitment to the rights of minorities can prevent such violence. Apart from the above mentioned common concerns of minority communities, Christians, in the recent past, experienced physical assaults, the vandalism of their houses, schools and places of worship, forceful closedown of churches, and the arrests of the Christian priests and community workers on the grounds of false allegations of inducing conversions.[18] Minority rights should be understood in this larger context.

CONSTITUTION AND MINORITY RIGHTS

The preamble to the Constitution of India says that India is a 'sovereign socialist secular democratic republic'. This identity reflects in the fundamental rights and other legal entitlements ensured in the Constitution. The Constitution guarantees justice, liberty and equality to all citizens and promotes fraternity among them. It promises to protect the dignity of every citizen irrespective of caste, creed, class and ethnicity.[19] This liberating and egalitarian framework of the Constitution protects the rights of all sections of the citizenry and aims to empower them in all aspects of their lives. The beauty of the Indian Constitution is its preferential treatment towards minorities (religious and linguistic)[20] and socially marginalized communities. For religious minorities, apart from certain specific minority privileges (Article 30), Article 15 of the Constitution emphatically denounces any form of discrimination based on religion in the social life of citizens.[21] It gives them a guarantee that they have equal access to shared resources of the nation. Article 25 allows the citizenry, including minorities, 'subject to public order, morality and health . . . to profess, practice and propagate religion' of his or her choice. Article 26 gives them the 'right to form and manage institutions for religious and charitable intents . . . and to manage its own affairs in the matter of religion. . .'.[22] The above mentioned articles recognize their freedom of conscience and management of their religion. Article 29 guarantees them the right to conserve their distinct culture, language and script and education in public institutions. Article 30 gives special protection to minorities by granting them 'the right to establish and administer educational institutions of their own choice'. It also stipulates the condition clearly that if the state acquires the property of the institution 'established and managed by a minority', the state should not discriminate against a minority institution in granting aid.[23] For Christians, this right is important for protecting their faith and culture in a pluralistic society. The State is the defender of the rights of minorities. It is the responsibility of the state to curtail any violation of these rights.

The Constitution establishes the importance of the protection of minorities very clearly and prevents possible majoritarian dominance over a minority. The protection of cultural, linguistic and educational interests of minorities is 'unparalleled in the constitutions of the world.'[24] Minority rights legally protect minorities from the 'majoritarian politics that seemingly pushes them into the periphery' today.[25] By guaranteeing fundamental rights, particularly minority rights, the Constitution allays the fear of minorities in a 'majoritarian' multi-religious social context and facilitates their empowerment and participation in national life. The purpose of minority rights is not to perpetuate 'minority-consciousness' among minorities but to overcome their social disabilities owing to majority-minority profiling.

MINORITY RIGHTS: PROTECTION AND PROBLEM

People look at minority rights positively and negatively. While some try to argue that minority rights are problematic in a secular state, others including minorities emphasize the protective potential of minority rights. The current socio-political atmosphere proves that the framers of the Constitution were right in their approach to foresee the future of minorities in the country and include minority rights in the Constitution. The Partition of India and its consequent religious polarization, the fear of religious minorities, the importance of religion and culture in the identity of minorities, the commitment and loyalty of minorities to the nation, etc., influenced them to ensure special rights for minorities.[26] They viewed minority rights as a medium to protect minorities and bring them up on an equal basis with other communities. They knew that the growth of the nation depends on the safety and progress of minorities also.[27] For minorities, minority rights protect their identity, culture and faith. It also gives them a 'sense of security and a feeling of confidence'[28] in a majoritarian politicized religious context. They are aware that minority rights are 'subject to regulations, but not extinction' as Justice Mukherjee construed.[29] In a democratic society where number matters for power, minorities may not have access to the corridors of power. In such a situation, minority rights not only empower them to claim their space but also call for those in power to even out the unequal space. However, for some, the protective nature of minority rights, particularly Article 30 violates the principle of equality in the Constitution.[30] They even argue that 'minority rights are a form of pandering to or pampering the minorities'.[31] These arguments do not hold water in the case of minorities in India. Their survival does not depend exclusively on minority rights. There were voices, particularly from Christian intellectuals, for 'the protection of human rights rather than minority rights'.[32] Minorities are not 'pampered' citizens who would misuse their rights at 'the cost of national integrity, sovereignty and unity'.[33] Due to historical and contextual reasons, minority rights complement the protection they enjoy along with co-citizens.

The fear of the critics of minority rights has historical antecedents. The introduction of separate electorates and reserved seats for different religious communities and depressed classes by the British to 'divide and rule' Indians[34] might be haunting the critics even today. The partition must have intensified their thought of possible internal fault lines because of minority rights. They evaluate minority rights in the light of separate electorates and argue that minority rights divide the citizens and obstruct the integration of minorities. On the pretext of secularism, without evaluating the historical reasons, they criticize minority rights as a violation of equality. For religious nationalists, minorities like Christians are an 'internal threat'.[35] They reject the constitutional provision of minority rights outright and stigmatize minorities. They consider minority rights a 'problem' because it may contribute to sub-nationalism. Some would interpret minority welfare measures in line with minority rights as 'minority appeasement' or 'vote-bank politics'.[36] Unfortunately, 'Secularism has become synonymous with being pro-minority. And anything pro-minority is seen as anti-Hindu today.'[37] According to Rajeev Bhargava, minority rights do not violate secular values. The pluralistic composition of Indian society and its history of intercommunity conflicts requires special rights for minorities. This is one of the distinctive features of Indian secularism. Minority rights envisage 'reasonable communitarianism' for the protection and empowerment of minorities.[38] They do not pose any threat to the nation but offer natural justice to the minorities having distinct religious and linguistic identities.

MINORITY WELFARE AND DEMAND FOR MINORITY STATUS

There are six religious communities-Muslims, Christians, Sikhs, Buddhists, Zoroastrians and Jains—officially notified as minority communities in India. The Constitution guarantees them protection by granting special rights. Apart from constitutional safeguards through minority rights, there are statutory and welfare programmes/mechanisms to protect the rights of minorities and address their grievances. National Commission for Minorities is a statutory body that works for the development of minorities and monitors the working of constitutional and legal safeguards for minorities and helps Central and State governments in addressing the issues of minorities, particularly their holistic development.[39] The National Minorities Development and Finance Corporation provides financial support to minorities for 'self-employment/ generation activities'.[40] Ministry of Minority Affairs was created 'to ensure a more focused approach towards issues relating to minorities. It monitors and implements various schemes and programmes for minority education empowerment (Scholarship Schemes), economic empowerment (PM VIKAS), infrastructure development (PMJVK), special needs, support to minority institutions, etc.[41] There are also state-specific schemes for minority empowerment.[42] However, minorities become anxious when the government discontinues any scholarship or scheme for their welfare. For example, Central Government discontinued Maulana Azad National Fellowship (MANF) because it, according to the Minority Affairs Minister, 'overlaps with other fellowship schemes'.[43] For Christians, any scheme/programme for empowering minorities and other weaker sections of society has the imprint of a life-affirming God. Divine care for minorities comes through such initiatives. They also believe that the State is a divine gift. It is an instrument to accomplish the divine purpose of protecting individuals and communities.[44] Therefore, while concerned about the welfare of minorities, the State should also be proactive to defending their rights in instances of infringement.

The Constitution recognizes religious and linguistic minorities. The identification of religious minorities is based on the national population. Recently, a petition[45] has reached the Supreme Court of India to declare Hindus as a minority community in Jammu & Kashmir, Lakshadweep, Mizoram, Nagaland, Meghalaya, Arunachal Pradesh, Manipur and Punjab. According to the petitioner, Hindus are a minority in these states/union territories. The Supreme Court directed the petitioner to approach the National Commission for Minorities (NCM). The main argument in the petition is that minority status should be decided on the basis of the state population. This is in line with the Supreme Court decision in the TMA Pai case (2002) that religious and linguistic minorities should be identified at the state level for the purpose of Article 30. While seeking time from the Supreme Court to submit its view regarding the minority status of Hindus, the Central Government said '. . . the matter is sensitive in nature and will have far reaching ramifications. . .'.[46] Though the decision on this issue involves judicial, legislative, and executive processes, if Hindus are a minority in a particular state, they should be considered as minority community and give minority privileges. It reminds one that 'We are all minorities in India, given our divisions of language, region, caste and cultural practices.'[47] The reality of minorities talks not just about 'number' but about dignity, recognition and social justice.

A CHRISTIAN PERSPECTIVE ON MINORITY RIGHTS

Minority Existence

The Bible tells the stories of the existence of minorities. For example, the people of Israel (Jews), God's chosen people in the Bible, experienced a 'minority condition' in Egypt.[48] Unlike minorities in India, they lived without social, cultural or religious rights. The Egyptians exploited their labour and restricted their freedom including religious liberty. The Pharaoh even ordered to kill their newborn sons to reduce their population and subdue them (Exodus Chapter 1) completely. However, God strengthened them to survive the systemic ordeal and liberated them from the bondage of the Pharaoh (Exodus Chapter 14). It means minorities are a part of God's creation plan. The existence of minorities informs one that their survival is not at the mercy of majority communities. During their stay in Egypt, the people of Israel enriched Egyptian society with their lifestyle, culture and faith. It became a plural society. The biblical God loves diversity. Therefore, minorities reflect the principle of diversity in God's work of creation.

God's approval for diversity in terms of people groups (minority or majority), languages, cultures and faith are implicit in the biblical story of Babel Tower (Genesis 11: 1-9). People in the story were proud of one language, one speech and the resources available in their hands. They decided to build a city and a tower and live there so that they would not be scattered. They wanted to establish one world order in which there was no space for diversity. But God wanted them to be diversified. When they resisted the divine plan of diversity, God confused their language and started the process of diversification.[49] The different languages that emerged out of a confused state are the evidence of God's approval of different languages whether spoken by the majority or minority. In today's language, the Babel tower refers to the attempt of promoting one language, one culture and one religion. This story says implicitly that absence of diversity means the absence of minorities. God wants every society to be enriched by the diversity of people, language, and cultures. An ecosystem of diversity is impossible without minorities.

In the Bible, there is another story (Acts 1: 1-13; 2: 1-39), that has implications for the existence of minorities. The story of the Day of Pentecost also affirms diversity. After Jesus' resurrection, his followers, who were a minority,[50] gathered in Jerusalem to receive the promised Spirit of God to spread His message in the world.

When the Holy Spirit came upon them, they began to speak in different languages known by others who witnessed the event. It proves that God loves, values and protects the diversity of languages. The existence of multiple languages corresponds to different communities including minorities. The story of Pentecost narrates not only the importance of diversity but also the need for unity. Though they spoke in different languages, they were united in vision and mission. The principle of 'unity in diversity' is very much evident in the Indian Constitution.[51] While recognizing different cultures, languages, people groups and faith, it emphasizes national unity strongly. It conveys the fact that the principle of diversity (the existence of minorities) cannot endanger the unity of the nation. Diversity is both a Biblical and a Constitutional principle. God does not want human beings to create a society without diversity which is characterized by the existence of minorities. By recognizing and protecting minorities, the majority honours and acknowledges the divine principle of diversity. The violation of the rights of minorities is the violation of the divine plan of diversity.

Care for Minorities

Christians believe that God is the creator and protector of minorities. The Bible very clearly instructs them to care for minorities because 'God administers justice for the fatherless and the widow, and loves the stranger, giving him/her food and clothing' (Deuteronomy 10: 18-19). The Biblical faith strongly affirms the rights of minorities (Deuteronomy 23: 7). The Bible even warns that God punishes those who afflict minorities (Exodus 22: 21-4; Deuteronomy 24: 17; 27: 19). It also instructs that a stranger[52] should not be mistreated. S/he should be treated as 'one born among you, and you shall love him/her as yourself' (Leviticus 19: 33-4). It is interesting to note that God, who liberated the people of Israel from the slavery of Egyptians, punished them and sent them into exile because they failed to do justice to the minorities among them.[53] One of the greatest commandments of Jesus Christ is 'You shall love your neighbor as yourself' (Matthew 22: 39). In this context, it can be rephrased that irrespective of religious identity, everyone should be loved and cared for. This love implies recognition of his/her religion, culture, language and fundamental rights. Marilyn Friedman aptly observed that care for persons primarily requires respect for their rights.[54] Otherwise, it is charity, not empowerment. Though biblical teachings on the care for minorities are primarily addressed to those who adhere to the biblical faith, they have implications for both Christians and their co-citizens of neighbouring faiths. If Christians are numerically majority in a context, they should care for their minority co-citizens and ensure their protection and empowerment. They should be model citizens to influence their co-citizens who would protect them in turn wherever they are a minority. As a minority community, they should also raise their voice for the concerns of other minorities. The Bible challenges every human being to care for minorities because God is the creator and protector of entire humanity.

Minority Rights: Rights to Serve the Nation

Christians are one of the religious minority communities in India. They are entitled to the special protection constitutionally accorded to minorities. According to the Constitution of India, they have the right to establish and administer educational institutions. Availing the minority rights, Christians have established many institutions and contributed to the educational advancement of the nation. They offer quality education to the community and the general public. For Christians, minority rights, particularly Article 30 of the Constitution, not only gives them protection but also offers the opportunity to serve people, particularly marginalized sections of society. However, the emphasis on minority rights has been reduced to protecting the rights and privileges of minorities, especially in the management of educational institutions. If the government interferes in the affairs of minority educational institutions to ensure transparency on admission and appointment, the minority communities especially the Christians have raised their voices on the pretext of minority rights. For instance, Churches in Kerala protested against the attempts of the government to control the self-financing professional colleges. They even issued pastoral letters against the government.[55] In the past, they protested against the Education Bill passed by the Communist government in Kerala in 1958. Minority communities of West Bengal also conducted mass rallies under the banner of the United Minority Forum against the government's interference in the management of minority institutions.[56] Though there are genuine concerns in protests, many educational institutions have lost their Christian testimony of service in society. If one looks at minority rights from a Christian perspective, one realizes that while granting protection to minorities, minority rights should serve others too. There are voices from the Christian community in this direction.

Paulose Mar Paulose interpreted minority rights in light of human rights. In the context of the Church's overemphasis on minority rights, he interpreted them in relation to the service of the people who are deprived of basic human rights. Mar Paulose argues that it is marginalized communities who need special privileges to get empowered in society. For him, a minority means people who are disempowered in life. They are socially oppressed, economically poor and politically powerless communities. In other words, minorities are marginal in existence. He was critical of the Church for using minority rights to protect their interests without equal concern for the weaker sections of the public. The crux of Mar Paulose's argument is that minority rights are granted to empower the whole community.[57] According to K.T. Thomas, former Supreme Court judge, 'Minority rights are not to be claimed as privileges; rather they should be taken as a protection offered by the constitution. And no one is to claim these as one's rights forgetting the responsibilities. . . .'[58] The responsibility of Christians is to serve everyone irrespective of religious traditions, particularly the downtrodden in society. Minority rights should not be used for vested interests. The privileges involved in the protection should be used to enrich the social, cultural and political life of the nation. If the Indian Church is not able to extend the benefits of minority rights to the wider community, it stands against the hopes and aspirations of the underprivileged whom Jesus accompanied.

Mar Paulose identified two dangers in the minority consciousness of the Indian Church because of obsession with minority rights. Firstly, the Church and the Christians are often afraid to get involved in the socio-political and economic struggles for social justice. Secondly, the Church is too concerned about its rights and privileges, and not equally concerned about the rights and privileges of the human community outside of the Church.[59] It must be noted that the insecure minority consciousness is anti-biblical.[60] Christians should relinquish minority 'victim' syndrome and must be courageous to look beyond community interests.[61] The minority status should be considered as God's will[62] to engage in dialogue with co-citizens of neighbouring faiths as co-pilgrims in the mission of building up the nation. They should use minority rights to achieve social equity and uphold democratic values in society.[63] The Church has been given the mandate to serve and liberate humanity, particularly the poor.[64] The Church in India can enjoy minority rights only in the name of Jesus Christ who stood for the rights of all. The Church, the community of Jesus, has no other option but to follow in His footsteps. In sum, minority rights should be rights to serve the people.

Minorities are an integral part of this nation. The existence of different minority communities enhances the beauty of the plural identity of India further. Though religious identity gives a particular community minority status, they are not 'outsiders'. They contribute to the progress of this nation equally. The constitutional provision of minority rights does not create an unequal society or communal fault lines but protects minorities in the context of majoritarianism. Minority rights function as a protective shield to minorities and assure them of a dignified life, particularly by preserving their faith, culture and language. The challenges minorities face today underline the importance of minority rights. For Christians, the Bible values the existence of minorities and their protection. They believe that minority rights in the constitution are biblically sound because of its liberating capital. The biblical faith teaches them to care for minorities. In the past, Christians have fought in the name of minority rights to protect their collective interests. Still, they have served the nation through the institutions established under the provision of minority rights.While minority rights protect minorities, a Christian perspective informs that minority rights should be used to serve the nation by empowering the poor and the marginalized (including the minorities). Minority rights remind the citizens of both minority and majority communities of their responsiblities regarding service and care towards every one. The State, the defender of citizens' rights, should address the concerns and aspirations of minorities within the framework of minority rights.

NOTES

1. https://www.census2011.co.in/religion.php, accessed on 7 April 2021.
2. James Massey, *Minorities and Religious Freedom in a Democracy* (New Delhi: Manohar & Centre for Dalit Studies, 2003) 42.
3. P.T. Chandi, 'Christian Colleges in India and Their Role in National Development', *International Journal of Christianity and Education*, vol. 14, no. 3 (December 1971): 126-31.
4. *The Constitution of India* (New Delhi: Ministry of Law and Justice, Government of India, 2011), 13.
5. Government Targets Delhi's Biggest Christian School', *Asia News*, 17 December 2018, http://www.asianews.it/news-en/Government-targetsDelhi% E2%80%99s-biggest-Christian-school-45760.html, accessed 14 January 2019.
6. Mita Mukherjee, 'Missionary Schools Seek Exit from Panel', *Telegraph* (Kolkata), 28 December 2017, https://www.telegraphindia.com/states/west-bengal/missionary-schools-seek-exit-from-panel/cid/1396723, accessed 14 January 2019; Ajayan, 'It Is Church *vs.* State in Kerala over Education', *Live Mint* (New Delhi), 30 July 2007, https://www.livemint.com/Politics/AxI5EYbaYrgup67rb2WphK/ It-is-church-vs-state-in-Kerala-over-education.html, accessed 14 January 2019.
7. Saji Thomas, 'Hindu Hardliners Try to Damage Mission Schools' Image', *Union of Catholic Asian* , 3 October 2017, https://www.ucanews.com/news/hindu-hardlinerstry-to-damage-mission-schools-image/80407, accessed on 14 January 2019.
8. Nikhila Henry, 'Church Properties Face Encroachment in TS, AP.' *The Hindu,* 14 July 2015, https://www.thehindu.com/news/national/andhra-pradesh/church-properties-face-encroachment-in-ts-ap/article7419019. ece, accessed on 7 April 2021; 'Encroachments on Gurdaspur Cemeteries Christians Livid', *The Tribune,* 14 February 2017, https://

www. tribuneindia.com/news/archive/features/encroachments-on-gurdaspur-cemeteries-christians-livid-363838, accessed on 7 April 2021.

9. Constitution of India, Article 26, http://legislative.gov.in/sites/default/files/coi-4 March 2016.pdf, accessed on 14 January 2019; Massey, *Minorities and Religious Freedom in a Democracy*, op. cit., 65.
10. http://archive.indianexpress.com/news/credit-for-minorities-govt-s-priority-no.1/31705/, Accessed on 7 April 2021.
11. Massey, *Minorities and Religious Freedom in a Democracy*, op. cit., 66.
12. 'BJP Terms Mamata's decision to construct dining halls for Muslim majority schools as "minority appeasement"', 28 January 2019, https://www. timesnownews.com/india/article/bjp-terms-mamatas-decision-to-construct-dining-halls-for-muslim-majority-schools-as-minority-appeasement/444990, accessed on 7 April 2021.
13. *National Commission for Minorities Act of 1992*, III.9.a, b, http://www.minorityaffairs.gov.in/sites/default/files/ncm_act1992.pdf, accessed on 16 January 2019.
14. Massey, *Minorities and Religious Freedom in a Democracy*, op. cit., 95 & 160.
15. Centre for Study of Science and Secularism and Minority Rights Group International, *A Narrowing Space: Violence and Discrimination against India's Religious Minorities* (London: Minority Rights Group International, 2017), 5, 6, 16.
16. https://www.hindustantimes.com/analysis/muzaffarnagar-riots-judicial-commission-fails-to-hold-up-the-light-to-the-truth/story-L58wKP4Ln9gTTr0c9myHIJ.html, accessed on 7 April 2021.
17. Massey, *Minorities and Religious Freedom in a Democracy*, op. cit., 111.
18. Ziya us Salam, 'Christians as Target', *Frontline* (28 August 2020): 58-9 at 58; 'Nuns accused of conversion, forced to get off train Jhansi', *The Hindu* (Lucknow), 24 March 2021, https://www.thehindu.com/news/national/other-states/nuns-accused-of-conversion-forced-to-get-off-train-in-jhansi/article34153286.ece accessed on 20 July 2022; idem, 'Christians at Receiving End', *Frontline*, vol. 39, no. 1 (1-14 January 2022): 56-8 at 56 & *The Indian Express* (Pune, 1 September 2022), 2.
19. *The Constitution of India* (Delhi: Ministry of Law and Justice, Government of India, 1989), 1.
20. The term 'minority' comes from 'minores' (Latin) which means 'the little ones, the weaker ones, the vulnerable ones, the powerless and the voiceless'. It refers to people who are marginalized because of 'their ethnic, social, economic and cultural situations.' Cf A. Pushparajan, 'Mission of the

Christian Community in the Present-Day Indian Context', in *Towards A Theology of Christian Minorities in the Indian Scenario Today,* ed. Roy Lazar and Shalini Mulackal (Bengaluru: Indian Theological Association & Asian Trading Corporation, 2017), 133.

21. *The Constitution of India* (New Delhi: Ministry of Law and Justice, Government of India, 1989, 7.
22. *The Constitution of India* (New Delhi: Ministry of Law and Justice, Government of India, 1989), 12.
23. *The Constitution of India* (New Delhi: Ministry of Law and Justice, Government of India, 2011), 12 & 13.
24. G.N. Joshi, *The Constitution of India* (Calcutta: Macmillan & Co., 1966 5th edn.), 102.
25. Shalini Mulackal, 'Towards a Theology of Christian Minorities in the Indian Scenario Today', in *Towards A Theology of Christian Minorities in the Indian Scenario Today,* op. cit., 2.
26. Rowena Robison, 'Introduction', in *Minority Studies,* ed. Rowena Robinson (New Delhi: Oxford University Press, 2013), 7 & 9.
27. M.T. Cherian, *Hindutva Agenda and Minority Rights: A Christian Response* (Bangalore: Centre for Contemporary Christianity, 2007), 268-9.
28. Sunita Gangwal, *Minorities in India: A Study in Communal Process and Individual Rights* (Jaipur: Arihant, 1995), 21.
29. Ibid., 151.
30. Cherian, *Hindutva Agenda and Minority Rights,* 273.
31. Robison, 'Introduction', op. cit., 19.
32. T.N. Madan, *Modern Myths, Locked Minds: Secularism and Fundamentalism in* India (New Delhi: Oxford University Press, 2009, 2nd edn.), 255.
33. Gangwal, *Minorities in India,* op. cit., 22.
34. Robison, 'Introduction', op. cit., 6.
35. M.S. Golwalkar, *Bunch of Thoughts,* 2nd enlrgd. and revd. edn. (Bangalore: Jagarana Prakashana, 1980), 248, 251 & 256.
36. https://zeenews.india.com/news/nation/cong-appeasing-muslims-to-retain-lost-glory-advani_234101.html, accessed on 29 October 2022.
37. Neerja Chowdhury, 'Taking Fight to BJP', *The Indian Express* (Pune, 29 October 2022), 15.
38. Rajeev Bhargava, 'Indian Secularism: An Alternate, Trans-cultural Ideal', in *History of Science, Philosophy and Culture in Indian Civilization,* vol. X, pt. 7, ed. V.R. Mehta and Thomas Pantham (New Delhi: Sage, 2006), 295-6.
39. http://ncm.nic.in/homepage/homepage.php, accessed 30 October 2022.

40. http://www.nmdfc.org/index1.aspx?lsid=59&lev=2&lid=32&langid=1, accessed 30 October 2022.
41. https://www.minorityaffairs.gov.in/en/schemesperformance, accessed on 30 October 2022.
42. http://www.minoritywelfare.kerala.gov.in/schemes-implemented.php?token=, accessed on 30 October 2022.
43. 'Centre Stops Maulana Azad Scholarship for Research Scholars from Minority Communities', *The Hindu,* New Delhi, 9 December 2022, https://www.thehindu.com/news/national/centre-stops-maulana-azad-scholarship-for-research-scholars-from-minority-communities/article 66238681.ece, accessed 9 December 2022.
44. Paulose Mar Paulose, *Swathanthryamanu Daivam,* (Malayalam) (Ariyannur: Patabhedam, 1996), 90-1 & Dietrich Bonhoeffer, *Ethics* (New York: Mac Millan Company, 1962), 297 & 305.
45. Akshay Deshmane, 'Demand for Minority Status', https://frontline.thehindu.com/cover-story/article24200995.ece accessed 11 October 2022.
46. Ananthakrishnan G., 'Minority Tag for Hindus: Govt seeks time. . .', *The Indian Express* (Pune, 2 November 2022), 1 & 2.
47. Shashi Tharoor, *Why I am a Hindu* (New Delhi: Aleph Book Company, 2018), 179.
48. S. Stanislas, 'Biblical Understanding of the Identity, Role and Rights of Minorities', in *Towards a Theology of Christian Minorities in the Indian Scenario Today,* 54-5.
49. Massey, *Minorities and Religious Freedom in a Democracy,* op. cit., 139; James Massey, *Caste-Class Victims and Their Assertion for Justice* (New Delhi: Centre for Dalit Studies, 2013), 28.
50. They represented minority faith, lifestyle and community life in the predominantly Jewish religious and Roman political context. They had gone through severe persecution by Roman and Jewish authorities. However, they also survived as Jews experienced in Egypt. The survival of minority communities in their respective contexts in today's world needs to be understood as God's care for them. It also calls for the majority to become instruments of God's care in the case of minorities.
51. Massey, *Minorities and Religious Freedom in a Democracy,* op. cit., 140; James Massey, 'Minority Rights', *NCC Review,* cxxi/2 (February-March, 2001): 119-44 at 137-8.
52. In the Old Testament, a stranger refers to one who does not follow the faith of the people of Israel. They are religious minorities today. S/he is an outsider in terms of religion, culture, language etc.

53. Stanislas, 'Biblical Understanding of the Identity, Role and Rights of Minorities', op. cit., 60-2.
54. Susan J. Hekman, *Moral Voices, Moral Selves: Carol Gilligan and Feminist Moral* Theology (Pennsylvania: The Pennsylvania State University Press, 1995), 22.
55. M.G. Radha Krishnan, 'Ire of the Minorities', *India Today*, vol. XXXIII, no. 1 (1-7 January 2008): 21. The Kerala Professional Colleges (Prevention of Capitation Fee, Regulation of non-exploitative Fee and other measures to ensure Equity and Excellence in professional education) Bill passed by the Kerala Legislative Assembly was opposed by the Mainline Syrian Christian churches in Kerala. Their protest against the bill was in different forms such as rallies, public meetings, litigation, the closing of schools, and issuing of Pastoral Letters. The Pastoral Letters were opposed in and outside the church because the new Bill was progressive and revolutionary that helps the economically marginalized sections to do professional studies. Rf. George Zachariah, 'The Grand Inquisitor and the Syrian Christian Primates in Kerala: Musings on the Pastoral Letter', *Gurukul Journal of Theological Studies*, vol. XVIII, no. 1 (January 2007): 40-1 & 47.
56. N.B. Mitra, 'Bishops Condemn Government Assault on Minority Rights', *People's Reporter*, vol. 20, no. 3 (10-25 February 2007): 3.
57. Paulose Mar Paulose, *Nisabdharayirikkan Ningalkkenthadhikaram* (Malayalam) (Noorannad: Fabian Books, 1998), 41, 68, & 86-7.
58. K.T. Thomas, 'Not an Article of Special Privilege but Only a Provision for Protection', reported by R.C. Thomas, *People's Reporter*, vol. 19, no. 14 (25 July-10 August 2006): 1.
59. Paulose Mar Paulose, *Spirituality for Struggle* (Thiruvalla: Christava Sahitya Samithi, 1999), 24-6.
60. Stanislas, 'Biblical Understanding of the Identity, Role and Rights of Minorities', op. cit., 74.
61. Mulackal, 'Towards A Theology of Christian Minorities in the Indian Scenario Today', op. cit., 4.
62. A. Alangaram, 'Self-Understanding of the Indian Church as a Minority and its Theological Implications', in *Towards a Theology of Christian Minorities in the Indian Scenario Today*, op. cit., 97.
63. Pushparajan, 'Mission of the Christian Community in the Present-day Indian Context', op. cit., 133.
64. Alangaram, 'Self-Understanding of the Indian Church as a Minority and its Theological Implications', op. cit., 100.

CHAPTER 5

Church and State in a Secular Democracy

In its popular and organized form, religion plays a role in a nation's life. The secular identity of the nation gives room for the positive participation of religions in society. Secularism in India does not separate religion and state practically. Though it proclaims neutrality and equal treatment, the state is not always unbiased. The ideological underpinning of the ruling dispensation influences the approach of the state towards religious communities. Historically, the relationship between religion and state in India has not always been smooth. On the one hand, religious communities watch over the policies and decisions of the state, the state on the other, is cautious when it comes to framing a policy or enacting a law, or implementing a judicial decision that directly or indirectly affects a religious community. The state is more watchful not to offend a particular religious community that holds a majority political constituency in a region. Religious communities also respond to the intervention of the state differently. They have no hesitation in fighting against the state if the intervention of the ruling dispensation does not satisfy the religious authorities. They ring the alarm of infringement of freedom of religion. Sometimes, on the pretext of reforms, the state intentionally interferes in the affairs of a particular religion and leaves the others. In a pluralistic society, religious communities may suspect the intention of the state if it fails to maintain neutrality.

Sadly, religious communities in India are more concerned about their interests and problems. In their actions and demands, they appear to be communal organizations that are politically irresponsive, neutral to the pertinent issues of poor people and averse to secular progressive movements. The Church is not much different from other religious communities in this regard. The Church in the present context also attempts to establish and safeguard its interests and privileges instead of standing for the people who are politically powerless and socially voiceless in protecting their rights. The Church has made strong protests when the state passed a law or introduced a bill apparently restricting the religious liberty of Christians. In a democratic society, the Church can represent the voice of Christians and remind the state about its constitutional commitment if the actions of the state violate their freedom. It is also true that Church has maintained (or situationally forced to maintain) silence against the struggles of other communities. For instance, except for some individual voices, the Church was largely silent during the emergency period and communal conflicts that victimized others. In India, religious communities rarely appreciate the state for its initiatives to empower the poor and the marginalized. But they go out of their way to support the state as long as they enjoy the favour of the state. Indeed, 'community gratification' defines the level of the relationship between the state and the religion. Unfortunately, both want to control each other and tend to bias in the secular state. They forget their roles in the empowerment of the disempowered.

Every religious community desires the state to listen to and implement its demands. As the chapter deals with the Church-State relationship, the examples from Christian community are given here. For instance, Christian organizations strongly protested against the draft of the Kerala Church (Properties and Institutions) Bill.[1] They demanded that the government should not consider it for legislation. The Karnataka Legislative Council passed the 'Protection of Right to Freedom of Religion' Bill despite the concerns raised by the Church.[2] Christian organizations, politicians, and ecclesiastical leaders constantly raise the issue of reservation for Dalit Christians to the government and are pursuing a legal struggle in the Supreme Court. The churches in north-eastern India have started a campaign for clean elections and corruption-free government.[3] Like other religious communities, the Church or its functionaries try to influence their constituency directly or indirectly during elections.[4] It is an altogether a different issue to assume that all Christians listen to the political advice of the Church leaders in the elections. The Church also approaches the state to consider its demands such as land allocation for worship places, permission for educational institutions, etc. There is a conflict when the state does not deliver according to the expectations of the Church. In this context, this chapter explains the Church-State relationship within the Christian religious framework informed by some representative voices like Dietrich Bonheoffer,[5] M.M. Thomas[6] and Paulose Mar Paulose.[7]

CHURCH: 'CHRIST EXISTING AS COMMUNITY'

The idea of 'Church' is illustrated by different biblical images such as the 'Body of Christ', 'People of God' and 'Bride of Christ', etc. In the Christian belief system, there is a doctrine that describes the being and nature of the Church. The study of the doctrine of the Church is called Ecclesiology. The term 'ecclesiology' comes from the Greek word *Ekklesia*, which means 'an assembly', 'called out', etc. Throughout the centuries, the doctrine of the Church has been explained and interpreted in different ways according to the changing context of the time. Isidore of Pelusium of the fifth century interpreted Church as 'the assembly of saints joined together by correct faith and an excellent manner of life'.[8] For Augustine of Hippo, Church is 'a mixed body' of both saints and sinners.[9] Martin Luther understood Church as the place where the 'Word of God is preached, believed, confessed and acted upon'.[10] These ecclesiological understandings developed in specific contexts, particularly the engagement of Christian faith with existing religious, ideological and philosophical thinking of the time. In the context of the emergence of secular societies, Christian theologians have redefined the relationship between the Church and the State. The Church that controlled the State in the medieval period had to take completely different pathways in its relationship with the State.

For me, Dietrich Bonhoeffer's description of the church provides a theological base for the discourse of the Church-State relationship.

According to him, the Church is a worldly reality. It must remain a temporal reality for the sake of people. It cannot claim any earthly security because Christ did not do so. It must renounce all privileges and possessions, but not the Word of Christ, for the wellbeing of the people. It should engage not only with the poor and the rich but also with the pious and the godless.[11] The Church is not a 'religious society'. Bonhoeffer argues that 'the Church can only defend its own space by fighting, not for space, but for the salvation of the world. Otherwise, the Church becomes a 'religious society' that fights in its own interest and thus has ceased to be the Church of God in the world'.[12] Therefore, the primary task of the Church is not to stand for its cause but to become the witness of Jesus Christ in society. For him, the witness of the Church means, 'The Church is the Church only when it exists for others.'[13] The Church derives its identity from Christ. In the words of Bonheoffer, 'the Church is "Christ existing as community", and is to be understood as a collective person'.[14] The word of the present Christ is the word of the Church to the people in the world. The word of the Church must address all realities of the world.[15] This is the calling of the community of Jesus. It is not simply a community of the worshippers of Christ but Christ takes form among them. 'The Church is the man (woman) in Christ and awakened to new life.'[16] It is the visible body of Jesus Christ.[17] As 'Christ existing as community', the Church is for preserving Christian piety and morality. It must be preserved to serve the people, order and State. It upholds sacrifice, prayer and forgiveness. It proclaims life in death, shares love in hate, brings the message of salvation in suffering and hope in despair.[18] The life of the Church is not limited to the so-called religious functions of human beings, but engages with their existential crisis in this world. Its engagement with the state is part of its existence as 'Christ existing as community'.

CHURCH AND STATE: A BIBLICAL VIEW

The Bible gives a framework for a Christian view of the Church-State relationship. According to the Bible, God establishes civil authorities. A civil ruler is an ordained servant of God. The ruler cannot act independently of God. Since s/he is ordained by God, everyone must submit to him/her. The ruler cannot violate the law of God and dominate the citizens. As God's servant, the ruler should do good to the citizens. The obedience to the civil authorities should come out of individual conscience, not from the fear of possible punishment. The citizens should pay taxes to the state faithfully (Romans 13: 1-7). The Westminster Confession says,

> God, the supreme Lord and King of all the world, hath ordained civil magistrates, to be, under him, over the people, for his own glory, and the public good: to this end, hath armed them with the power of the sword, for the defense and encouragement of them that are good, and for the punishment of evildoers . . . Civil magistrates may not assume to themselves the administration of the Word and sacraments; or the power of the keys of the kingdom of heaven; or in the least, interfere on matters of faith.' (Westminster Confession, article 23: 1, 3).[19]

It draws a functional line between the Church and the State.

The relationship between civil government and God shows that there cannot be a strict separation between Church and State. Both receive validation from God. In responsibilities, the Church and the State are equally answerable to God. The State cannot always expect the Church to be obedient to its orders. The prophetic criticism of the Church is not intended to defame the state but to remind 'the state to be state as God ordained it and rules over it'. The prophets in biblical history questioned the rulers whenever they violated the law of God and failed to deliver justice to the people. The state must protect the rights of citizens. The Bible advises Christians to be obedient to the state if it does not demand them to do that which God prohibits.[20] According to Martin Luther, in the secular authority, the emperor does not need to be a Christian. The role of the secular authority is to manage worldly affairs but not otherworldly matters. Christians should be subjected to secular authority as long as they are responsible rulers.[21] The Christian attitude to the state is also defined by the practice of the love commandment of Jesus (John 13). Moreover, Christians must pray for the civil authorities (1 Timothy

2: 1-2).[22] Biblically, Church and State are not two separate entities but complementary institutions because as Bonheoffer puts it, 'Christ is present to us in a double form as church and as state' (1 Corinthians. 8: 6, Colossians 1: 16, 17, 20, John. 1: 3).[23] The Church and the state have the same area of function: human beings.[24] Though they may have functional demarcations, Christians believe that, they are instruments of God to fulfil God's purpose of governing and preserving the creation.

BOUNDARIES, EXPECTATIONS AND MUTUALITY

Dietrich Bonhoeffer argues that Church and State represent the presence of Christ. Though both are working for the betterment of humanity, they correct each other and are expected to execute their God given tasks. The State expects the Church not to interfere in the affairs of the secular office. For him, the State can interfere in the spiritual office in matters of justice.[25] It goes in line with the Constitution of India. The Church has the task of testifying before the State to their common master—Jesus Christ. It does not mean that the role of the Church is to force the State to follow a Christian policy or enact Christian laws. But the Church can insist that the State be faithful to its responsibilities. The State should give protection to the public Christian proclamation against violence and blasphemy, protection for the institution of the Church against arbitrary interference and protection for Christian life in obedience to Jesus Christ.[26] In the Church-State relationship, there must be mutual knowledge of boundaries and responsibilities in a secular state. In the Indian context, religious communities and the state need to maintain a relationship that demonstrates mutual respect and enabling practically through not manipulation and dominance.

The 'Religious' Responsibility of the State

In a secular society, theoretically, the state cannot be 'religious'. But Christians believe that the State has 'religious' responsibilities (responsibilities related to religion). In his theology of State,

Bonhoeffer explains that the State should not allow religion to influence its policies for the citizenry. It does not mean that the State should not listen to religious people or has the right to frame any policy to control a religious community that questions its ideological framework. The calling of the State is to protect the righteous actions of the religious communities and be neutral in dealing with matters of religion. If the State prefers one religion over another or establishes a new one, it suffers from being religiously neutral. The 'religiously' preferential actions of the state lead to communal conflicts. It not only affects the functions of the State but also disturbs the secular fabric of society. Therefore, the 'religious' responsibility of the State is to defuse 'religiously' communal conflicts. In such an eventuality, the State should protect the victims of communalism. The State must also regulate the fundamentalist approach of religious communities. The religious (personal) identity of civil authorities is not a direct or indirect approval for the communal agenda of a particular religious community. The proclamation or propagation of the faith does not need a sword or political power but word and deed.[27] The protection of religious communities and the combat against communalism constitute the 'religious' responsibility of the State. The protection of religious communities means safeguarding their rights and privileges. If the State is faithful to its vocation, being religiously neutral but equally protective, it can resist religious conflicts. The task of the Church is to proclaim the divine character of the State and live out its faith in society.

The Political Responsibility of the Church (Religion)

The political responsibility of the Church is multi-faceted. Since the Church and the State are the two fold forms of the presence of Christ on earth, the Church has the political task of supporting and challenging the State. It has the so called 'positive' and 'negative' roles related to the affairs of the State. For Bonhoeffer, the Church should call 'sin' by its name and warn people against it. It is the responsibility of the Church to bring the attention of the ruling dispensation to its errors and shortcomings that disrupt the functions of the State. If the State does not listen to the voice of the Church in any context, the only political responsibility that remains with the Church is to maintain and encourage the order of justice at least among its members. By doing so, the Church is being faithful to its tasks.[28] Political participation for nation building is another political responsibility of the Church. Through its members, the Church should participate in building up the State that upholds democratic political values. According to Bonhoeffer, 'the Church which may not enter the political struggle must nevertheless enjoin its members to study social questions with the ultimate aim of act'.[29] In a pluralistic context, the institutional participation of Church in politics may lead to communalism. Therefore, the Church should encourage its members to contribute to the nation through political involvement but remain aloof from it as a body.

The Church has a prophetic role in its relationship with the State. Bonheoffer observes that 'so long as the State acts to maintain justice and order, the Church as such may not engage in direct political action against the State. This does not mean that the Church takes no interest in political affairs, for it is the responsibility of the Church to ask the State again and again whether it is fulfilling its duties as a State'.[30] It may happen in both situations, i.e. when there is 'too little order' and when there is 'too much order'. 'Too little order' means allowing a group to violate the laws. 'Too much order' means suppressing the freedom of religion.[31] While the Church has to support and appreciate the State for protecting the rights, promoting the welfare of all, and delivering justice, it must challenge the State for restricting citizens' freedom. The Church, 'Christ existing as community', is called upon to become a corrective and prophetic force that participates in the life of the State. Instead of engaging with the State through the eyes of communal interest, every religious community should cultivate a value oriented, issue based, and participatory political approach.

CHURCH AND STATE: DIVINE PURPOSE

Christians believe that there is a divine purpose for religious and democratic institutions. Every community exists with a divine purpose. The divine purpose has to be materialized not by rejecting the social life of human beings but by recognizing it.[32] So Paulose Mar Paulose opines that it is the responsibility of the Church to evaluate whether any community or system works for the realization of the divine purpose or creates any hindrance to the welfare of human beings. In that sense, the interests of the Church are spread out in all aspects of society. The State is also included in it. The State is a divine gift. It is an instrument to fulfil the divine purpose of individuals and society. Here the role of the Church is to observe the activities of the State whether it works for the welfare of humanity or not. The involvement of the Church in the affairs of the State is not for establishing minority rights and privileges, but for realizing the purpose of God in this world.[33] The Church should become a corrective force when the State goes against the interests of people. It should consider resistance as a form of Christian obedience when the people are denied justice. Human welfare is the aim of any government. When the State fails in this mission, it automatically negates the divine purpose. At this juncture, the responsibility of the Church is to resist the State when it becomes a means of oppression.[34] As a religious institution, the Church has to persuade the State to fulfil the divine purpose-the welfare of all citizens.

POLITICAL ENGAGEMENT AND STATE: AN INDIAN CHRISTIAN THEOLOGICAL OUTLOOK

The Christian faith endorses political engagement. Christian involvement in politics is based on the essence of Christian social and personal ethics: obedience to God and love of neighbour.[35] Political engagement is one of the means to transform society. The Christian understanding of salvation is both a social and other-worldly experience. It requires political participation to facilitate the empowerment of communities in a democratic society. It is not limited to safeguarding religious liberty alone.[36] Many Christians hesitate to participate in politics because of the influence of otherworldly spirituality. The main factor which prevents them from political engagement, particularly participation in political struggles, according to M.M. Thomas, is that 'there are many who sincerely maintain that the movement of church unity, evangelistic mission and even Christian social service will lose their spiritual integrity, if it is mixed up with politics'.[37] This non-political Christianity hampers the vision of Church as New Humanity in Christ. The Church cannot be a mute spectator in the political sphere.[38] It should represent a voice for social change. Paulose Mar Paulose claims that the distinctive feature of Christianity is that God, whom the Christians worship, is the one who suffered with humanity and still participates in the suffering of His creation.[39] This God is present in the ongoing struggles of the people striving to establish their rights. The becoming flesh of such a God in Jesus Christ attacked the religious institutionalism that supported injustices, denounced dehumanizing systems, and made the socio-cultural religious customs subservient to higher values.[40] This God leads the revolutions of the time to preserve human dignity and prosperity. So, Christians cannot say that they are not interested in politics.[41]

What is the nature of the political engagement of the Church? Political engagement, for Christians, is an act of witnessing to the values of Christian faith and tradion in society. It does not necessarily mean joining political parties. The political witness of the Church refers to the participation in the ongoing liberating struggles of people to transform the existing sinful socio-economic structures and human relations. According to Paulose Mar Paulose,

> The response of love toward God and the neighbour requires participation in the political process. Along with other citizens, Christians have a responsibility to confront, understand, and attempt to solve the problems like providing food for the hungry, alleviating poverty and unemployment; grappling with deadly issues like environmental pollution; finding ways to control the population explosion; and building up a world of peace with justice.[42]

This political engagement is an expression of Christian spirituality. It is called spirituality for struggle:[43] identifying with the hopes and fears of people and challenging the evil structures of society. God, who participates in people's movements, cannot be limited to the rites and sacraments of the Church. God is beyond the traditions and creedal definitions of the Church.[44] It implies that the source of the political witness of the Church is God, who struggles along with humans to renew the whole creation.

The political involvement of the Church should uphold secularism because an open secular state alone can deliver justice to human freedom in the context of religious and ideological pluralism.[45] M.M. Thomas suggests that Christians should promote an inclusive approach and create secular human fellowships to prevent religion as a tool of politics in secular society. The participation of the Church in the political process requires the discrimination between humane and inhumane activities. Corruption, violation of democratic rights and negation of freedom of speech are inhuman practices.[46] There must be a difference in the political approach of the Church while dealing with ecclesiastical matters and non-ecclesiastical affairs as well.[47] The political participation is not limited to the election and other political benefits but to conscientize illiterate people about their political rights, duties, and privileges. It challenges the corruptibility of power because, according to him, 'the corruptibility of power is the main cause of injustice'.[48] To participate actively in politics, the Church should encourage and train its members because the political participation of the Church occurs through its members. Every member of the faith community must understand his or her place as Christ's witness in everyday life.[49]

In political involvement, the Church cannot support one particular political party because the Church has members having different political and ideological persuasions. However, the Church may extend issue or programme-based support to a political party for the larger interests of the nation.[50] A Christian, who involves himself or herself in politics, must uphold Christian values in every aspect of the political process. S/he needs to follow a constructive approach that endorses the government's progressive policies but challenges what is not democratic and constitutional in the behaviour of the State.[51] S/he must have a political opinion and express his/her disagreement through democratic ways. Moreover, the Church cannot form a political party and assert political power. It can teach moral teachings to the people and uphold human dignity, human rights and the welfare of all.[52] The formation of a political party would promote the idea that 'Christianity implies a particular political program'. It would also strengthen the communal forces in the context of minority-majority political profiling. The Church can contribute to nation building through political actions as mentioned earlier rather than forming a political party. For Christians, political participation is a religious obligation[53] to transform society than get political power.

There is a 'communal' element in the political involvement of the Church. It happens with other religious communities too. For instance, instead of striving to protect the rights of all citizens, particularly the marginalized, the Indian Church—in the name of minority rights—has attempted to protect its rights and privileges. Unless and until their interests are endangered, the churches do not encourage people to participate in the political process.[54] M.M. Thomas aptly observed that the 'Church is not just to look after their communal interests but also perhaps primarily the interests of all men, women and children in the country as human beings.'[55] In the past, the Church had used its political influence to protect its 'communal interests' such as establishing schools, colleges and other institutions.[56] Like other religious communities, the Church also does political lobbying with the State today. It becomes communal when it serves the interests of a particular community. 'Communal' political engagement is not a Christian witness. The privileges and resources of the religious communities should serve society.

The Church's political witness has a preferential location. The public engagement of the Church through political actions is incomplete without addressing the issues of marginalized communities. Paulose Mar Paulose argues that the Church should prioritize the marginalized in its political struggles. For him, the Church is not qualified to proclaim the Gospel if it does not participate in the sufferings of the marginalized and identify with them. The Gospel compels the Church to stand for the afflicted and take sides with the oppressed in their struggles.[57] The decisive factor is not the numerical strength of the Church but its readiness to suffer with God in the world.[58] The Church cannot be neutral in its political approach. It must have a 'preferential option' for the oppressed. The political involvement may situate the Church in conflict with the State. Because as long as the Church stands for a common cause, particularly the cause for the marginalized, the Church has to face the opposition of the ruling class. It is the destiny of the Church in this corrupt world. According to M.M. Thomas 'the church has every Christian reason to stand for a path of social development which does not deny men and women the dignity of freedom. So long as the church is true to its mission of confessing Christ's "New Humanity" in society and state, some tensions between church and society, between church and state are inevitable.'[59] The political witness of the Church cannot be blind to the social realities because concern for others is the expression of Christian spirituality. The political engagement of the Church becomes 'Christian' when it stands for the voiceless, the powerless, and the marginalized. The disempowered human realities demand a shift in approach: communalism to communitarianism. The political engagement of every religious community should shun communal agenda and strive for equal and mutual empowerment of communities.

In a religiously pluralistic society, the State cannot ignore religions/religious communities completely. They have contributed to the development of the nation by sharing their social and spiritual capital. Despite the natural tensions between State and Religion, there are many areas where they can converge and work together for the sake of citizens. Both State and Religion have a divine mandate to support and correct one another and maintain functional boundaries. The Christian understanding of the Church and State relationship gives a framework for a healthy relationship between State and Religion. For Religion, State is the custodian of rights including, the freedom of religion. A secular State expects religious communities to transcend communal thinking and support the State for the welfare of citizens. Indian secularism with its distinctive character acknowledges the role of Religion in a secular society and enjoins the State not to treat Religion as a threat. Christianity affirms the divine character of the State. As long as the State is not biased against religion and works for the common good, it maintains its divine identity. The approach of people, who represent the State and Religion, determines the future of the relationship between the State and Religion. For Christians, State and Religion are partners in the mission of empowering communities.

NOTES

1. T.A. Ameerudheen, 'Under Pressure from Christian Community, Kerala Government decides not to back Church reform bill', *Scroll.in,* 7 March 2019, https://scroll.in/article/915654/under-pressure-from-christian-community-kerala-government-decides-not-to-back-church-reform-bill, accessed on 8 November 2022.
2. Christian Community dismayed over passing of anti-conversion bill in Karnataka', *Hindustan Times,* Bengaluru, 17 September 2022, https://www.hindustantimes.com/cities/bengaluru-news/christian-community-dismayed-over-passing-of-anti-conversion-bill-in-karnataka-101663382749928.html, accessed on 8 November 2022.
3. Wasbir Hussain, 'The Church: Tackling Politics', *Outlook,* 3 February 2022, https://www.outlookindia.com/website/story/the-church-tackling-politics/218361, accessed on 8 November 2022.
4. Church denies involvement in Mizoram elections', *Business Standard,* 22 November 2018, https://www.business-standard.com/article/news-ani/church-denies-involvement-in-mizoram-elections-118112201290_1.html, accessed on 8 November 2022.
5. Dietrich Bonheoffer (1906-45) was a German theologian known for his theological views and actions during the Nazi regime. He emphasized the creative relationship of the Church with the state especially the political participation of the Church in society.
6. M.M. Thomas (1916-96) was an ecumenical lay theologian of international repute. He was a former Governor of Nagaland (1990-2).

7. Paulose Mar Paulose (1941-98), Bishop of the Chaldean Syrian Church, was a radical Indian theologian of the twentieth century.
8. Alister E. Mcgrath, *Christian Theology, An Introduction* (Oxford: Blackwell Publishing, 2001, 3rd edn.), 476.
9. Ibid., 479.
10. Ibid., 481.
11. Dietrich Bonhoeffer, *A Testament to Freedom: The Essential Writings of Dietrich Bonhoeffer*, ed. Geffrey B. Kelly and F. Burton Nelson (San Francisco: Harper- Sanfrancisco, 1995), 86-7, cited by Carla Barnhill, *A Year with Dietrich Bonhoeffer* (New York: HarperCollins, 2005), 178-80.
12. Dietrich Bonhoeffer, *Ethics* (Minneapolis: Fortress Press, 2005), 63-4, cited by Carla Barnhill, *A Year with Dietrich Bonhoeffer*, 21.
13. Dietrich Bonhoeffer, *Letters and Papers from Prison* (New York: Macmillan Publishing, 1972), 382.
14. Dietrich Bonhoeffer, *No Rusty Swords* (New York: Harper & Row Publishers, 1965), 33.
15. Ibid., 161.
16. Dietrich Bonhoeffer, *Ethics* (New York: Macmillan Company, 1962), 21.
17. Dietrich Bonhoeffer, *The Cost of Discipleship* (London: Student Christian Movement Press Ltd, 1959), 223-6.
18. Bonhoeffer, *No Rusty Swords*, op. cit., 154-5.
19. R.C. Sproul, *Essential Truths of the Christian Faith* (Illinois: Tyndale House Publishers, 1992), 338.
20. Sproul, *Essential Truths of the Christian Faith*, op. cit., 338-9.
21. Gerhard Ebeling, *Luther, An Introduction to His Thought* (Philadelphia: Fortress Press, 1980), 183-7.
22. S. Stanislas, 'Biblical Understanding of the Identity, Role and Rights of Minorities', in *Towards a Theology of Christian Minorities in the Indian Scenario Today*, ed. Roy Lazar and Shalini Mulackal (Bengaluru: Indian Theological Association & Asian Trading Corporation, 2017), 72.
23. Dietrich Bonhoeffer, *Christology* (London: Collins, 1966), 66.
24. Bonhoeffer, *Ethics*, op. cit., 315.
25. Ibid., 310.
26. Ibid., 311.
27. Ibid., 312-13.
28. Ibid., 314.
29. Bonhoeffer, *No Rusty Swords*, op. cit., 294.

30. John D. Godsey, *The Theology of Dietrich Bonhoeffer* (London: Student Christian Movement Press Ltd, 1960), 110.
31. Godsey, *The Theology of Dietrich Bonhoeffer*, op. cit., 110.
32. Paulose Mar Paulose, *Swathanthryamanu Daivam* (Malayalam) (Ariyannur: Patabhedam, 1996), 89.
33. Ibid., 90-1.
34. Ibid., 93.
35. Herbert Jayasingh, 'The Christian Community in a Secular State', in *Secularism: Collection of Articles,* compiled by Vincent Rajkumar (Bangalore: Christian Institute for the Study of Religion & Society, 2018), 99.
36. Herbert Jayasingh, 'The Christian Community in a Secular State', op. cit., 102.
37. M.M. Thomas, *Church and Human Community* (Delhi: Indian Society for Christian Knowledge (ISPCK), 1985), 11.
38. M.M. Thomas, *New Creation in Christ* (Delhi: ISPCK, 1976), 75.
39. Paulose Mar Paulose, *Vithakyappetta Vithukal* (Malayalam), Collection by K.J. Thomas (Trissur: Paulose Mar Paulose Foundation for Socio-Cultural Development, 2005), 78.
40. Paulose Mar Paulose, *Spirituality for Struggle* (Thiruvalla: Christava Sahitya Samithi, 1999), 40.
41. Mar Paulose, *Swathanthryamanu Daivam*, op. cit., 92.
42. Paulose Mar Paulose, *Church's Mission* (Bombay: BUILD, n.d.), 12.
43. Mar Paulose, *Spirituality for Struggle*, 83-5.
44. Paulose Mar Paulose, *Nisabdharayirikan Ningalkkenthadhikaram?* (Malayalam) (Noorannad: Fabian Books, 1998), 109.
45. Thomas, *Church and Human Community*, op. cit., 47.
46. M.M. Thomas, *Some Theological Dialogues* (Madras: The Christian Literature Society, 1977), 71.
47. M.M. Thomas, *Bharathathil Christava Sabhayude Samuhika Dharmam* (Thiruvalla: The Theological Literature Committee, 1981), 142.
48. M.M. Thomas, *Ideological Quest within Christian Commitment* (Madras: The CLS for CISRS, Bangalore, 1983), 42.
49. Mar Paulose, *Church's Mission*, op. cit., 15.
50. Jayasingh, 'The Christian Community in a Secular State', op. cit., 106.
51. Ibid., 107.
52. Thomas, *Bharathathil Christava Sabhayude Samuhika Dharmam*, op. cit., 142.
53. Jayasingh, 'The Christian Community in a Secular State', op. cit., 110.
54. Mar Paulose, *Nisabdharayirikkan Ningalkkenthadhikaram*, op. cit., 42.

55. M.M. Thomas, 'The Churches and the Future of Indian Democracy', National Council of Churches Review, vol. XCVII, nos. 6-7 (June-July 1977): 343.
56. M.M. Thomas, *Parivarthanathinte Daivasasthram* (Thiruvalla: The Theological Literature Committee, 1982), 134.
57. Mar Paulose, *Nisabdharayirikkan Ningalkkenthadhikaram*, op. cit., 31.
58. Mar Paulose, *Spirituality for Struggle*, op. cit., 41-2.
59. M.M. Thomas, 'The Churches and the Future of Indian Democracy', op. cit., 343.

CHAPTER 6

Religious Communalism: A Christian Response

Religion is not a bad thing. How one uses it matters in the religiously plural world. Love for his/her religion/community is also not a bad idea, but it is deplorable if it happens at the cost of disliking others. Religious communalism emerges when religion becomes an excuse for furthering temporal interests. It does not build up a nation but breaks the unity of people. Everyone is a victim in a communalized society: victim of hatred, victim of 'communal mind', victim of violence, victim of false 'religious pride', victim of 'communal politics'. India has historical wounds of communalism that have remained unhealed even today. The political use of religion has become 'normal' in our generation. But there are different religious and ideological resources to overcome the evil of communalism. This chapter deals mainly with the issue of communalism from a Christian theological perspective. It also explains the ideological underpinning of communalism and engages with the current communal polarization of society.

COMMUNALISM: IDEOLOGY, POLITICS AND POWER STRUGGLE

Communalism, particularly its religious form, has historical antecedents in India. It began with the British idea of the periodic census which defined Indians in terms of religion, caste, tribe or ethnicity. The notion of Hindus and Muslims as 'two different nations'[1] (two-nation theory advocated by the Muslim League and Hindu Mahasabha) communally divided people. It provided content for majority minority profiling.[2] The British policy of divide and rule and subsequent partition of the country[3] added fuel to the fire of communalism. The impact of the 'two-nation theory' continued in the political life of post-independent India. The nation witnessed periodical communal conflicts between different religious communities and heard disturbing communal voices/demands from different corners. Communal politics thrived on communal conflicts, controversial legislations like the Muslim Women (Protection of Rights) Act in 1986, demand for Khalistan, demolition of Babri Masjid, legislations on religious conversion, communal ideologies and movements, etc. Today, communalism has different religious tags: Hindu, Muslim, Sikh, Christian. It is not a spontaneous reaction that comes out of wounded religious sentiments. It has an ideological and religious framework.

According to Gyanendra Pandey, in the Indian context, 'the word "communalism" refers to a condition of suspicion, fear, and hostility between members of different religious communities'. It has more or less political meaning[4] in the context of the organized political assertions of religious communities. For Bipin Chandra, communalism is an ideology. It looks at socio-political-economic realities through the lens of a particular religion or caste/tribe.[5]It teaches that followers of religion have common economic, political and social interests. They constitute a religio political community having shared dreams and aspirations. In a communal framework, religion serves the political agenda of the community. Communal conflict/violence is not 'communalism' per se but an outcome of the spread of communalism.[6] Religious profiling of majority minority is the language of communalism.[7] For Jawaharlal Nehru, 'In neither case (Hindu and Muslim communalism) was it even *bone fide* communalism (i.e. the stirrings and demands of a community), but . . . political and social reaction hiding behind the communal mask.'[8] Communalists present 'communalism as nationalism'[9] and get validation from the larger community. Communalism, irrespective of its form and origin, is equally dangerous, victimizes people, and creates faultlines in society.

Communalists glorify their religious identity and assert superiority over others. For instance, Hindutva proponents, according to Prabhat Patnaik, attempt to homogenize Hindus and claim cultural and religious pre-eminence of Hinduism and stay on the past injustice experienced by the community to strengthen their communal appeal. They interpret history from a communal perspective and refute contrary claims.[10] Some communalists do not endorse violence but agree with the argument of typical communalists. They dwell on the numerical strength of the community and its cultural and historical origin and identity. In the words of Amartya Sen, they are 'proto-Hindutva enthusiasts'.[11] Such enthusiasts can be seen in every religious tradition. They are silent ideological supporters of communalism.

There would be historical or contemporary social, political, economic and religious factors or reasons for communalism in the society. One of the reasons is the 'faulty education about members of other communities'.[12] Sometimes, it emerges as a reaction to an imagined threat posed by another community.[13] The threat perception 'requires' political involvement to protect the interests of the religious community.[14] Another common factor that allows communalism to thrive in our society is that non-communal and liberating elements/teachings of religion get less attention among believers.[15] Communal ideologies choose the issues or beliefs which have emotive value to a particular community, for example, a ban on beef consumption, cow protection, conversion, personal laws, places of worship, etc.[16] Economic reason also gets the religious form in communal conflicts.[17] In a multi religious democratic context, who controls power matters. The competition for political power, one of the chief reasons for communalism, finds shelter in the political abuse of religious sentiments. Today, communalism is the natural ally of many power hungry politicians. They do not tolerate any criticism of communalism. They even interpret such criticism as an attack on religion.[18] Thapar aptly said, 'it (communalism) is fundamentally a hunt for power'.[19] Some blame religion for communalism. In reality, religion has nothing to do with communalism but the misuse of religion for power and hegemony[20] creates communal divisions in society. From a theological perspective, 'dogmatism, legalism and institutionalism'[21] contribute to the emergence of religious communalism.

Communalism is not a new phenomenon. Stories in religious Scriptures explain its mechanism. For example, two narratives in the Bible vividly describe the interplay of religion, politics and economy. The story in Acts 19: 23-40 shows how religion is misused to protect economic interests. In Acts 24: 1-23, politics serves religion.[22] This interplay continues unabated.

Communalism devalues a particular religion and its rich heritage of faith and service to humanity. It kills the spirit and liberating essence of religion. As Samuel Rayan said, 'when I kill and commit arson in a religious frenzy or brutal greed, I destroy whatever is sacred, beautiful and venerable in my own cultural and religious heritage'. Therefore, he calls communalism 'a crass exhibition of unfaith and unspirituality'.[23] Religions nurture God-human and human-human relationships. Communalism distorts the spirituality of relationships and perpetuates enmity and irreligious mentality among people. A devout Hindu/Christian/Muslim/Sikh cannot become 'communal'. Mahatma Gandhi is an example of a non communal Indian. He valued all religions. His prayer meetings witnessed the reading of the Scriptures of all religions. He said, 'My Hinduism is not sectarianism. It includes all that I know to be best in Islam, Buddhism and Zoroastrianism. I approach politics, as everything else, in a religious spirit. Truth is my religion and ahimsa is the only way to its realization'. (*Harijan,* 30 April 1938).[24] His statement reflects the mind of many devout people who counter communalism in their religious and social lives. Likewise, 'secular' and 'communal' cannot stay together in a secular democratic society. We need politicians like Nehru who would publicly challenge the menace of communalism. He boldly said, 'So far as I am concerned, I am prepared to lose every election in India but to give no quarter to communalism or casteism'.[25] As an ideology, a political tool and a means of power struggle, communalism has already (mildly or extremely) gripped the psyche of the majority of the Indians. Today, communal polarization is more visible in Indian society.

COMMUNAL POLARIZATION

The Preamble of India's Constitution declares the nation to be a 'SOVEREIGN SOCIALIST SECULAR DEMOCRATIC REPUBLIC'.[26] In the West, of course, secularism is associated with the strict separation of religion and state. In India, though, reflecting its very different context, secularism means the equal support of the State for and acceptance of all religions. In other words, 'secularism' in India became synonymous with 'pluralism'.[27] The Dalai Lama has said, 'India is a living example of religious harmony and secular ethics. The Indian Constitution is based on secularism.'[28] Currently, though, Indian society is increasingly polarized in terms of caste and religion. Religious polarization has had especially disastrous consequences, contributing to the upsurge of religious intolerance, which has led to the condoning and even initiation of violent crimes against members of minority communities. What might be called the political use of religion has distorted the very idea of secularism, also leading to its caricature as a kind of 'minority appeasement'.[29]

Communal polarization in the name of religion is a serious threat to India's secular fabric. It threatens the pluralistic heritage of the nation and destroys communal harmony. The destruction of the Babri mosque in Ayodhya, Uttar Pradesh, in December 1992; the burning of the Sabarmati Express train in Godhra, Gujarat and subsequent communal riots, in February 2002; the violent clash of the Hindu and Muslim communities of Muzaffarnagar, Uttar Pradesh, in August-September 2013; the communal riots in Delhi in 2020—are few among many such incidents that have polarised the nation communally in the recent past. These incidents are repeatedly invoked by desperate politicians who hope to preserve and even enlarge their vote banks through appeals to 'the politics of hatred'.[30] They also take pride in their decisions that have a religious impact. For example, recent elections in Gujarat and Himachal Pradesh (2022) have witnessed the claims of BJP politicians on the construction of the Ram Temple in Ayodhya and the renovation of the Kashi-Vishwanath temple corridor. The politicians, who do not invoke controversial religious issues, go for 'soft' religious appeals like inscribing the images of Hindu deities, Lakshmi and Ganesha on Indian currencies.[31]According to T.R.S. Subramanian, 'India's vote banks are still based on religion and community rather than performance and economic interests. . . .'[32] The political parties directly or indirectly promote vote bank politics and blame each other for abetting it.[33]

The country also witnesses 'an abrasive intrusion of religion onto the public square'. Though there is no state religion, the religion of the majority gets 'unofficial' state patronage more than other religions. The 'othering' of religious minorities has become the new normal in contemporary society. It echoes the call for the genocide of Muslims, the disruption of the religious activities of minorities, etc. The recent eviction initiatives in minority populated areas have communal overtones.[34] The communalists draw new social, religious, and political boundaries between the minority and the majority communities[35] and perpetuate religious identities for vested political and economic interests. Whether minority or majority, all religious communities have contributed to communal polarization in India. Majority communalism emerges as a reaction to minority communalism and vice versa. Communal polarization causes people to look at everything through the eyes of communal interests. The continuation of communal riots, the assemblage of people on communal lines over local issues, etc., shows that the forces of communalism have succeeded, to a large extent, in polarizing the people on religious grounds. However, in a democratic society, the communalization of politics affects the citizenry badly.

COMMUNALIZATION OF POLITICS

Indian political life has always involved the interplay of religion and politics since Independence. However, the intensity of this interplay has been increasing steadily. Today it has reached a dangerous level, with recent general and state elections seeing blatant attempts to polarize voters along communal lines.[36] The founders of this nation aimed at creating an alternative society based on the principles of justice, equality, liberty and fraternity. They envisioned a community in which these values would prevail over caste hegemony and religious majoritarianism. Today communal politics threatens the nation's secular polity. It poses a challenge for all citizens, irrespective of their religious affiliation.[37] Communal politics promotes religious differences to obscure other differences and employs strategies such as labelling, scapegoating, spreading misinformation and narrating distorted stories.[38] It has multiple layers. If religious differences do not work, then group/

sect identities emerge as a tool to play a negative power struggle. For instance, in electoral politics, wherever mixed religious communities exist in equal or slightly different proportions, the religious sentiments of the majority community in the constituency are evoked. In case, a particular religious community constitutes a majority in a constituency, caste or denomination/sect tag is employed to ensure electoral victory. This polarization is not an innocent process but a product of a calculated and vicious plan to achieve the goal of power. The politicians are the priests of the communalization of politics. It is aptly said that 'The temple and the mosque lovers of today's India are, first and foremost, power-hungry politicians. In their hands, religion no longer is concerned with value, but only with instrumentalism; that is, religion is a means among others for the achievement of whatever goals are adopted'.[39] When religion becomes an instrument for political campaign, it loses its purpose and contributes to the divisive agenda of communalists. Many religious leaders also join with communal politicians and give tacit support to the politicization of religion. Political parties like the Indian Union Muslim League, the BJP, the Akali Dal, Kerala Congress, etc., have religious preferences[40] in their manifestos and policies even though they claim to be democratic and inclusive. The communalization of politics results in framing communal policies, legislating communal laws, and executing communal strategies. The 'other', who are outside of a particular communal ideology, are the victims of communal politics. Religion teaches a different 'politics'.

RELIGION AND LIBERATIVE POLITICS

There is an exclusivist polemic and inclusivist humanitarian dimension in the theology and praxis of every religion. The former produces a fundamentalist and communal mindset, the latter the compassionate and humanitarian outlook that encourages people to work for communal harmony, justice and national integration. The polemic dimension is conservative and anti-rational. It divides people on religious lines and causes communal conflicts. The humanitarian side has a prophetic and liberative intention: standing for the cause of the poor and the vulnerable.[41] In a religiously plural context, particularly threatened by religious communalism and fundamentalism, according to Paulose Mar Paulose, religion has a prophetic and liberative rather than communally 'political' role. What makes a religion relevant? 'A religion becomes relevant if it relinquishes its conservatism, and becomes revolutionary and partakes in the struggle for a new earth and new heaven, by standing up for the oppressed'.[42] It calls for religion to be prophetic against injustice, corruption, the influence of money and caste, wrong priorities of the state, communalism. It should raise its voice against the forces that victimize people in the name of religion, caste and ideology. The basis for such prophetic and liberative engagement is human dignity. The political role of religions is to support the struggle of people to affirm their rights.[43] The liberative intent of this role reminds us that religion/religious communities should support liberative politics rather than communal politics. In communal politics, the interests of a particular group are protected and encouraged; whereas in liberative politics, the agenda of political engagement is the well being of the wider community. In liberative politics, people are the centre of political activity, whereas, in communal politics it is the vested interests of the rich and powerful who dominate the political sphere. Liberative politics is prophetic and sensible to the issues of people. Communal politics is defensive and creates hatred and enmity among communities. In liberative politics, religion functions as a corrective force that transforms society. But in communal politics, religion becomes an instrument to polarize society for political mileage. It creates a mindset of 'we' and 'them' and perpetuates 'othering'.

CHURCH/RELIGION IN COMMUNAL CONTEXT: COMMUNITY AGAINST 'OTHERING'

Every religious community has a moral responsibility to combat communalism. The location sometimes redefines the role of a particular religious community to address societal issues of the time. The menace of communalism calls for every religious community to rethink its identity in terms of inter-community relationships. M.M. Thomas, referring to the Christian community, observes that a religious community should shape its self-understanding as a community against 'othering' in a communally charged context. He suggests that the faith communities should come out of their isolated existence and embrace dialogical life.[44] It requires religions to dialogue with one another and to strive for 'secular koinonia'.[45] For Christians, 'secular koinonia' is not 'secular' *per se* but an expression of their faith commitment. The dialogical existence of religions helps counter religious fundamentalism and communalism that distort devout minds for vested motives. The dialogue renews communities[46] and prevents communal profiling and 'othering'. There may not have been any theological hindrance for religious communities to participate in dialogical life. For Christians, dialogue is biblically valid because the Christian faith teaches that Jesus Christ abolishes all walls of separation among humans.[47] The entry point of the dialogical life of religions is common challenges[48] like religious communalism that have far reaching ramifications in society. In the dialogical engagement, religious communities are called to redeem the human values of freedom, equality, and justice and to uphold the quality of national fraternity.[49] Reconciliation and social communion are the final goals of dialogical life.[50]

In line with dialogical life against 'othering', religious communities should take some proactive steps to counter communalism. Though Paulose Mar Paulose identified six important points for the Church, they are significant for other religious traditions too. Firstly, to defeat communalism and to protect secular nature of society, the Christians/religious communities should stand for the cause of the weak and the voiceless rather than for the communal interests in the name of minority rights or under the pretext of numerical strength. Secondly, the Church/religious communities should not run for political power. They can spiritually and morally serve people only if they consciously maintain distance from the corridors of power.[51] Thirdly, Christian ecumenism/religious fraternities should not be a hindrance to the unity of human communities in a particular context. Fourthly, the Church/religious communities must support secular ideologies if they work for the welfare of humanity. Fifthly, the Churches/religious communities should cooperate with Social Action Groups involved in activities for socio-economic and political justice. Finally, the Church/religious communities should resist decisions and policies of the governments that directly or indirectly encourage communalism.[52] The Church as New Humanity in Christ has a mandate of renewing and transforming human communities.[53] As a transforming force, the Church is not a community that strengthens the walls of social and religious separation but an inclusive community that breaks those walls to prevent 'othering' in society. Every religious tradition is an inherently inclusive community having theological and social capital to embrace 'others' to proclaim that 'you are no more other'.

CHRISTIAN COMMUNALISM

In India, communalism cannot be attributed to one particular religion/sect alone. All religions, directly or indirectly, have contributed to the upsurge of communalism.[54] Social, religious, political and economic interests of faith communities have been instrumental to the communalization of society. Some may wonder about Christian communalism because they are familiar only with the narratives of Hindu, Muslim or Sikh communalism. One of the reasons is that comparatively speaking, there are very few communal clashes between Christians and other religious communities, particularly those initiated by Christians. Geographically, the political influence of Christians is very much restricted, compared to that of other religious communities. Also they are not united to have common political and economic interests. The Churches concentrate more on establishing educational, health and social service institutions and engaging in mission activities.[55] However, like any other religious community, Christians also have a communal inclination. The communal elements are implied in some of their theological assertions and activities.

The theological roots of Christian communalism lie in the absolutist revelatory claim and Christ centred inclusivist approach of Christians.[56] The biblical affirmation of one God and negation of other gods create an exclusive mindset among Christians. They are taught that Jesus is the ultimate revelation of God, and they alone possess this truth. It is their religious duty to defend and spread the revealed truth. This understanding motivates many Christians to initiate missional activities among non-Christians. The crusades, the persecution of heretics, the inquisition, the forced conversion of Jews and other non-Christians, etc.,[57] are examples of the impact of theological exclusivism in the past. Theological exclusivism provides the basis for communal thinking. However, the biblical faith neutralizes theological exclusivism through its advocacy of openness and universality. The biblical understanding of covenant God who cares for the entire humanity, the approach of Jesus towards non-Jews (Mt 8: 5-13; Mk 7: 24-30), the positive attitude towards non-Christian religions (Acts 17: 22-31) speak against communal behaviour of Christians.[58] If Christians think and act communally, then theological exclusivism shapes their mindset. The whole message of the Bible is anti-communal though exclusive faith affirmations of people in a particular historical context are also recorded.

Christian ecumenism is one of the expressions of the communal nature of the Christian community in India. Ecumenism refers to the unity of churches for the welfare of the Christian community. It primarily addresses common issues related to Christians in their respective contexts. Though ecumenism has a positive side in terms of sharing resources, spiritual fellowship, social service, establishing and managing educational institutions, etc., its approach seems to be communal sometimes. It is more obsessed with safeguarding the rights and privileges of the minority status of Christianity in India. It seldom raises the issues of the people of neighbouring faiths. The unity of churches cannot be a communal enterprise for it is rooted in Jesus Christ, who is not communal, in his approach and actions. Therefore, its scope goes beyond the concerns of Christians. The unity with communal intent is against the vision of Jesus.[59] This unity should neither be against the people of neighboring faiths nor to get privileges; but a unity against the powers and principalities of injustice and marginalization. Jesus' prayer for unity (John 17: 20-6) will be more meaningful in the Indian context if Christians understand ecumenism as a unity to engage with people, particularly the weak and the vulnerable in society. For that, Christians should enlarge their ecumenical vision and join with other religious traditions and secular movements. It has the potential to translate ecumenism as a life-affirming endeavour. This approach removes the communal tag of ecumenism. According to M.M. Thomas, 'Christian Ecumenism has truth and meaning only as it becomes the ground and pillar of a New Humanism which can provide the framework of understanding and critical participation in the revolution of our time'.[60] For him, Church is not a communal organization or institution destined to look after the concerns and interests of Christians alone but the interests of all citizens irrespective of religion, gender, ethnicity. [61] This is the essence of ecumenism.

Some of the evangelistic activities of Christians have a communal character. For example, discrediting the customs and beliefs of other religious traditions has contributed to communal tensions between religious communities. It comes out of the influence of theological exclusivism. It portrays all Christians in communal frame and compels others to respond communally. The antagonistic nature of evangelism makes others offensive and even dissuades them from respecting the Christian faith. Gandhi shares how his dislike towards Christianity developed:

> In those days, Christian missionaries used to stand in a corner near the high school and hold forth, pouring abuse on Hindus and their gods. I could not endure this. I must have stood there to hear them once only, but that was enough to dissuade me from repeating the experiment. . . . I also heard that the new convert had already begun abusing the religion of his ancestors, their customs, and their country. All these things created in me a dislike for Christianity.[62]

Gandhi might have had other reasons to dislike Christianity. But there is truth in his comments. However, the Bible does not endorse any form of evangelism that condemns other religious traditions.

Denominationalism among Christians has characteristics of communalism. Denominational (sect) rivalry is common in Christianity. Denominations covertly or overtly compete with each other and practise 'mutual exclusion'. Every denomination attempts largely to safeguard its privileges and raise its voice for the concerns of the respective group. It reflects in the social and political outlook of Christians. Denominationalism claims that a particular Christian sect has common political, economic, social, and religious interests. It prepares many Christians to think communally about other Christian communities and religious traditions. Denominationalism also defines the nature of the political involvement of a sect, particularly in electoral politics. The leaders directly or indirectly communicate the political preference of a particular denomination and attempt to influence its members during elections. Many of them campaign for the candidate if s/he belongs to the denomination. On the political front, if one takes Christians in general, like any other religious community, they are also responsible for communal politics in the areas where they constitute a substantial constituency. Some Christian religious and political leaders openly demand Christian candidates for a particular constituency. Many Christians cast votes on communal lines. Communal elements are noticeable in the social and political outlook of many Christians but it is a myth that all Christians follow the political guidelines of denominations. In reality, Christian and 'communal' are theologically incompatible. This principle applies to other religious traditions also. A Christian theological response is given in the following section to enrich the responses of Christians and other religious communities to communalism.

NON-COMMUNAL COMMUNITY: A CHRISTIAN PERSPECTIVE

In a communally polarized context, every religious community should become a non-communal community. To resist communalism, religious communities have to redefine their mission and self-understanding as well as evolve as non-communal communities. There are a few things involved in the process of becoming non-communal communities. Often, the response of the religious communities becomes 'communal', which strengthens the communal forces. For Christians, according to Athyal, a religious response to communalism should not be 'communal' because God involves Godself in the process of the transformation of human communities and the Church is the natural partner of God in this process.[63] Other religious traditions are also equal partners in the process that includes combating communalism. This consciousness will create non-communal communities in society.

Every religion should be subject to prophetic criticism.[64] It is very much needed to shape the outlook of the religious community towards communalism. Religious communities/persons should ask whether his/her religious thinking or religion has contributed to the rise of communalism. The biblical faith teaches that prophetic critique is divine. For instance, the Bible tells the stories of prophets sent by God to remind people about their duties in relation to God and fellow human beings and make them sensitive to the world. In a communal context, prophetic critique would tell religious communities that being communal is not their divine destiny in this world. Therefore, the prophetic critique calls for the repentance of our 'communal' mistakes[65] and sanitizing our thinking process towards building up non-communal communities. It is impossible without an experience of 'radical tolerance, the death of all communalism'.[66]

The life and practices of religious communities should become the antidote to communalism. They should uphold 'nobler sentiments' and denounce 'aggressive tendencies' in respective religions. It helps to cultivate communal harmony in society. Since communal disharmony emerges in a socially and economically unequal society, the struggle for a just and humane society is imperative for the struggles against communalism.[67] This is possible if religious communities come together based on secular ethos and address the concerns of peace and justice.[68] The convergence of non-communal communities is the only remedy for the communalization of society.

Indian Christians cannot become communal because of historical and theological reasons. Historically, they gave up their communal electoral safeguards and upheld the secular ethos of the Constitution. They cannot practise communal politics because the Christian faith teaches them tolerance, inclusiveness, and openness

(Gal. 3: 28;1 Cori. 12: 12; Col. 3: 11). The love commandment of Jesus (Matthew 22: 39) rejects all boundaries erected by communalists. Christians cannot look at socio political economic realities through the eyes of religion but through love. The outlook of love is non-communal and egalitarian. It means communalism is the absence of love among human beings. Love is not the monopoly of Christians. Every religion teaches love in different ways. Therefore, no religious person can become a communal being. A non communal community emerges when adherents of a religion become the embodiment of love that transcends all human made boundaries.

God is Not Communal[69]

According to Samuel Rayan, God is the creator of 'the other', and loves them and protects their existence. Therefore, faith in God requires one to accept the identity of 'the other' as God does. Human beings are destined to embody love because they are created by the love of God. The Christian faith affirms that the other person is also the image of God. It implies that both God and human beings cannot become 'communal'. For God, human beings are not objects of communal interest. As the image of God, human beings are 'holier' than any religious place/object/ritual. God is concerned about every human being because s/he carries the image of God. In the story of Cain and Abel (Genesis 4), God asked Cain, who killed his brother, Abel, 'where is your brother (Gen 4: 9)?' This question is very significant in the context of communalism. He responded to God with another question, 'Am I my brother's keeper?' This is the response of a communalist who is least concerned about brother/sister in another tradition. When one kills another person, the image of God, one is lost to God. This story in the communal context reminds one that s/he is responsible for 'the other' who is also the image of God but a member of another community. If God is not 'communal' in creating and protecting human beings then religious communities ought to become non-communal.

Humans are not for Religion

Religion plays an important role in human life. But human beings are not created to satisfy 'religion'. Religions are not custodians of humans. Unfortunately, human beings are victims of institutionalized, politicized and communalized religions. In such a context, the words of Jesus come as a counter narrative to placing religion above humans (communal strategy). He said, 'The Sabbath was made for man (woman), and not man (woman) for the Sabbath' (Mark 2: 27). The Sabbath symbolizes religion in today's context. The implied meaning is that worship places, Scriptures, theologies, religious political social institutions, etc., are for human beings and their liberation.[70] Therefore, religion should serve humans by guiding them to the divine and the hungry, the needy, the marginalized, the victims of communalism, but not preparing them to look at fellow beings through the lens of the doctrinal system. While being committed to the faith, every religious community must be aware of the fact that religion is for humans but not vice versa. This outlook enables them to become non-communal in a communal context.

Jesus is not Communal

Christians believe that Jesus is the saviour of humanity. His divine identity is essentially non-communal and all embracing because everything was created through him. His life and work tell all that he was anti-communal in his approach, teachings, and relationship with others. He had no enemies even though many considered him an enemy. For him, no one was a profane, outsider or unholy pagan. All human beings, irrespective of their faiths, were brothers and sisters.[71] He rejected religious laws that defined people.[72] Jesus respected the religiosity of others (Mt 8). He identified with the socially and religiously other (Mk 2).[73] He is a model of a non-communal person. Every religion may have such divine personalities/iconic figures. They cannot be viewed through a communal lens because their divine essence is not 'communal'. They embrace everyone. People who follow them or believe in them also cannot live communally.

Every religious community has theological and Scriptural capital to affirm its inherent non-communal identity. Religious people should emulate non-communal values and practices of their respective religions. They should proclaim the truth that they are not 'communal' and a threat to others. They should not allow the communal forces to misuse their rich religious heritage for vested political and economic interests. Religious communities should resist communalism in the name of religion.

INCLUSIVE-PROPHETIC APPROACH AGAINST COMMUNAL APPROACH

Christian faith teaches an inclusive approach to life, not excluding or discriminating against anyone because of his or her religion (Matt 13: 24-30; Luke 9: 51-6; John 18: 33-8; 1 Cor 5: 12-13; etc.). This approach has nothing to do with traditional community centric, vote bank based politics. Instead, one should take a more holistic approach. Christian political engagement should be in the tradition of the Old Testament prophets and Jesus Christ himself. The Bible (Isa 61: 1-3; Luke 4: 18-19; etc.) offers valuable insights regarding the nature of Christian political engagement. For example, the book of Isaiah, especially Chapters 9, 11 and 53, provides a political engagement model that might be called 'prophetic politics'.

The prophetic approach to politics demands two things. First, the system should protect the poor and the weak from the domination of the ruling class. Prophetic politics stands against all economic exploitation, political discrimination and social marginalization. When one sees politicians taking advantage of the poor to further their own designs, one must insist that the actual needs of the poor be not only addressed but prioritized. Second, rulers must acknowledge that God is the sovereign 'Lord of lords' (Deut 10: 17; Ps 136: 3; cf. Dan 2: 47) so that all human authorities are subject to God's overarching power. This means that rulers should govern according to the revealed will of God, whose intent is to protect every citizen's rights, particularly the poor and members of minority communities (Ps 82: 3; Prov. 31: 8-9; Isa 1: 17; etc.).

Prophetic politics requires that rulers who do not uphold their responsibility in this regard be reminded of their duty. With the nation facing a crisis brought about by the communal politics of vote banks, one must urge the ruling class to look beyond the narrow interests of one or another religious community and defend the principles of secular democracy enshrined in the Constitution.

An extension of prophetic politics might be called 'messianic politics'. Isaiah speaks of a messianic ruler who 'with righteousness . . . shall judge the poor, and decide with equity for the meek of the earth' (Isa 11: 4), and Christians recognize that this ruler prophesied by Isaiah is Jesus Christ. The life and ministry of Jesus show that he stood for an alternative model of politics, informed by his consciousness that he was a 'suffering servant' (Isa 53). He came to serve others even though he was their Messiah. Rather than conforming to the exploitative, oppressive politics of his time, he aimed to establish a society based on justice and righteousness. Though he did not make a direct attempt at gaining political power (John 18: 36), his actions and teachings shaped the socio political and religious mindset of his people. He showed them that the political class must engage with the issues of ordinary people. Like him, rulers should become suffering servants who attend to people's needs, irrespective of caste or creed; this must be the approach of all who engage in politics.[74] When serving the people becomes the motto, it will be hard to pursue communal interests.

Christian faith endorses democratic government. The values of democracy are inherent in the Christian understanding of human beings, the world and the political order.[75] The question is whether political democracy alone is enough to establish and maintain a just order in society. Although India is often described as 'the world's largest democracy' many forms of inequality are still deeply entrenched.[76] Dalits, tribals, and members of other so-called 'backward' communities face especially difficult social conditions. It seems clear that political democracy cannot establish the social equality necessary for a just society; for this, it must be joined to social democracy, the establishment of a social order in which everyone is equally valued.[77] In the Indian context, social democracy is fundamental because the caste mentality still captivates the thinking of most citizens. Yet the Old Testament prophets and Jesus Christ himself emphasized the need for social equality. They questioned the ruling class of their day, which ignored the social conditions of the poor, the weak and members of minority communities, much like the ruling class of our day. Christian political engagement must focus on social democracy while supporting and strengthening political democracy. Without social democracy, it seems inevitable that traditional communal politics will lead to the eruption of social disorder and even violence.

Political education can play an essential part in our struggle against the communalization of politics. One should take the initiative to educate our fellow citizens about democratic values, the Indian political system, the ideological basis of political parties, the citizen's constitutional rights and duties, etc.[78] This information must reach the weaker elements of society, as those are especially vulnerable to and often implicated in the communal conflict. Political education should aim to make all citizens aware of the threat posed by traditional communal politics. This should be part of Christian engagement in Indian society.

To resist communalism, religious communities should create inter faith groups for reconciliation, mutual protection, rehabilitation of victims of communalism, etc.[79] Everyone has the right to proclaim the truth of his/her religion. It has to be exercised with much care and accountability. The proclamation may contribute to communalism if it does not consider the theological and cultural sensitivity of the people.

In India, there should be no place for communalism and religious intolerance. Despite a few aberrations, for many centuries, India upheld the value of tolerance. A beautiful expression of this point is the famous statement of Swami Vivekananda to those assembled in the World's Parliament of Religions, held in Chicago in 1893:

> I am proud to belong to a religion which has taught the world both tolerance and universal acceptance. We believe not only in universal toleration, but we accept all religions to be true. I am proud to tell you that I belong to religion into whose sacred language, the Sanskrit, the word 'exclusion' is untranslatable.

I am proud to belong to a nation which has sheltered the persecuted and the refugees of all religions and all nations of the earth.[80]

Yet today, this land of tolerance has become a land of religious intolerance because of communal bigots who capitalize on the religious prejudices to protect their political and economic interests. However, one has not lost hope. No religious community can become 'communal' because God is not communal. Everyone is the image of God though s/he belongs to a different religious tradition. 'Othering' is not religious but communal. Therefore, communalism is anti religious.

NOTES

1. Hindus and Muslims constitute two separate nations.
2. T.N. Madan, *Modern Myths, Locked Minds: Secularism and Fundamentalism in* India (New Delhi: Oxford University Press, 2009, 2nd edn.), 252.
3. Ram Puniyani, *Communal Politics* (Mumbai: J & P Publishers, 2003), 46.
4. Gyanendra Pandey, *The Construction of Communalism in Colonial North India* (New Delhi: Oxford University Press, 1990), 6.
5. Bipin Chandra, *Essays on Contemporary India* (revd. edn., Delhi: Har-Anand Publications, 1999), 23.
6. Ibid., 125-6.
7. Madan, *Modern Myths, Locked Minds*, op. cit., 251.
8. Pandey, *The Construction of Communalism in Colonial North India*, op. cit., 240.
9. Chandra, *Essays on Contemporary India*, op. cit., 85.
10. Shashi Tharoor, *Why I am a Hindu* (New Delhi: Aleph Book Company, 2018), 187.
11. Amartya Sen, *The Argumentative Indian* (London: Penguin Books, 2005), 53.
12. Paulose Mar Gregorios, *The Secular Ideology: An Impotent Remedy for India's Communal Problem* (Delhi: Indian Society for Promoting Christian Knowledge/Mar Gregorios Foundation, 1998), 70.
13. Ibid., 45.
14. Jesudas M. Athyal, 'The Return of the Sacred: An Indian Christian Perspective on Religion and Politics', *Nationalism and Hindutva: A Christian*

Response (Delhi: Centre for Mission Studies/Union Biblical Seminary/ Indian Society for Promoting Christians Knowledge, 2005), 146.
15. Ibid., 159.
16. Romila Thapar, *The Past as Present: Forging Contemporary Identities Through History* (New Delhi: Aleph, 2014), 122.
17. George M. Soares-Prabhu, 'Religion and Communalism: The Christian Dilemma', *Responding to Communalism,* ed. S. Arokiasamy (Anand: Gujarat Sahitya Prakash, 1991), 141.
18. Thapar, *The Past as Present: Forging Contemporary Identities Through History,* op. cit., 116-17.
19. Ibid., 125.
20. Bosco Puthur, 'Mission of the Church in the Context of Communalism', in *Communalism in India: A Challenge to Theologizing,* ed. S. Arulsamy (Banglore: Claretian Publications, 1988), 182.
21. Paul Puthanangady, 'Communalism: A Theological Reflection', in *Communalism in India: A Challenge to Theologizing,* op. cit., 157.
22. R.J. Raja, 'Communal Conflicts in the Nascent Church', in *Responding to Communalism,* op. cit., 233-7.
23. Samuel Rayan, 'The Other and the Theologian', in *Responding to Communalism,* op. cit., 134.
24. P.L. John Panicker, *Gandhi on Pluralism and Communalism* (Delhi: Indian Society for Promoting Christians Knowledge, 2006), 189.
25. Chandra, *Essays on Contemporary India,* op. cit., 149.
26. *The Constitution of India* (New Delhi: Ministry of Law and Justice, Government of India, 1989), 1.
27. Wendy Doniger, 'The Hindu Code in Vanishing Ink', *Outlook* (24 February 2014, New Delhi), 16-18.
28. Quoted in 'Corruption in India a Big Contradiction: Dalai Lama', *Times of India* (Mumbai), 21 March 2014, 6.
29. Doniger, 'The Hindu Code in Vanishing Ink', op. cit., 18.
30. Aroon Purie, 'From the Editor-in-Chief', *India Today,* 23 September 2013, 1. & Avinash Nair, 'Rioters given lesson in 2002. . .', *The Indian Express* (Pune, 26 November 2022), 1 & 2.
31. Badri Narayan, 'Winning Gujrat', *The Indian Express* (Pune, 26 November 2022), 12.
32. Quoted in Kunal Pradhan, 'Riot for Vote', *India Today,* 23 September 2013, 26.
33. https://www.newindianexpress.com/nation/2021/mar/29/congress-used-minorities-as-commodity-exploited-their-sentiments-for-vote-bank-politics-jitendra-2283188.html, accessed on 5 April 2021.

34. Abdul Khaliq, 'Crisis of Fraternity', *The Indian Express* (Pune, 24 February 2022), 11.
35. Drego Pearl, 'Communal Politics and Violence: Towards a Theological Response', in *Indian Secularism: A Theological Response*, ed. Antony Kalliath and Raj Irudaya (Banglore: Indian Theological Association, 2011), 90.
36. General Election, 2019 and State Elections 2021.
37. James Massey, 'Inter-Play of Religion, Politics, and Communalism in India', in *From Truth to Truth, A Journey through Faiths: A Selection of Representative: Essays by Dr. James Massey*, ed. Deepak Seth (New Delhi: Centre for Dalit Studies and NOIDA: Academy Press, 2008), 224.
38. Pearl, 'Communal Politics and Violence: Towards a Theological Response', op. cit., 94.
39. Madan, *Modern Myths, Locked Minds: Secularism and Fundamentalism in India*, op. cit., 261.
40. Mar Gregorios, *The Secular Ideology: An Impotent Remedy for India's Communal Problem*, op. cit., 48.
41. Ibid., 67-8.
42. Paulose Mar Paulose, *Nisabdharayirikkan Ningalkkenthadhikaram?* (Malayalam) (Noorannad: Fabian Books, 1998), 143.
43. Paulose Mar Paulose, *Swathanthryamanu Daivam* (Malayalam) (Ariyannur: Patabhedam, 1996), 35, 22-4 & 36.
44. M.M. Thomas, *Risking Christ for Christ's Sake: Towards an Ecumenical Theology of Pluralism* (Geneva: World Council of Churches Publications, 1987), 1.
45. M.M. Thomas, *New Creation in Christ* (Delhi: Indian Society for Promoting Christian Knowledge, 1976), 48.
46. M.M. Thomas, *Man and the Universe of Faiths* (Madras: The Christian Literature Society, 1975), 145.
47. M.M. Thomas, *The Gospel of Forgiveness and Koinonia* (Delhi: Indian Society for Promoting Christian Knowledge and Thiruvalla: CSS, 1994), 9.
48. Thomas, *Man and the Universe of Faiths*, op. cit., vi.
49. M.M. Thomas, *The Church's Mission and Post-Modern Humanism* (Delhi: Indian Society for Promoting Christian Knowledge and Thiruvalla: Christava Sahitya Samiti, 1996), 29.
50. M.M. Thomas, *Religion and the Revolt of the Oppressed* (Delhi: Indian Society for Promoting Christian Knowledge, 1981), 69.
51. Mar Paulose, *Nisabdharayirikkan Ningalkkenthadhikaram*, op. cit., 101-2.
52. Ibid., 103.

53. Thomas, *Risking Christ for Christ's Sake*, op. cit., 119.
54. Athyal, 'The Return of the Sacred: An Indian Christian Perspective on Religion and Politics,' op. cit., 150.
55. Soares-Prabhu, 'Religion and Communalism: The Christian Dilemma', op. cit., 144.
56. Panicker, *Gandhi on Pluralism and Communalism*, op. cit., 80-6.
57. Illickamury, 'Judaeo-Christian Tradition and Communalism', in *Communalism in India: A Challenge to Theologizing*, op. cit., 91-3.
58. Ibid., 97-101.
59. Paulose Mar Paulose, *Spirituality for Struggle* (Thiruvalla: Christava Sahitya Samiti, 1999), 62-3.
60. M.M. Thomas, *Towards a Theology of Contemporary Ecumenism* (Madras: The Christian Literature Society, 1978), 164
61. M.M. Thomas, 'The Churches and the Future of Indian Democracy', National Council of Churches Review, vol. XCVII, nos. 6-7 (June-July 1977): 343.
62. M.K. Gandhi, *An Autobiography or The Story of My Experiments with Truth* (Ahmedabad: Navajivan Publishing House, 1927, rpt. 1996), 28-9.
63. Athyal, 'The Return of the Sacred: An Indian Christian Perspective on Religion and Politics', op. cit., 147-8.
64. Puthanangady, 'Communalism: A Theological Reflection', op. cit., 158-9.
65. Puthiadam, 'Communalism: An Analysis and a Christian Answer,' in *Responding to Communalism*, op. cit., 269.
66. Soares-Prabhu, 'Religion and Communalism: The Christian Dilemma,' op. cit., 162.
67. Mar Gregorios, *The Secular Ideology: An Impotent Remedy for India's Communal Problem*, op. cit., 61.
68. Athyal, 'The Return of the Sacred: An Indian Christian Perspective on Religion and Politics', op. cit., 159.
69. Rayan, 'The Other and the Theologian', op. cit., 128-32.
70. Ibid., 132.
71. Soares-Prabhu, 'Religion and Communalism: The Christian Dilemma', op. cit., 145-8.
72. Ibid., 162.
73. Rayan, 'The Other and the Theologian', op. cit., 130.
74. Massey, 'Inter-Play of Religion, Politics, and Communalism in India', op. cit., 225.
75. Michael Novak, *The Spirit of Democratic Capitalism* (New York: Simon and Schuster, 1982).

76. Dibyendu Chaudhuri and Parijat Ghosh, 'Why Inequality is India's Worst Enemy', *Downto Earth*, 5 March 2021, https://www.downtoearth.org.in/blog/economy/why-inequality-is-india-s-worst-enemy-75778, accessed on 6 April 2021.
77. Massey, 'Inter-Play of Religion, Politics, and Communalism in India', op. cit., 226.
78. Ibid.
79. Pearl, 'Communal Politics and Violence: Towards a Theological Response', op. cit., 91.
80. Swami Vivekananda, 'Speech of Mr. Vivekananda', in *The World's Parliament of Religions: An Illustrated and Popular Story of the World's First Parliament of Religions, Held in Chicago in Connection with the Columbian Exposition of 1893*, ed. John Henry Barrows, 2 vols. (Chicago, Ill.: Parliament Publishing Co., 1893), 1: 102.

CHAPTER 7

Nationalism and Christians

India has citizens who belong to different religious, cultural and caste/ethnic traditions. Despite differences in lifestyle, food, language and cultural practices, the spirit of Indianness runs through the veins of citizens. Together they constitute the nation and serve her with utmost devotion. As a nation, India embodies the hopes and aspirations of every citizen. Her existence explains the loyalty of her citizens. However, nationalism has become one of the sensitive issues in the nation with its multi religious citizenry today. Nationalist ideologies based on religious identities have defined nation, citizenship and loyalty to the nation on religious lines and challenged secular nationalist thoughts that united every Indian to fight against colonial rule. Sectarian nationalist ideas, particularly those derived from majoritarian religious traditions, suspect the nationalism of minorities who are sons and daughters of this land. It pushes them into the periphery of society. Though the Constitution of India affirms inclusion and equality of all citizens in national life, contemporary nationalist discourses dominated by religion factor speak the language of exclusion.

CONTEXT

In India nationalism has roots in the nationalist movement against colonial rule. The nation has witnessed the emergence of different nationalist discourses throughout the centuries. Different ideologies and contextual factors shape them. Some advocated inclusive, composite national identity of citizens, while others promoted exclusive, religious nationalism in a religiously pluralistic society. The nation has experienced the consequences of both majority and minority religious nationalism. Religious nationalism has defined the loyalty and love of the citizens to the nation based on their religious or ethnic identity. It profiled the citizens: the loyal and the disloyal. Citizens, who adhere to majoritarian religion, were portrayed as 'national' whereas citizens, who belong to minority religious traditions, were 'anti-national' or 'threat' to the nation. The former were considered sons/daughters of this soil, the latter the 'other', or the 'stranger'. The religiously shaped 'national' profiling of citizens produced the culture of 'othering', triggered communal conflicts and mutual hatred and led to the Partition of the nation. Religious nationalism continues to suffocate the secular social life of the nation. It appears in newer forms and asserts its space through political power, economic systems and cultural symbols. Though every form of religious nationalism is fundamentally dangerous, majoritarian (religious) nationalism is hegemonic and authoritarian. Minorities are the victims of religious nationalism in any context. The people who oppose religious nationalism are also targets of religious nationalists.

In India, majoritarian (religious) nationalism is advocated mainly by the Hindutva movements. It is better to call it 'Hindutva' nationalism than 'Hindu' nationalism. One hesitates to call it 'Hindu' nationalism because though 'Hindutva' nationalism derives its religious framework from Hinduism, the majority of the Hindus are opposed to majoritarian (religious) nationalism in the name of their religion. In that case, religious nationalism (majority or minority) is not endorsed by the majority of the particular religious tradition. However, the proponents of religious nationalism mislead the citizens and propagate nationalist thinking in a religious framework. The 'Hindutva' nationalism claims that it promotes cultural nationalism. In reality, it practises religious nationalism in a cultural garb. Today, religious minorities, particularly Muslims and Christians, face the challenges of 'Hindutva' nationalism in their social, religious and cultural life. Despite their contributions and sacrifice for the nation, they are labelled as people having extra-territorial loyalty.

Religion continues to shape the nationalist thinking of many citizens. Though the idea of India, according to a recent study, meant 'community of communities' for the majority of Indians, 'being a Hindu' is part of Indian identity for many Hindus. This study also says that the majority of Indians irrespective of religious traditions are proud of their states and religion.[1] If religion is an important factor in defining nationalism or national identity, majoritarian religious ideas, icons, and symbols become synonymous with 'nationalism'. It excludes minorities from the frame of nationalism and places them in 'second-class citizen' status. Their social vulnerability begins with religiously framed exclusionary nationalist discourses.

While majoritarian religious nationalism attempts to profile minorities as disloyal to the nation or a threat to the nation, there are voices within the ideological stream of Hindutva that claim that all Indians are Hindus by culture and ancestry. Mohan Bhagwat, RSS chief, recently said,

> The basis of unity is our motherland and our glorious tradition. For us, the word 'Hindu' is the synonym for the motherland, ancestors, and the legacy of Indian culture. The word 'Hindu' does not denote any caste or linguistic definition, but it is the name of a culture that guides the development and uplift of every human being. All those who accept this, irrespective of any caste, creed, religion or language, are Hindus, and in this backdrop, we consider every Indian a Hindu.[2]

Though he spoke about Hindus and Muslims, 'every Indian' in the statement includes Christians also. A majority of Indian Christians are descendants of culturally and religiously 'Hindus'. For minorities, the cultural and ancestral description of 'Hindu' identity is appealing in the context of 'religious' nationalism. It may mitigate anti-minority nationalist propaganda. However, it does not translate into an inclusive identity on the ground. Minorities are treated as the 'other' because of their religious identity. The religion factor also determines the destiny of their loyalty.

Religious nationalism, particularly 'Hindutva' nationalism, has reached out to the diaspora Indians also. The Hindutva movements like VHP, Hindu Swayamsevak Sangh (HSS, the diasporic version of RSS) have started their branches aboard and attracted many Hindus towards Hindutva nationalist agenda.[3] Though diasporic nationalism has religious identity, it is conveniently called 'cultural nationalism'.[4] The diaspora 'Hindutva' Hindus support their counterparts in India.[5] Their connecting point is 'religion' than culture. It has political, economic and cultural implications both at home and foreign lands. Sikh nationalism also has a diasporic facet. Benedict Anderson calls diasporic nationalistic engagement and identification 'long distance nationalism'.[6] The religion factor plays crucial role in diasporic or long distance nationalism. The proponents of diaspora nationalism get political patronage in their home country.

Today, banning books, rewriting history, hyper nationalism, hate speech, anti conversion laws, minority assault, mob lynching, demonizing minorities, romanticizing historical heroes/icons, attack on artists, restrictions on questioning authorities, legislating citizenship laws such as Citizenship (Amendment) Act,[7] etc., have the direct or indirect influence of religious nationalism. Everything is interpreted through the eyes of 'religion'. Dissenting voices are countered by violence and legal actions. In this context, this chapter addresses the issue of nationalism, particularly religious nationalism, from a Christian perspective.

INDIAN NATIONALISM

Nationalism has taken different ideological forms in India. According to Bipin Chandra, anti colonialism defined nationalism during colonial rule. Anti colonial thinking and participation in national movements were considered signs of nationalism. After Independence in 1947, nation building became a form of nationalism. It attracted many to participate in the nation building process. Some Indian Marxists argued that nationalism was a bourgeois ideology, and it was not relevant to the marginalized and exploited classes. Chandra observes that in post independent India, there are three models of nationalism: religious nationalism (he calls it Hindu nationalism), the liberal model that emphasizes the democratic state as the instrument of nation building, and the national popular that understands nation building as the empowerment of the ordinary citizens.[8]

The history of Indian nationalism shows that initially, nationalism was not a 'religion mixed' ideology. The national movements, particularly Indian National Congress, promoted the spirit of nationalism that transcended religions and cultures. However, religion began to define nationalism with the thinking and initiatives of Bal Gangadhar Tilak, Bipin Chandra Pal, and Lala Lajpat Rai, the extremists in the Congress, who emphasized India's glorious past and culture, particularly the Vedic civilization, in the nationalist thinking of the time. They defined Indian culture as Hindu culture. Tilak popularized the Ganapati festival to unite Hindus against British rule.[9] Thus, the extremists sowed the seeds of religious (Hindutva) nationalism.

Hindutva nationalism and other kinds of religious nationalism emerged during the colonial period. With the partition of the nation, Hindutva nationalism became more vocal and dominant. V.D. Savarkar provided a ideological foundations to Hindutva nationalism. He argued that this land belongs to the people who consider it as their fatherland and holy land. For him, Christians and other non Indic religious minorities may fulfil the first clause (fatherland), but they fail to prove that India is their holy land. In the case of Christians, Palestine is the holy land. Mecca is the holy land for Muslims. Therefore, naturally, their love and loyalty are divided. However, the 'choice of love' invites them into the Hindu fold.[10] In his schema of nation and nationalism, Christians, Muslims and others, who do not fulfil his national criterion, stand outside of the landscape of India, and therefore are not nationalists.

While Savarkar placed Christians and other minorities outside of Hindustan ideologically and gave 'choice of love' to the Hindu fold, M.S. Golwalkar demanded them to be 'wholly subordinated to the Hindu claiming nation nothing, deserving no privileges, far less any preferential treatment—not even citizens' rights'.[11] For him, Christians, Muslims and Communists are 'internal threats'. Christians are an 'internal threat' because they are involved in proselytization. They are disloyal and anti national and with the change of religion, their love and devotion for this nation disappeared.[12] His religious outlook demanded that Christians and other minorities be submissive to the Hindus (a majority of them least expect it) and prove their national loyalty. For him, religious identity alone defines the loyalty of a citizen. His disciple,

Pandit Deen Dayal Upadhyaya, another Hindutva ideologue, strongly endorsed his views on religious minorities, particularly Muslims and Christians. He opined that 'the Muslim problem is the oldest, the most complicated and it assumes ever-new forms. This problem has been facing us for the last twelve hundred years.'[13] He advocated for Hindu *rashtra* (nation) and demanded that Muslims and Christians must identify with Hindu culture.[14] According to Aakar Patel, 'structurally, we have already arrived at a Hindu *rashtra*. What is happening today is the use of the existing law (laws restricting freedom of religion and banning cow slaughter, etc.) to brutalize India's minorities in innovative ways.'[15] What disturbs the minorities is that the views of the pioneers of Hindutva ideology continue to reflect in the intimidating and provocative statements and actions of many Hindutva exponents.[16] Though they may represent a minority view, their impact casts feelings of anxiety, fear and pain on the life of religious minorities today. The Hindutva ideology opposes secular nationalism and envisions a nation where minorities live without special rights and acknowledge the cultural, political and religious supremacy of Hindus.[17]

Mahatma Gandhi, Jawaharlal Nehru, Sardar Vallabhbhai Patel and Rabindranath Tagore rejected religious nationalism, particularly Hindutva nationalism, and emphasized secular nationalism. Gandhi opposed the sectarian understanding of nationalism and asserted that India belongs to all born in this land. For him, religion does not define the national identity of citizens. They are Indians first, then Hindus, Muslims, Christians, Parsis, etc.[18] Nehru's nationalist thinking comes from his understanding of this notion. According to him, '. . . what counted ultimately were people, the people of India, people like them and me, who were spread out all over this vast land. *Bharat Mata,* Mother India, was essentially these millions of people, and victory to her meant victory to these people'.[19] It means that one particular community or people group does not constitute this nation. He hoped that 'The Indian people, freed from the terrible sense of oppression and frustration, will grow in stature again and lose their narrow nationalism and exclusivism. Proud of their Indian heritage, they will open their minds and hearts to other peoples and other nations. . . .'[20] His view of nationalism was neither religious nor exclusive. Sardar Patel categorially affirmed that,

> Ours is a secular state. We cannot fashion our policies or shape our conduct in the way Pakistan does it. We must see that our secular ideals are actually realized in practice. . . . Here every Muslim should feel that he is an Indian citizen and has equal rights as an Indian. If we cannot make him feel like this, we shall not be worthy of our heritage and of our country.[21]

Tagore dreamed of a nation with no walls of separation, where people live and think without fear. This nation should be a 'heaven of freedom' and open to other cultures.[22] Secular nationalism resonates in the writings of these national leaders and icons.

Romila Thapar very clearly explains the nature of Indian nationalism in the context of religious nationalist narratives. She argues, 'Nationalism is secular, and the term should refer only to the one Indian nationalism'.[23] It has a shared history of all citizens who form this nation.[24] Nationalism of communal organizations is not Indian nationalism. No religious community can appropriate Indian nationalism solely.[25] According to her, 'The identity and consciousness of being Indian did not need to be defined. We understood nationalism to be Indian nationalism, and not Hindu or Muslim or any other kind of religious or other nationalism'.[26] The 'consciousness of being Indian' is the benchmark of nationalism, not religion. It speaks about a citizen's loyalty and love towards the nation.

Indian nationalism, being secular nationalism, underlines the principle of 'unity-in-diversity' of cultures, communities, traditions, religions, and ethnicities.[27] It upholds tolerance, integration and loyalty to the nation. It promotes the national spirit while enabling citizens to celebrate local culture, participate in respective community life, preserve traditions and follow any creed.[28] Indian nationalism affirms the spirit of 'Indianness and the composite Indian culture'.[29] It embraces the diverse cultures, traditions and aspirations of every Indian. The loyalty of a citizen is not defined by his/her religious identity but by his/her consciousness of being Indian and participation in nation-building.

CHRISTIANS AND NATIONAL MOVEMENT

Christian participation in the initial stage of the national (freedom) movement against colonial rule was minimal. Therefore, many nationalists wrongly perceived Christians as a de-nationalized community or supporters of colonial oppressors. They viewed that Christians sided with the rulers because of their common religious identity. They also believed that the growth of Christianity on Indian soil might endanger the cause of the nationalist movement.[30] There were a few reasons for the minimal participation of Christians in the national movement. Missionaries generally criticized nationalism and discouraged Christian participation in Indian National Congress (INC) and other political movements. But missionaries like T.E. Slater, C.F. Andrews, E. Greaves, Jack C. Winslow and Stanley Jones supported the participation of Christians in the national movement. Some of them attended the sessions of INC and signed a statement against the Jallianwala Bagh massacre in 1919.[31] Minority consciousness is another factor that restricted their participation in the freedom movement.[32] Many Christians also believed that they would be marginalized in independent India ruled by the Hindus. They were suspicious of the nationalist appeal garbed by the religious symbols and festivals promoted by revolutionary leaders like Bal Gangadhar Tilak.[33] From a Christian mission point of view, British rule was a natural supporter of the propagation of the Christian faith. Thus, native Christians appeared to be supportive of colonial rule.[34] Theology of obedience to the authority (then British rule) [35] also conditioned the minds of Christians to be passive towards the national movement.

Despite missionary discouragement, many native Christians participated in the national movement. Christian leaders like K.T. Paul advocated the active participation of Christians in the national struggle.[36] J.A. Saldanha, a Catholic politician, criticized the disinterest of Christians in the national movement strongly and opined that 'Because we are Christians, we have not ceased to be Indian citizens'.[37] He encouraged the Christian community to give their best effort to free the nation from colonial rule. For many Indian Christians, the nationalist thinking and participation in the national movement were not in contradiction to their faith. Aloysius Soares asked, 'What prevents a good Christian being a good Indian as well, when we see that good Christians can be thoroughly good, thoroughly patriotic, American, Frenchman, German?'[38] It reflects the nationalist mindset of many Christians during the national movement. If Christians were called a denationalized group because of their minimal participation in the national movement then many Hindus, Muslims, and other religious people were also 'denationalized' citizens. They were part of the British administration and enjoyed the privileges of colonial rule. Like other communities, Christians also participated in the national movement against colonial rule.

Christians' participation in the national movement happened at different levels. They were actively involved in the activities of the INC. Some of them like R.S.N Subramania, Kali Charan Banerji, Madhusudan Das, G.G. Nath, Peter Paul Pillai, etc., attended the early annual meetings of INC. Christian women such as Pandita Ramabai, Ms. Trimbuck and Ms. Nikambe also participated in some of the INC sessions. Rajkumari Amrit Kaur, S.M. George, George Joseph, J.C. Kumarappa, and H.C. Mookerjee were other prominent Christians who participated in the national movement, particularly under Mahatma Gandhi. S.K. Dutta, V.S. Azariah, Sushil K. Rudra, K.T. Paul, B. Rallia Ram, Augustine Ralla Ram, V. Chakkarai, etc., were vocal nationalists though they were officially not part of INC. The leaders of the All India Conference of Indian Christians (AICIC) were devoted nationalists.[39] Indian Christians also participated in Civil Disobedience movement. Joseph Bennie, K. Jacob Louis and Vincent Joseph Gomez were arrested because of their involvement in the movement. It is recorded that Frederick Michael Pinto of Mahim participated in the Salt Satyagraha.[40] Many Christian students were imprisoned during the Quit India movement.[41] Nationalist Christians like V. Chakkarai and P. Chenchaiah attempted to make the Indian Church national in thinking, theology (Indian) and life. A few Christians also participated in the London Round Table Conferences (1930-2).[42]

The nationalist thinking of Indian Christians was evident in their opposition to the formation of the Nationalist Christian Party in 1930. It was founded by Joachim Alva, a Catholic, to give voice to the national ambitions of the Christians. But many Christian leaders openly criticized it and rejected its scope in the context of the national movement.[43] When a proposal for a League of Minorities surfaced, Christians rejected it as well.[44] For them, the Nationalist Christian Party and League of Minorities had communal intent that was detrimental to the goal of the national movement and the future of Indian Christians.

The participation of Christians in the Constituent Assembly, which framed the Constitution of India, is noteworthy. Raj Kumari Amrit Kaur, Joseph Alban D'Souza, P.K. Salve, H.C. Mukherji, J.J.M. Nickols Roy, J.N.P. Roch Victoria, and Jerome D'Souza were prominent Christian members in the Assembly. They renounced separate electorates and reservation for Christians and did not demand any specific privilege for the community. [45] They stood for the cause of national integration and communal harmony. Being a minority community, they could have asked for certain safeguards. But they prioritized national interests over communal concerns and put their trust in the safeguards guaranteed for all citizens in the Constitution. This approach was the continuation of their nationalist position and participation in the national movement.

The national movement and its influence on Christians resulted in interpreting Christian faith from the Indian perspective. Theologically educated Christians articulated Christian faith in Indian religious and cultural categories (Indianizing Christian faith). A new stream of Christian Theology emerged in India.[46] For example, some called Jesus an *Avatar, Sat Guru* and interpreted Trinity as *satcitananda.* Christianity was defined as *Bhakti Marga* in the Indian context. The Biblical God was interpreted in light of *Parabrahman* in Hindu scriptures.[47] Today, there are socially, religiously, and culturally indianized contextual theologies like Dalit, Tribal, and Indian feminist theologies. There were also attempts to Indianize (indigenize) Christian worship, liturgy, dress code of priests, etc. For instance, sitting on the floor, prostrations of various types, use of materials like oil lamp and camphor and gestures like the waving of the lights and flowers and using *bhajans, kirtans, kathakalashempam* and *villupathu,* etc., were encouraged by Catholic and Protestant denominations. Some Bishops wear saffron cassocks and *rudrakshamala* as a part of their affinity to Indian culture.[48] Their participation in the national movement, rejection of communal privileges, nationalist thinking, efforts of indinizing Christian faith and lifestyle, etc., prove that Christians were/are never denationalized. Though initially, their involvement was minimal, they participated actively in the later stage of the national movement. They continued their commitment to the nation through their participation in the nation building process in the post Independence era. Christian participation in the national movement and nation building process is an outcome of their awareness that they are primarily Indians whose religious faith is not an obstacle to their love towards the nation.

CONVERSION AND NATIONALISM

The national loyalty of Christians has been questioned for a long time. During the time of the freedom movement, many nationalist ideologues and even leaders of the national movement doubted the nationalism of Christians. In their minds, the question of the nationalism of Christians revolved around the issue of conversion. They assumed that with the change of religion, Christians lost their national consciousness. The religious identity of Indian Christians and colonizers strengthened the doubt of nationalists. They reacted differently according to their ideological persuasions. The reaction of Mahatma Gandhi is a case in point. Gandhi, a pluralist in orientation, was not in favour of conversion. He insisted that every religious person should try to become a better follower of his/her faith. He was skeptical about the national loyalty of converts, particularly Christians. He observed in social, cultural and political context that after conversion, Christians abandoned their eating habits, national (cultural) dress, mother tongue and cultural practices. They always tried to identify with the lifestyle of colonizers. He was concerned that conversion should not denationalize the converts.[49] Though the concern was genuine, his contextual observation was not true for all Christians in the nation. Christians in south India and Tribal Christians in north-east India and central India have not abandoned their cultural practices and socio-familial customs. Conversion has not denationalized Indian Christians. Indeed, like other communities, they also preserve their 'Indianness'.

The nationalist suspicion of conversion finds its place in Hindutva nationalist discourses also. According to M.S. Golwalkar, Christians are not loyal to the nation because they have changed their religious identity. They have abandoned their ancestral religion, the religion of the land, and embraced a foreign religion, the religion of the oppressor. Moreover, they are involved in conversion activities.[50] For him, religion defines love and loyalty of citizens to the nation. But participation of Christians in the national movement and their sacrifice and service to the nation disproved his 'nationalist' characterization of Christians. The present Hindutva movements, which continue the ideological legacy of Golwalkar, propagate the same myths and question the national loyalty of Christians.[51] They are accused of breaking the nation through conversion, promoting separate identities, and for engagement with socially weaker sections.[52]

Jawaharlal Nehru, the first prime minister of India, gave an apt reply to the anti-national profiling of Christians. According to him,

> Indian converts to some of these religions (non-Indic religions) never ceased to be Indians on account of a change of their faith. They were looked upon in other countries as Indians and foreigners, even though there might have been a community of faith between them. . . . An Indian Christian is looked upon as an Indian wherever he may go. . .[53]

This is the essence of Indian nationalism. Religion does not define national loyalty. Conversion does not make a Christian less Indian. If conversion to a particular religion makes a citizen disloyal as Hindutva ideologues believed and Gandhi worried then it is logical to assume that Christians who convert to Indic religions in Europe and America must have extra territorial loyalty. The conversion question must also challenge the national loyalty of the followers of Indic religions who migrated to Christian majority countries. If an American or European Hindu (converted or migrated) is not less American or European then an Indian Christian is also not less than an Indian Hindu or Indian Buddhist in his/her national pride. For an Indian Christian, religion or conversion is a personal choice, not a matter related to nationalism. It does not dilute his/her passion for national integrity and sovereignty.

'RELIGIOUS' NATIONALISM: 'UNTENABLE' IN SECULAR INDIA

India has a history of religious nationalism. She has experienced the brunt of religious nationalism throughout the centuries. In India, religious nationalism has appeared in the name of Hinduism, Sikhism, Islam and Ethnicity. Some argue that ethnic nationalism in north-eastern India has a religious character, particularly Christianity. Instead of identifying a particular 'religious nationalism' with the movement or ideology that advocates it, the proponents of religious nationalism define it as a socio-political expression of a religion and a religious community. For instance, 'Hindu' nationalism. The so called 'Hindu' nationalism, advocated by the Hindutva movements, is not endorsed by the majority of Hindus. This exclusive nationalism does not have doctrinal support from Hinduism that teaches non violence, inclusion, and tolerance to the world and affirms *Loka Samastha Sukino Bhavandhu* (May All Beings Everywhere Be Happy and Free), *Vasudhaiva Kutumbakam* (The World is One Family) and *Atithi Devo Bhava* (A guest is akin to God). This reasoning applies to all 'religious' nationalisms. 'Religious nationalism' is not an obligation of believers. It is a distorted social and political use of religion by the communalists for vested interests. Therefore, in India, religious nationalism should not be attributed to religion but to the movements that evoked religious feelings for their version of nationalism. All Hindus, Muslims, Sikhs and Christians are not promoters of nationalism in the name of their religions. The Hindutva, Khalistan, Muslim communal and Christian ethnic national (north-eastern India) movements are votaries of religious nationalist ideologies in India.

Historically religious nationalists, particularly Hindutva and Muslim nationalists, were influenced by the two nation theory of Hindu Mahasabha and Muslim League during the national movement against colonial rule. Hindu Mahasabha claimed that India belonged to Hindus. Muslim League argued that Muslims constituted a separate nation, and a Muslim majority country was the only solution to protect their interests. It resulted in the partition of the country.[54] The partition strengthened the nationalist claims of the Hindutva movements and questioned the nationalism of Muslims in India. Muslim communalism continued as a reaction to Hindutva nationalism in independent India. Though a separate nation is far impossible, Muslim communal/separatist movements still define the community as a separate race having nationalist ambitions. Minority religious nationalisms (Khalistan, Muslim Separatism and Christian Ethnic Nationalism in the north-east) emerged out of the fear of exclusion by the majority community and the possible preferential treatment of the majority community.[55] Majority nationalism (Hindutva) has mild and extreme approaches to contain minority nationalism: accommodation and subordination. The former attempts to accommodate Indic religious traditions like Sikhism, Buddhism and Jainism into Hindu tradition and demands Christianity and Islam to be more syncretic and indigenized.[56] The latter assigns subordinate position to non Indic religious communities.[57]

Hindutva nationalism emerged in the 1920's in the context of the Khilafat movement, particularly the Hindu Muslim conflicts. Savarkar gave an ideological framework for Hindutva nationalism and argued that pan-Islamism was a threat to Hindus. It rejected the national movement's view of the nation as an amalgamation of different religious communities and defined India's national and cultural identity as Hindu. It promoted common religious identity (Hindu), a common language (Hindi) and a nation (Hindustan).[58] Hindutva nationalism attempts to 'de-secularize the Indian polity and re-sacralize the nation-state by essentializing certain religious tenets'.[59] It brings rituals and deities of Hinduism into the nationalist frame and attempts to make Hinduism a civil religion.[60] Hindutva nationalists claim that they are real nationalists.[61] They have no problem with Indic religious communities because they consider them as Hindus[62] despite differences in theological convictions. But they are suspicious of Christians for their shared religious identity with the colonial rulers in the past and the ongoing missionary activities. This negative attitude, to some extent, is mitigated by two factors. Like Muslims and Sikhs, Christians have not defined themselves as separate nation. The separatist claim of Christians in north-eastern India is primarily ethnic rather than religious in intent. Secondly, though there is a deviation today, Christians have not approached the state with specific demands in the name of religious identity. But many factors contributed to the negative attitude of Hindutva nationalists against Muslims: vote bank politics, Muslim neighbourhood Pakistan and Bangladesh, partition of India, separate racial (national) consciousness, the secessionist movement in Kashmir, communal riots, involvement of communal Muslims in terrorist activities, etc.[63]

Khalistan nationalism is another religious nationalism that emerged in the name of Sikhism. The Akali movement demanded a separate state to protect the religious, cultural, economic and political rights of Sikhs. The Akali nationalists believed that a separate state or nation ruled by Sikhs would give them protection to practise their religion without any potential restrictions under any non-Sikh ruling dispensation. In the 1980s demand for Khalistan, an independent Sikh nation, was raised strongly by the Khalistan nationalists.[64] It led to insurgency in Punjab and even caused the death of Mrs. Indira Gandhi, then prime minister of India. Demand for Khalistan developed tensions between Sikhs and Hindus. Many of them were killed during the insurgency period. The Khalistan movement has sympathizers in Punjab and abroad even today. Sikhs for Justice is a case in point. It conducts Khalistan referendum among Sikhs in foreign countries.[65] Religion was also used by Muslim nationalists. Pakistan was the product of religious nationalism promoted by Muslim nationalists who had separate political and economic interests garbed in religious passion. Muslim communalism today is the continuation of the pre-partition religious nationalism of Muslims. Religious nationalism is evident in ethno nationalism in north-eastern India as well.

For example, A.N. Phizo evoked Christian religious sentiments to get support from Christian majority nations for an independent Nagaland, a nation of Nagas. Though Naga nationalism was/is based on ethnic identity, religion also contributes to their nationalist thinking. T. Muivah, a Tangkhul Naga, co-founder of NSCN acknowledged the role of religion in their fight for a separate nation.[66] The loyalty to ethnic identity (ethno-nationalism) led to the emergence of insurgent movements in north-eastern India. Like minority religious nationalism, ethno nationalism in north-eastern India is also a reaction to the fear of 'domination and assimilation by the assimilative Indic culture'.[67] Though ethno nationalism of Christians in north-eastern India has a religious connotation, Christian majority states in that region are not 'Christian theocracies'. They are ruled as part of the nation.[68] It is not the Church or its theology that guides them but the Constitution of India. It demonstrates that ethno-religious nationalism has limited influence among Christians. The Christians in other parts of India neither consider them a separate nation nor express religious nationalist inclination.

These religious nationalisms have certain commonalities. They are exclusive ideologies. They teach their votaries to exclude others. They use religion to consolidate a potential constituency. They are driven by a communal, political and economic agenda framed by the elite in respective communities. They are a threat to the secular ethos and the pluralistic heritage of India. Religious nationalisms identify the 'other' and depict them as threat to the religion. They propagate the myth that religion is in danger under a particular ruling dispensation. The consequences of religious nationalism are fear of domination and exclusion, mutual suspicion, communal violence, disintegration of the nation, intolerance and the degeneration of religion and its values. It is observed that 'A nationalism imbued with the spirit of militant religious revivalism is not likely to lead to a secular independent state'.[69] In the words of Romila Thapar, religious nationalisms are 'not nationalisms but fundamentalist religious identities. . . . Nationalism of a (any) religious community is not Indian nationalism. . .'.[70] Is religious nationalism tenable? Should we promote it?

According to T.K. Oommen, religious nationalism is untenable in a pluralistic or mono religious context. The Muslim nationalists in Pakistan do not consider their co-religionists, particularly Indian migrants, equal to them. For them, Indian migrants are outsiders, not nationalists. Oommen also explains that the Urdu language is one of the cultural symbols that has the potential to preserve religious nationalist thinking among Indian Muslims. But the majority of Indian Muslims do not speak Urdu. They are divided also on doctrinal grounds. When Khalistan nationalists claim that Punjab is their homeland based on religion, they reduce the Sikhs outside Punjab and non-Sikhs as outsiders.[71] This approach is not sustainable in the light of the demographic realities of Punjab. Hindutva nationalism is also untenable because of the heterogeneous nature of Hindus. The marginal Hindu communities would not approve of the Hindutva project for the nation which would be ultimately ruled by upper caste Hindus. The ethno nationalisms among Christians in north-eastern India also face the challenge of sustainability because of growing denominational differences.

Religious nationalism cannot survive without cultural and religious homogenization. It is impossible in a pluralistic context like India. Homogenization of a religious community is also a difficult task because of the differences in theological and doctrinal orientation, lifestyle, language, caste identity, etc. Religious nationalism also requires doctrinal, cultural, and ethical conformism over liberalism.[72] It keeps many away from religious nationalism. The inseparability of homogenization and religious nationalism informs one that the latter eventually 'establishes the hegemony of the dominant'. It threatens diversity, pluralism, and democracy. In the globalized world, context where openness, tolerance, and difference are valued, religious nationalism is irrational and indefensible.[73] Moreover, in a democratic society, citizens cannot live with religious nationalism because religious nationalists value community rights and morality over individual rights, desires and opinions. Religion, not Constitution, defines national and individual morality.[74] Christians cannot support religious nationalism because of its exclusive nature and impracticality in a multi religious context. For them, it is socially, culturally and theologically untenable. It is against their religious conviction that every human being is the image of God. Therefore, every citizen has the right to exist with dignity in the nation where God has placed him/her.

CHRISTIANITY AND NATION BUILDING

Christianity in India has contributed a lot to the progress of the nation. Unfortunately, Christianity is known only for the conversion and expansion of the Church. This characterization is the product of the propaganda of right wing nationalists. The contributions of Christianity to the social, economic, educational and cultural life of nation do not get the positive attention of the larger society. Many do not look at the contributions of Christianity from a nation building point of view. John Barla, the Union Minister of State for Minority Affairs, rightly said,

> After so much contribution, there is no respect (recognition). Why are there allegations that we convert people? No, we don't convert people. . . . There are Christian schools in the remotest area of the country where there are no government institutes. . . . Businessmen and politicians send their children to Christian schools. . . .[75]

His statement reflects two realities: the sacrificial service of Christians to the nation and the negative perception of their contributions. The conversion bogey conceals the nation building efforts of Christians in India.

Christians have participated in nation building through their services to the social, economic, educational, political, and cultural life of nation. They 'were pioneers in the field of education, female education, literature, printing press, steam engine, paper mills, and contributed much to the enrichment of Indian languages, culture, and the abolition of several social evils such as widow burning and child marriages'.[76] Christian mission organizations and churches established schools, colleges, and professional institutions to provide quality education. Education has transformed the social condition of many communities, particularly socially weaker sections. Christian educational institutions have been instrumental in producing loyal and talented citizens for the nation. The hospitals started by missionaries and native Christians, particularly in remote villages, contributed to the development of the health care system in India. The social intervention of missionaries, and later Christian NGOs, contributed to the social empowerment of oppressed communities. For example, London Missionary Society (LMS) missionaries questioned oppressive caste practices and social evils such as untouchability, restrictions on dress code, slavery, and the denial of access to public spaces and amenities in south India. The Serampore Missionaries were instrumental in abolishing *sati* (widow burning). The Catholic and Protestant missionaries worked to empower many Tribal, Dalit, and Backward communities. They also contributed to the development of Indian languages and developed calligraphy for languages. As citizens, individually and collectively, Indian Christians continue to contribute to developing the nation.

Participation in nation building, for Indian Christians, is not only the duty of a citizen but also a biblical mandate. There is no religious reason not to participate in the nation building process. They are 'called to participate in the life and development of the nation, in order to witness to Jesus Christ as Lord and Saviour of humankind'.[77] They believe that the nation is a divine instrument of God's rule in the world.[78] God's love for the world obligates Christians to serve a nation where they reside as citizens. By participating in nation building, they participate in the 'creative action of God' in the nation's life.[79] The goal of nation building is inherent in the spirituality of Christians. It is part of the praxis of their faith in society. For them, nation building happens when they serve fellow citizens and lead them to empowerment.

NATIONALISM: AN INDIAN CHRISTIAN PERSPECTIVE

The discourses of nationalism in India are dominated by religio cultural nationalism of the Hindutva movements. Religious nationalism is a threat to any secular, pluralistic society. The ideological framework of religious nationalism is discriminatory and aggressive toward minorities. It defines them as 'others' in their homeland. For religious nationalists, Christians are 'others' who have a different religious identity, nationalist thinking and ambitions. But Christian participation in the national movement and their contributions to the nation does not substantiate the allegation. For Christians, nationalist thinking has doctrinal and scriptural support. According to M.M. Thomas, Christians should participate in national life because they believe that Christ is the Lord of the world, including their nation, its history, culture and present progress. If they are obedient to Christ, who is present in the life of nation, they should strive to help the nation grow 'truly a nation' and protect its integrity and sovereignty.[80] Loyalty to Christ and loyalty to the nation do not contradict each other in Christian faith. God cares for every nation and participates in its history through its citizens. Love for one's nation is a natural response to this conviction.

Jesus is the model of nationalistic thinking and praxis. Jesus had a critical attitude toward the imperial power (Roman Empire) and the aggressive nationalist movement of Zealots. It does not mean that Jesus was not nationalist in today's language of nationalism. He loved his 'nation' and its people under colonial rule. His ministry of empowerment benefitted the people who constituted his 'nation'. Empowerment of people is a sign of nation building. However, Jesus stood for an 'open society', an open nation, which was inclusive and egalitarian, where everyone would enjoy equality. It means he did not envision a society (nation) that has space only for a particular religious community. His teachings of love, particularly love for neighbour and enemy, give space for those who disagree with one's nationalist ideology. The beauty of Jesus' approach is that he embraced the people whom Jews did not consider as part of their nation. Samaritans were a case in point. His perspective always was guided by the values of the Kingdom of God.[81] Therefore, Jesus defined nation and love for the nation within the framework of the Kingdom of God. In that nation, ethnicity, religion, culture, language and ideology did not define citizens.

The life and ministry of Jesus gives another religious rationale for Christians to become nation builders and patriots. The Nazareth declaration of Jesus (Luke 4: 18-19) shows that Jesus is a 'builder of humanity'.[82] He said 'The Spirit of Lord is on me, because he has anointed me to preach good news to the poor. He has sent me to proclaim freedom for the prisoners and recovery of sight for the blind, and to release the oppressed and to proclaim the year of the Lord's favor.' The social, political, economic and religious implications of this declaration point to nation building because it empowers people, particularly the vulnerable. The progress of citizens is the nation's growth. When they enjoy freedom, justice, and equality, the nation manifests signs of inclusivity and development. Jesus set an example for Christians to work for the nation by empowering its citizens. When they participate in nation building, they express their commitment to Jesus, who taught them to sacrifice their lives for others, and express their love for the nation that gives them a home in the world. For Christians, nation building is nationalism. It involves love, sacrifice, selfless service and pride for nation.

Christians cannot endorse any nationalist thinking that excludes fellow citizens in the name of his/her religion or ethnicity because the language of exclusivism is not the language of the Christian faith. Jesus never approved of any ideology that has potential elements of authoritarianism. Any nationalist ideology that speaks the language of exclusivism is anti national because it does not help nation building. In India, religious nationalism, particularly Hindutva nationalism presented in cultural garb, is a discriminatory and sectarian project. It is not compatible with Christian view of nationalism. For Christians, all citizens are equal stakeholders in the process of nation building. Indian nationalism embraces every citizen with his/her rich cultural or religious heritage. Nationalism is not the monopoly or burden of a particular religious community with its majoritarian appeal. The expression, 'WE THE PEOPLE OF INDIA' in the preamble of the Constitution of India, vividly explains the spirit and content of Indian nationalism.

NOTES

1. Priyadarshini Singh, 'Ideas of Indian-ness', *The Indian Express* (Pune, 1 February 2022), 11.
2. 'Indian Hindus, Muslims share same ancestry: RSS Chief Mohan Bhagwat', *Hindustan Times*, 7 September 2021, https://www.hindustantimes.com/

india-news/indian-hindus-muslims-share-same-ancestry-rss-chief-mohan-bhagwat-101630952385870. html, accessed on 21 October 2022.

3. Christophe Jaffrelot, ed., *Hindu Nationalism A Reader* (Delhi: Permanent Black, 2007), 361-3.
4. Romila Thapar, *The Past As Present: Forging Contemporary Identities Through History* (New Delhi: Aleph, 2014), 113-14.
5. Abhik Bhattacharya, 'Hindutva in Indian Hindu Diaspora. . .', *Outlook,* 31 October 2022, https://www.outlookindia.com/national/hindutva-in-indian-hindu-diaspora-where-the-far-rights-back-home-meet-their-global-cousins—news-233586, accessed on 19 January 2023.
6. Raqib Hameed Naik and Divya Trivedi, 'Sangh Parivar's US Funds Trails', *Frontline,* 4 July 2021, https://frontline.thehindu.com/the-nation/sangh-parivars-us-funds-trail/article35117629.ece, accessed on 19 January 2023.
7. Citizenship Amendment Act 2019 (CAA) was enacted to give citizenship to Hindus, Sikhs, Parsis, Christians, Buddhists and Jains from Pakistan, Afghanistan and Bangladesh who came to India before 31 December 2014. Muslims are excluded from the list of beneficiaries because they are, according to the government, not persecuted minorities in those countries. Though, there were strong protests from political parties and civil societies, the NDA government passed the Act in Parliament. This Act has also been challenged in the Supreme Court of India.
8. Bipin Chandra, *Essays on Contemporary India* (revd. edn., Delhi: Har-Anand Publications, 1999), 91-101.
9. P.L. John Panicker, *Gandhi on Pluralism and Communalism* (Delhi: Indian Society for Promoting Christian Knowledge, 2006), 163-4.
10. V.D. Savarkar, *Hindutva* (Bombay: Veer Savarkar Prakashan, 5th edn., 1969), 113-16.
11. M.S. Golwalkar, *We or Our Nationhood Defined* (Nagpur: Bharat Prakashan, 1947), 55-6. Today many Sangh Parivar organizations disown this particular position and the book. But their outlook is already shaped by it. It is very much evident in their approach to religious minorities.
12. M.S. Golwalkar, *Bunch of Thoughts*, 2nd revd. and enlargd. edn. (Bangalore: Jagarana Prakashana, 1980), 248, 251 & 256.
13. B.N. Jog, *Pandit Deendayal Upadhyaya: Ideology and Perception-Politics for Nation's Sake*, vol. VI (Delhi: Suruchi Prakashan, 2014, 73), quoted in Shamsul Islam, 'Suitable Heroes!', *Indian Currents*, vol. xxviii, no. 41 (10-16 October 2016): 20-2 at 21.
14. Pavan Kulkarni, 'Deendayal Upadhyaya, Bigoted "Guiding Force" of a Hindu Rashtra', *The Wire,* 30 October 2017, https://thewire.in/history/

deendayal-upadhyaya-guiding-force-hindu-rashtra, accessed on 31 March 2021.

15. Ziya us Salam, 'Interview with Aakar Patel, former director of Amnesty International India', *Frontline,* vol. 38, no. 6 (26 March 2021): 95-7 at 95.
16. For instance, Rajeshwar Singh, an RSS Pracharak and leader of Dharam Jagran Samiti (an organization involved in reconverting Christians and Muslims to Hinduism) said, 'Muslims and Christians will be wiped out of India by 31 December 2021.' https://sabrangindia.in/article/muslims-and-christians-will-be-wiped-out-india-december-31-2021-bjp-leader-rajeshwar-singh accessed on 31 March 2021. During the general election in 2019, K.S. Eshwarappa, a BJP leader, said, 'Christians are not loyal and honest citizens of India. Loksabha (Parliament) tickets (candidature) cannot be distributed to Muslims and Christians under quota. Tickets should be given to those who are loyal to the country.' https://www.mangalorean.com/bjp-leader-eshwarappas-remarks-christians-are-not-loyal-honest-citizens-of-india-fumes-christians/ accessed on 31 March 2021.
17. Rowena Robison, 'Introduction', in *Minority Studies,* ed. Rowena Robinson (New Delhi: Oxford University Press, 2013), 19.
18. M.T. Cherian, *Hindutva Agenda and Minority Rights: A Christian* Response (Bangalore: CFCC, 2007), 106-9 & Gyanendra Pandey, *The Construction of Communalism in Colonial North India* (New Delhi: Oxford University Press, 1990), 233.
19. Jawaharlal Nehru, *The Discovery of India* (New Delhi: Oxford University Press, Centenary Edition, Sixth Impression, 1994), 60.
20. Ibid., 523.
21. Chandra, *Essays on Contemporary India,*op. cit., 182.
22. Amartya Sen, *The Argumentative Indian* (London: Penguin Books, 2005), 98 & 108.
23. Romila Thapar, *The Past as Present: Forging Contemporary Identities Through History* (New Delhi: Aleph, 2014), 110.
24. Ibid., 109.
25. Ibid., 111.
26. Ziya us Salam, 'Unfazed by Attack', *Frontline,* vol. 33, no. 18 (16 September 2016): 123-5 at 123.
27. Aditya Nigam, *The Insurrection of Little Selves: The Crisis of Secular-Nationalism in India* (New Delhi: Oxford University Press, 2006), 315.
28. Pandey, *The Construction of Communalism in Colonial North India,* op. cit., 261.

29. Chandra, *Essays on Contemporary India*, op. cit., 22.
30. Mary John, *Indian Catholic Christians and* Nationalism: *A Study based on the Official Catholic Journals of the Period (1857-1947)* (Delhi: ISPCK, 2011), 17 & 41.
31. D. Arthur Jeyakumar, *History of Christianity in India: Selected Themes*, revd. and enlargd. edn. (Chennai: The Author, 2014 rpt.), 96 & 100.
32. John, *Indian Catholic Christians and Nationalism*, op. cit., 14.
33. Jeyakumar, *History of Christianity in India: Selected Themes*, op. cit., 96-7.
34. John, *Indian Catholic Christians and Nationalism*, op. cit., 15.
35. Ibid., 104.
36. Jeyakumar, *History of Christianity in India: Selected Themes*, op. cit., 98.
37. John, *Indian Catholic Christians and Nationalism*, op. cit., 79.
38. Ibid., 141.
39. Jeyakumar, *History of Christianity in India: Selected Themes*, op. cit., 94-5 & 101-3.
40. John, *Indian Catholic Christians and Nationalism*, op. cit., 164-5.
41. Jeyakumar, *History of Christianity in India: Selected Themes*, op. cit., 104.
42. Binu John, *Christian Contribution to Nation Building* (Delhi: ISPCK, 2004), 41.
43. John, *Indian Catholic Christians and Nationalism*, op. cit., 64.
44. Jeyakumar, *History of Christianity in India: Selected Themes*, op. cit., 105.
45. Binu John, *Christian Contribution to Nation Building*, 43-4 & Mary John, *Indian Catholic Christians and Nationalism*, op. cit., 92.
46. Robin Boyd, *An Introduction to Indian Christian Theology*, Revised Edition (Delhi: ISPCK, 1975, rpt. 2004).
47. Michael Amaladoss, *Becoming Indian: The Process of Inculturation* (Bangalore, Rome: Centre for Indian and Inter Religious Studies & Dharmaram Publications, 1992), 63-8.
48. Aylward Shorter, *Toward a Theology of Inculturation* (New York: Orbis Books, 1997), 150; Michael Amaladoss, *Beyond Inculturation* (Delhi: ISPCK/Vidyajyoti, 1998), 8; D.S. Amalorpavadass, 'Efforts Made in the Roman Catholic Church towards Indigenization', *Bangalore Theological Forum*, vol. V, no. 1 (January-June 1973), 21 & Anthony Nariculam, 'Incarnation and Inculturation', *The Living Word*, vol. 100/6 (November-December 1994): 432.
49. M.K. Kuriakose, *History of Christianity in India: Source Materials* (Madras: CLS, 1982), 321-3, 343-4.

50. M.S. Golwalkar, *Bunch of Thoughts*, 2nd revd. and enlargd. edn. (Bangalore: Jagarana Prakashana, 1980), 248, 251 & 256.
51. R. Sahayadhas, *Hindu Nationalism and the Indian Church: Towards an Ecclesiology in Conversation with Martin Luther* (New Delhi: Christian World Imprints, 2013), 30.
52. Rajiv Malhotra and Aravindan Neelakandan, *Breaking India: Western Interventions in Dravidian and Dalit Faultlines* (New Delhi: Amaryllis, 2011), xii.
53. Jawaharlal Nehru, *The Discovery of India* (London: Meridian Books Limited, 3rd edn., 1951), 46.
54. Ram Puniyani, *Communal Politics* (Mumbai: J. & P. Publishers, 2003), 48.
55. Mark Juergensmeyer, *Religious Nationalism Confronts the Secular State* (New Delhi: Oxford University Press, 1994), 179.
56. Juergensmeyer, *Religious Nationalism Confronts the Secular State*, op. cit., 181.
57. Puniyani, *Communal Politics*, op. cit., 120.
58. Jaffrelot, ed., *Hindu Nationalism A Reader*, op. cit., 4-17.
59. Sahayadhas, *Hindu Nationalism and the Indian Church*, op. cit., 6.
60. Suryakant Waghmore, 'Whose Hinduism', *The Indian Express* (Pune, 14 February, 2023): 15.
61. Akeel Bilgrami, 'Secularism, Nationalism and Modernity', in *Secularism and Its Critics*, ed. Rajeev Bhargava (New Delhi: Oxford University Press, 1988), 385.
62. According to V.D. Savarkar, a Hindu is one who considers India as his/her father land and holy land. This definition locates Indic religious communities with the Hindu fold.
63. T.K. Oommen, 'Religious Nationalisms and Democratic Polity in India: Impossibility of Reconciliation', in *Nationalism and Hindutva: A Christian Response,* ed. Mark T.B. Laing (Pune, Delhi: Centre for Mission Studies/Union Biblical Seminary/Indian Society for Promoting Christian Knowledge, 2005), 39.
64. T.N. Madan, *Modern Myths, Locked Minds: Secularism and Fundamentalism in India*, 2nd edn. (New Delhi: Oxford University Press, 2009), 87-91.
65. 'Brawl breaks out over Khalistan referendum in Australia. . . .', *The Economic Times,* 30 January 2023, https://economictimes.indiatimes.com/news/india/brawl-breaks-out-over-khalistan-referendum-in-australia-india-raises-concerns-with-authorities/articleshow/97439452.cms, accessed on 31 January 2023.

66. Ramachandra Guha, *India After Gandhi* (New Delhi: Picador India, 2017, Tenth Anniversary Edition), 108 & 320.
67. Pachuau, 'Nationhood in Conflict: Ethnonationalism and (Indian) Political Nationalism in North East India', in *Nationalism and Hindutva: A Christian Response*, op. cit., 63.
68. Sahayadhas, *Hindu Nationalism and the Indian Church*, op. cit., 375.
69. Smith, 'India as Secular State', in *Secularism and Its Critics*, op. cit., 190.
70. Thapar, *The Past as Present: Forging Contemporary Identities Through History*, op. cit., 111.
71. Oommen, 'Religious Nationalisms and Democratic Polity in India: Impossibility of Reconciliation', op. cit., 42-4.
72. Ibid., 46-9.
73. Ibid., 50-1.
74. Juergensmeyer, *Religious Nationalism Confronts the Secular State*, op. cit., 197-9.
75. 'Why are Christians attacked, accused of conversion. . .'. *The Indian Express*, Kolkata, 21 January 2023, https://indianexpress.com/article/political-pulse/christians-attacked-accused-of-conversion-modi-advice-union-minister-john-barla-8396398/, accessed on 22 January 2023.
76. Binu John, *Christian Contribution to Nation Building*, op. cit., 70.
77. P.D. Devanandan, Korula Jacob and M.M. Thomas, 'Preface', in M.M. Thomas, Comp., *Christian Participation in Nation-Building* (Bangalore: NCCI and Christian Institute for the Study of Religion and Society, 1960), III.
78. Thomas, Comp., *Christian Participation in Nation-Building*, op. cit., 3.
79. Ibid., 113.
80. M.M. Thomas, 'Indian Nationalism: A Christian Interpretation', in *Secularism: Collection of Articles*, compiled by Vincent Rajkumar (Bangalore: Christian Institute for the Study of Religion and Society, 2018), 148.
81. John, 'Jesus and Nationalism: Some Insights from the Synoptic Gospels', in *Nationalism and Hindutva: A Christian Response*, op. cit., 278.
82. John, *Christian Contribution to Nation Building*, op. cit., 72-3.

CHAPTER 8

Reservation and Social Justice

India is home to communities having different social and economic standing in society. Many factors have contributed to the historical empowerment of communities (caste groups). After Independence, the reservation system played an important role in enhancing the social, educational, and economic status of many communities, particularly the lower castes, in the caste hierarchy. Reservation gave representation to Scheduled Castes (SC),[1] Scheduled Tribes (ST),[2] and Other Backward Classes (OBC)[3] in the services of the government and higher education, where once they lagged behind because of their social disabilities caused by the caste system. Reservation has upheld social justice and attempted to compensate for the historical victimhood of socially marginalized communities. Today, different categories of reservations provide representation to diverse groups of people. With social justice, the original goal of reservation, economic justice has also become one of the goals of the reservation in the current reservation policy. Though reservation has a well intended aim of social and economic justice, it has not responded to the social realities of all communities. Dalit Christians are a case in point. They are excluded from the reservation category, which they are socially entitled to avail. The exclusion of Dalit Christians from Scheduled Caste reservation is an issue of social justice. This chapter looks at the reservation system from the point of view of Dalit Christians.

RESERVATION IN INDIA

The idea of reservation in India emerged in the context of the inadequate representation of lower castes, particularly Scheduled

Castes and Scheduled Tribes, in jobs and higher education. The question of reservation was discussed in the Constituent Assembly that drafted the Constitution of India, and provisions were included in the Constitution to provide reservation to SCs/STs and other socially backward communities. Initially, social backwardness caused by caste was taken as the basis of reservation.[4] The under-representation of these communities in education and the services of the State was primarily caused by their historical victimhood of caste. They were/are historical victims of caste. They had/have no sufficient cultural and social capital. The historical 'displacement from public social locations due to the concepts of impurity and pollution associated with the religious ideologies. . .'[5] blocked the upward social, educational and economic mobility of the victims of caste. The lack of social and cultural capital left the Dalits, Tribals, and other backward Communities in a disadvantaged/under represented position in the services of the state. A majority of them did not have social capital in the form of politicians, high level bureaucrats, educationalists, etc., in their families or respective communities. They also lacked cultural capital, a favourable environment within the home to develop skills or facilities for shaping a promising career.[6] The reservation was introduced to compensate historical exclusion of lower castes from the services of the state and bring them into the mainstream of national life.

As an affirmative action, according to Felix Wilfred, 'reservation is one of the tools to arrive at the goal of social justice in favour of the under privileged and discriminated in the society'.[7] It is an 'action that is designed to assure fairness of treatment in the absence of any specific legal finding of discriminatory practices whose consequences are to be remedied'.[8] Through reservation, the opportunities negated by the discriminatory practices of the caste system are compensated. It aims to provide adequate opportunities to the under represented or underprivileged sections, in proportion to their population, in society.[9] Though caste was the main factor for providing reservation, the social backwardness of non-Hindu religious communities was also considered for reservation. For example, reservation policies in the states like Kerala, Tamil Nadu, Andhra Pradesh, Karnataka and Telangana give reservation to

Muslims.[10] In Kerala and Tamil Nadu, some Christian communities also get reservation based on their social backwardness and caste status. There is a shift in the basic principle of reservation, from (exclusively) caste to class, in the Constitution (One Hundred and Third Amendment) Act 2019, which provided 10 per cent reservation to the Economically Weaker Sections (EWS) based on their economic backwardness.[11]In the recent Supreme Court judgement, which confirmed the EWS reservation, Justice Dinesh Maheshwari said,

> Reservation is an instrument of affirmative action by the State to ensure an all-inclusive march towards the goals of an egalitarian society while counteracting inequalities; it is an instrument not only for inclusion of socially and educationally backward classes to the mainstream of society, but also for the inclusion of any class or section so disadvantaged as to be answering the description of a weaker section.

Justice J.B. Pardiwala, who was also part of the Bench, observed that 'reservation is not an end, but a means, a means to secure economic and social justice'.[12] Now, economic justice has also become the goal of reservation. The EWS quota 'takes reservation debate beyond caste'.[13]

The Court Order on EWS reservation aroused different reactions to class/economic criteria for reservation. Mr. M.K. Stalin, Chief Minister of Tamil Nadu, said, '. . . judgment should be considered as a setback in the century-long struggle for social justice'.[14] BJP leaders described the EWS quota as 'a form of social justice for the economically marginalized'.[15] For some, economic criteria would further drive historically marginalized communities into the periphery. They argue that economic backwardness does not contribute to social discrimination or exclusion in the Indian social setting.[16] According to Manuraj, 'income is a variable factor and not a structural or systematic tool for discrimination. On the other hand, caste is structural and systemic discrimination, and poverty is consequence of such discrimination'. Therefore, the economic condition cannot be the basis of reservation. The majority of the poor belong to OBC, SC, and ST communities.[17] Their economic condition is because of caste. The irony of the EWS quota is that the economic criterion for reservation has excluded the economically poor from SC, OBC, and ST communities. P. Chidambaram, former Finance Minister of India, observed that 'excluding the poor from SC, ST, and OBC from EWS quota will deny equality and justice to the poorest among the poor'.[18] The journey from caste to class has opened new pathways for including more people groups into the Indian reservation system.

The Hindutva nationalists and political parties are not in favour of caste based reservations. They promote economic (class) reservation. For them, caste based reservations exclude the upper castes and perpetuate caste identities, which is detrimental to the idea of a Hindu Rashtra. The RSS was critical of the implementation of the Mandal Commission report, which recommended OBC reservation in jobs and education. Though BJP has not publicly questioned the existing caste based reservations, it has always promoted economic reservation.[19] It is evident in its support of the EWS quota.

Initially, reservation was designed to ensure the representation of the SCs and STs in employment and higher education. Later, the OBC were included in the reservation system.[20] Now, economically weaker sections other than SC/ST/OBC are the latest beneficiaries of the reservation system.[21] Articles 15(4), 15(5), 15(6), 16(4), 16(6) 330 and 332 of the Constitution of India allow the State to frame laws and policies to provide reservation.[22] Currently, India has a reservation system that covers large sections of citizenry: SC 15 per cent, ST 7.5 per cent, OBC 27 per cent, EWS 10 per cent, Persons with Disabilities 4 per cent.[23] There are state-specific reservation systems that grant reservations to socially and economically backward communities. For example, in Kerala, the OBC category enjoys 40 per cent reservations. It includes Muslims and Dalit Christians.[24] Though the Indian reservation system has attempted to achieve social and economic justice for socially and economically disadvantaged groups of people, it has not addressed the social justice concerns of all communities fully, particularly socially marginalized communities like Dalit Christians and Dalit Muslims. Instead of including them in the SC quota based on their social identity (caste), Dalit Christians are denied

SC status and reservation because they profess Christianity, a non-Indic religion. They continue to endure social injustice because of their religious identity. The exclusion of Dalit Christians questions the aim and spirit of reservation.

RESERVATION, RELIGION AND DALIT CHRISTIANS

India is a Sovereign Socialist Secular Democratic Republic.[25] It does not have a state religion, and all religions are treated equally by the Constitution. Article 15(1) of the Constitution denounces any form of discrimination on the grounds of religion. It says 'The State shall not discriminate against any citizen on grounds only of religion, race, caste, sex, place of birth or any of them.'[26] Article 25(1) guarantees religious freedom, 'Subject to public order, morality and health and to the other provisions of this Part, all persons are equally entitled to freedom of conscience and the right freely to profess, practice and propagate religion'.[27] Though these two Articles are well meant in the content, they could not prevent orders or legal enactments that discriminated citizens like Dalit Christians because of their religious affiliation. The best example is the Constitution (Scheduled Castes) Order, 1950, commonly known as 'Presidential Order 1950'. According to this Order, Scheduled Caste status (SC status) can be given only to the person who professes the Hindu religion. Later, it was amended by the parliament to extend the SC status to the Sikh in 1956 and to the Buddhist in 1990.[28] Thus, at present, the Dalits who belong only to Hinduism, Sikhism, and Buddhism can get SC status. It means the Dalits, who profess to Christianity and Islam, do not legally come under SCs. Therefore, they cannot benefit from the welfare schemes of the government, reservations, and legal protections granted to the SCs.[29] The Constitution of India says there must not be any discrimination in the name of religion, but the Presidential Order 1950 excludes Dalit Christians and Dalits Muslims from getting the privileges of Scheduled Caste status.

In reservation policy, religion is a defining factor only for SCs, not for STs, OBCs,[30] and EWS. Religious identity is an obstacle for Dalit Christians and Muslims to get the benefits of SC reservation. However, it does not affect the reservation prospects of tribals and other backward communities. For example, Nadar Christians, who belong to the OBC category, have state specific reservations in Kerala and Tamil Nadu. Muslims in Kerala belong to the OBC category, but they have state specific reservation. If religion excludes a community from the reservation, Dalit Christians and Dalit Muslims are victims of such exclusion. Though they follow a different religious path, they are victims of the caste system. As Deshpande observed, 'In India, every Hindu, Muslim, Christian or Sikh also has a caste identity, whether chosen or imposed. In every community without exception, the Dalit *vs* non-Dalit divide is the most intensely and brutally patrolled border between social groups'.[31] It counters the argument that religion should be a criterion for Dalit reservation. In a petition seeking an inter caste certificate by a convert, the Madras High Court recently ruled that '. . . conversion from one religion to another religion will not change the caste of a person. . .'.[32] The One Hundred and Third Amendment of the Constitution granted reservation for EWS.[33] The supporters of the EWS quota argue that class, not caste, should be a criterion for reservation. The question is 'if class and not caste—as the anti-reservationists argue—can be the basis of determining beneficiaries, why not religion?'[34] Dalit Christians are discriminated against because of caste, class and religious identities. Unfortunately, religious identity obscures the social (caste) and economic (class) conditions that qualify them for SC reservation. If caste or class can give a rationale for a reservation today, religion also can be the basis to include Dalit Christians among Scheduled Castes for benefiting SC reservation.

DALIT CHRISTIANS: INTERPLAY OF CASTE AND RELIGION

In India, the socio economic political standing of a community is decided by many factors. Among them, caste plays a 'historical' role in the advancement of communities. While caste identity opens up new opportunities for progress for some communities; it works against the prospects and possibilities of others in the process of empowerment. Some make use of their numerical strength and bargain with the political system and create their space in society. Whereas religious identity works for some to improve their socio economic political standing; it does not happen with others. Many communities could not come up the socio economic and political ladder of society because of their caste and faith identities. Dalit Christians, Christians of SC origin, are one such community that suffers from the interplay of religion and caste. Their religious identity has more ramifications in their claim of reservation.

According to 2011 census, 16.6 per cent of the Indian population is SC or Dalits. It records that only 21.9 per cent of Dalit houses have concrete rooftops. While 58.2 per cent of the houses are floored by mud, 46.6 per cent of the houses have only one room.[35] This data shows one of the aspects of the unequal life condition of Dalits in India. Among them, Dalit Christians suffer more discrimination and exclusion.[36] Though they constitute substantial membership in many of the Indian Churches,[37]the caste identity of Dalit Christians hinders their advancement not only in society but also in multi caste (racial) churches. Unfortunately, the religious identity of Dalit Christians excludes them from all constitutional rights and privileges, welfare programmes and policies of the government, which they are entitled to enjoy as people of SC origin. The social, economic and educational, political conditions[38] of Dalit Christians justify their demand for reservation.

Social Status

Dalit Christians are converted from historically deprived communities in caste society. They were called 'untouchables'. Several factors have contributed to their conversion to Christianity: aspiration for a dignified life, religious quest, emancipation from the bondage of caste, educational help, etc.[39] Though some changes have taken place in their lives because of conversion, Dalit Christians continue to experience the stigma of caste. They are treated as socially inferior to the upper castes in Church and society. Conversion has not changed their social status substantially.[40] They are still Pariahs, Pulayas, Mahars, Mangs, Chamars,[41] etc., in social relations. Social identity (caste) of Dalit Christians takes precedence over their religious identity in the eyes of many non-Dalits.[42] There are separate Churches and cemeteries for Dalit Christians in south India.[43] The interplay of caste and religion is the cause of Dalit Christian discrimination in society, in the Church, by non-Christian Dalits, and by the government. While Dalit Christians are discriminated against in Church and society because of their caste, they are ignored by the non-Christian Dalits and the government because of their religion. Despite the negation of space and resources, they have not renounced their religious identity.

Education Status

Like other disadvantaged communities, Dalit Christians have limited access to education opportunities to develop life skills and job skills in the changing economic scenario. It hinders their social and economic empowerment. They also face discrimination that Dalits experience in educational institutions, such as denial of admissions, separate seating arrangements, physical and emotional harassment, caste profiling, etc. The percentage of dropouts among them is higher than co-religionists and fellow Dalits of Indic religious traditions. The number of graduates and professionals among Dalit Christians is also disproportionate to the number of Christian educational institutions.[44] They do not have the resources to afford quality education offered by educational institutions of a high standard.[45] Despite the best schools and colleges run by the Church, the educational status of Dalit Christians has not improved as compared to other Christian communities.The Church cannot evade its moral responsibility for the present educational status of Dalit Christians.[46] The government is also equally responsible for the unequal educational status of Dalit Christians. Since Dalit Christians are not entitled to SC reservation benefits, they are excluded from various scholarships offered by the government for higher education. The past and present governments have failed to take legal and legislative measures to address the issue of reservation for the educational empowerment of Dalit Christians. While education functions as a tool of empowerment for other communities, Dalit Christians have to be content with limited educational resources because of caste and religious factors.

Economic Status

The caste system, which defined the status of Dalits Christians in society and church, continues to decide their economic condition. Like their forebears, Dalit Christians also carry the stigma of economic deprivation. The caste people treated the ancestors of Dalit Christians as slaves, squeezed their labour power, and deprived them of land and resources. It has a huge impact on the economic life of Dalit Christians.[47] Most Dalit Christians are economically poor, suffering from a shortage of resources and struggling to meet their daily needs of life.[48] Since they don't fall under the reservation category, Dalit Christians have limited access to government jobs. A majority of them work in the private sector. Except for a few educated Dalit Christians, most of them work as daily wagers, plumbers, electricians, drivers, household helps, agricultural labourers, and do menial jobs, etc.[49] Regarding the possession of land, a majority of Dalit Christians own less than one acre of land. That too is dry land.[50] They do not have proper houses. They don't have regular income to meet the basic needs and educational expenses of their children. Most of the banks are not ready to give them loans for education or housing or other job oriented initiatives. They are trapped in debt by moneylenders. They are exploited in mines, construction sites, and other sectors where hard labour is needed.[51] They also face occupational segregation because of caste prejudices in an economically liberalized society.[52]

On the one hand, lack of education restricts many Dalits only to agricultural jobs; on the other, they are 'forced' to do their traditional jobs even if they have proper education. It is sad to note that neither the Church nor the government is concerned sincerely about the economic emancipation of Dalit Christians. They continue their journey as economical 'outcastes' in the economically liberalized global context of the twenty-first century. They are 'outside' the 'box of development' due to lack of education and the neglect of governments. One of the main reasons for the disempowered condition of Dalit Christians is that they are outside of the reservation system.

Political Disempowerment

In a democratic country like India, participation in politics and the decision-making process is imperative for the advancement of any community. It is a fact that all government decisions, policies, and welfare programmes are 'political' in nature. Those in the decision-making bodies/structures are either politicians or bureaucrats/government officials who naturally plan and execute the programmes in line with the policies of political parties/coalition in power. The decisions, they take, are sometimes positive for some communities/groups and negative for others. Therefore, participation in the decision-making process plays an important role in empowering a community, particularly disadvantaged communities like Dalit Christians.

Dalit Christians face discrimination in electoral and party politics because of their caste and religious identities. In many rural/urban locations, the upper castes do not appreciate their leadership in political meetings/election campaigns. Most of the time, mainstream political parties do not consider Dalit Christians as candidates in general or reserved constituencies. Even if they get elected from any constituency, the dominant castes either suppress their voices or ignore their demands. In many places, Dalit Christians have experienced intimidation to cast their votes in favour of a particular political party or candidate. Both high caste Hindus and upper caste Christians obstruct the political empowerment of Dalit Christians.[53] Since, they are not entitled to reservation; they cannot try their political fortunes in the reserved constituencies. While an upper caste Christian can get elected from a Christian dominated constituency or a general constituency, it is almost impossible for a Dalit Christian to become an official candidate of a mainstream political party. The political entry of Dalit Christians is blocked mainly by their caste and religion. Thus, reservation is crucial for the political empowerment of Dalit Christians.

The social, political, economic and educational realities of Dalit Christians prove that the interplay of religion and caste has disempowered them and denied them legitimate entitlements like reservation. The denial of reservation is virtually the denial of justice to them.

DALIT CHRISTIANS AND RESERVATION: AN ISSUE OF SOCIAL JUSTICE

Reservation has been a tool for the socio economic upliftment of the weaker sections in Indian society. In the case of Dalits, Scheduled Caste status and reservation are interrelated for the preferential treatment of Dalits in government jobs, welfare programmes and higher education. Many factors contribute to the continuous exclusion of Dalit Christians from the SC reservation. One of the main factors is that they do not have official SC status accorded by the President of India. SC status, as per the existing reservation policy, qualifies a Dalit community to avail of the benefits of SC reservation. According to the Presidential Order of 1950,[54] SC status can be given only to Hindus who were formerly considered untouchables. Later, it was amended to include Dalit Sikhs and Dalit Buddhists in 1956 and 1990 respectively.[55] Accordingly, the Presidential Order, which defines SC status based on religion, has deprived Dalit Christians of their SC status and excluded them from SC reservation. Though they share the same social status as Hindu/Sikh/Buddhist Dalits, Dalit Christians are denied SC status and reservation because of their religious identity. However, the religion factor was contested by the commissions that studied the socio economic and educational status of backward communities. Kaka Kalekar Commission (1955) and Mandal Commission (1980) have acknowledged caste discrimination among Christians and have categorically recommended scheduled caste status for Dalit Christians. The Report of the National Commission for Religious and Linguistic Minorities, popularly known as Justice Ranganathan Misra Report (2007), has reiterated that socio economic backwardness should be the criteria of reservation, not religion.[56] It also recommended removing religion as an essential factor for determining SC status.[57] Now, reservation for Dalit Christians has become a lawsuit pending before the Supreme Court of India.

The religion factor in the SC reservation has been used by the supporters of Hindutva to communalize the issue. It has divided Dalits on religious grounds. The Hindu, Sikh and Buddhist Dalits are afraid (feel anxious) that the inclusion of Dalit Christians or Muslims would reduce their share in jobs, educational or legislative (reserved seats in state assemblies and the parliament) opportunities available under the present reservation policy. Therefore, they do not extend their moral and political support to the cause of Dalit Christians. They also believe that the inclusion of Dalit Christians would make the competition difficult for them because they assume that educated Dalit Christians would take away their share.[58] The communalists attempt to reap political dividends by communalizing the genuine demand of Dalit Christians for social justice. They evoke religious arguments to consolidate their constituency to oppose the inclusion of Dalit Christians in the SC reservation.

The demand of Dalit Christians for reservation is countered by the argument that reservation was introduced to empower the historical victims of the caste system, an institution in Hindu society. The proponents of this argument view that reservation intends primarily to address the marginalized condition of Hindu communities, particularly the lower castes. Therefore, religion is important for reservation, particularly the SC reservation. For instance, in February 2010, the national executive of BJP criticized the Ranganathan Misra Report and passed a resolution that the

> Commission (Ranganathan Misra Commission) cannot dictate or thrust its opinion on the Christian Pope or Muslim Maulvis. . . . Reservation would amount to a formal introduction of a caste system in Islam and Christianity, thus changing the basic tenets of these religions, which is outside the jurisdiction of both Parliament and the Judiciary, and also contrary to the provisions of the Koran and the Bible.

The resolution conveniently argues that Christianity and Islam have no caste system. They teach the value of equality. Therefore,

Dalit Christians/Muslims do not face discrimination because of their social (caste) identity in Christian/Muslim communities. Thus, they do not deserve reservation that is based purely on social status defined by the caste. The RSS has the same view. The Akhil Bharatiya Pratinidhi Sabha (ABPS) of RSS said, in the context of extending reservation to Dalit Buddhists in 1990, that 'the Constitution makers envisaged these concessions only to remove caste-based discrimination and inequality prevalent in Hindu society. . .'.[59] The resolution of BJP and statement of RSS proposes two reasons to negate reservation to Dalit Christians. According to the BJP resolution, reservation contradicts the basic tenets of Christianity. But SC reservation has been extended to Dalits in Buddhism and Sikhism, which also doctrinally reject the caste system. In line with the RSS view, if reservation aims to remove inequality in Hindu society, it should not have been extended to Dalit Sikhs and Buddhists who do not consider themselves Hindus. But for Hindutva ideologues, they are Hindus because of their Indic religious and cultural identity. Dalit Christians are excluded because they are not followers of Indic religions. Though religious identity is emphasized for SC reservation, caste is considered while granting reservation for Dalits in non-Hindu Indic religious traditions. Ironically, the caste reality of Dalit Christians is not considered under the pretext of the belief system of Christianity. It denies social justice to Dalit Christians. A Dalit Christian represents 'the unique plight of a person who is not only low caste, but also a religious minority, poor, rural, and a woman, for example'.[60]

Though religious identity was a factor in defining SC status according to the Government of India (Scheduled Castes) Order, 1936, during the colonial rule, it did not affect the opportunities of Dalit Christians then because they were getting the benefits of separate representation reserved for Christians. After Independence, when Christian representatives in the Constituent Assembly renounced separate electorate and other privileges enjoyed by Christians, Dalit Christians lost their opportunities for social empowerment.[61] Both the Christian community and the government failed to address the loss of Dalit Christians who were neither part of Scheduled Castes nor the beneficiaries of any specific affirmative action. According to Deshpande, there is no constitutional, rational, or moral reason for the government to look at Dalits and their issues from a religious point of view. 'Politics' is behind the approach of the government towards the reservation for Dalit Christians. Instead of dealing with this issue from the point of view of social justice and taking sides with the marginalized, the government delays the process by appointing commissions to study the issue.[62] For instance, when the Supreme Court of India asked for the opinion of the central government on granting SC status to Dalit Christians in the pending petitions filed by organizations like the National Council of Dalit Christians (NCDC), the government appointed a three member commission under the leadership of K.G. Balakrishnan, former Chief Justice of India, to study the possibility and the implications of granting SC status to Dalits who do not belong to Hinduism, Buddhism and Sikhism.[63]

The new commission, according to NCDC, is a 'delaying tactic'. Vijay George, President of NCDC, said,

> This is a delaying tactic by the Government, which clearly does not want to see a conclusion to this case. What was the need for another commission when there have been numerous commissions and committees in the past that have submitted its reports to the government, including the Misra Commission that ruled in favour of awarding such a reservation. When Buddhists and Sikhs were accorded SC status, there were no commissions. This move is politically motivated and discriminatory on the basis of caste and religion.

But the appointment of the commission was justified by Vijay Sampla, chairperson of the National Commission for SCs. He said, 'We need to see the parameters for reservation of these communities. We need to verify if they indeed face the discrimination that they claim to face.'[64] The recent developments, pending litigations and appointment of the commission point to the fact that Dalit Christians have to wait for a long time to get social justice.

Conversion to Christianity has excluded Dalit Christians from Scheduled Caste reservation even though their social and economic conditions, as narrated in the previous section, qualify them for it.

However, based on the recommendations of the Mandal Commission, they are included in the OBC category, a group of communities that are socially and educationally backward. Currently, Dalit Christians are included in the OBC reservation category of twenty states.[65] The inclusion of Dalit Christians in the OBC category is a negation of their socio economic status and social justice. They are included in the category of communities that are socially and economically advanced and numerically and politically powerful compared to them. They have to compete with comparatively advanced communities to get the benefits of the OBC reservation. They get fewer opportunities in employment and education because of the limited resources available for the OBC quota in the reservation system.[66] They have to wait for their turn in the limited OBC quota. Unlike the SC quota shared by only SC communities, the OBC quota is distributed among communities having different social, economic and educational status. Therefore, Dalit Christians demand their inclusion in the SC list of communities for reservation.

Denial of Scheduled Caste status and reservation to Dalit Christians is an issue of social justice. They have been denied justice because of their religious faith. By this denial, the fundamental right to profess any religion guaranteed by the Indian Constitution has been violated. It also violates the principles of natural justice and fairness. Indeed, it is a violation of human rights.[67] For Dalit Christians, this issue has not been addressed adequately by the government and the Church.[68] They allege that the Indian Church/ Christian community has not extended its full support and cooperation to address the issue of reservation. The Church is neither united nor able to garner political support for the cause of Dalit Christians.[69] Unfortunately, Dalit Christians are opposed by their brothers and sisters in other religious traditions. Lack of solidarity within the community also affects their demand for reservation adversely. Moreover, the government's religious and political outlook obstructs social justice for Dalit Christians, who are disempowered among Dalits. The Constitution of India guarantees social justice. For Dalit Christians, granting SC status and reservation is one of the manifestations of social justice.

RESERVATION: A CHRISTIAN RESPONSE

Reservation is not a biblical word. But the idea of reservation as affirmative action is biblically rooted. The poor get preferential treatment in the liberative design of God. In the Old Testament of the Bible, God defends the rights of the poor. In the language of reservation, the poor are socially, economically and educationally vulnerable in society. They are victims of caste in the Indian context. God gave laws to protect the rights of slaves (Leviticus 25: 39 ff), and defended minorities, widows and orphans (Deuteronomy 10: 18-19). The Bible says, 'He (God) administers justice for the fatherless and the widow, and loves the stranger, giving him food and clothing' (Deuteronomy 10: 18). Today, God protects the poor and the vulnerable and ensures social justice through affirmative action like reservation. Reservation offers them jobs and educational opportunities, which give them 'food and clothing'. Reservation is also a form of social justice that corrects historical wrongs committed against the poor.

Jesus also stood for the cause of social margins in society. He raised his voice against the oppressive structures that marginalized the people. He defended the poor and enlarged the space of the downtrodden. The ministry of Jesus gave freedom and dignity to people who could not celebrate life in its fullness. God appreciates any attempt directed toward human empowerment. Reservation is a divine provision that delivers social justice to the victims of oppressive social structures like the caste system in India. It affirms the life of the powerless and voiceless and brings the poor into the mainstream of society as God did through the prophets and Jesus Christ. It is one of the revolutionary tools in the hands of God to liberate the people from their wretched condition. Therefore, it is spiritual and biblical for Christians to support reservation. But the negation of reservation to any weaker section of society because of their religious identity is a contradiction of divine providence that cares preferentially for the weak and the marginalized irrespective of their religious traditions. Christian faith affirms social justice. Thus, Dalit Christians look at reservation from the perspective of social justice. Social justice is the underlying principle of reservation. Denial of reservation to Dalit Christians is a denial of social justice. Though there may be communities or people groups who deserve reservation, preferential treatment should be given to those who are cumulatively disempowered like Dalit Christians.

Reservation is a life affirming policy because it contributes to the empowerment of marginalized communities. The framework of justice brings reservation closer to the Christian faith, which affirms justice as an ethical expression of faith in God. In the current understanding, reservation aims to achieve not only social justice but also economic justice. But for Dalit Christians, reservation is more of social justice than economic justice. Reservation compensates historical denial of social justice caused by the caste system. The economic deprivation of Dalit Christians is the result of the denial of social justice in the past. They are yet to get social justice through reservation because of their religious identity. Though the Constitution of India guarantees equality to citizens, Dalit Christians are unequal citizens because of the religious framework of Scheduled Caste reservation. Reservation does not achieve its goal of social justice as long as Dalit Christians are deprived of the benefits of reservation enjoyed by their counterparts in other religious traditions. Social justice demands reservation for Dalit Christians.

NOTES

1. The Term Scheduled Castes (SC) officially refers to socially and economically disadvantaged or marginalized communities in India. They belong to the lower strata of the caste hierarchy. They were known as the Depressed Classes during British colonial rule. Mahatma Gandhi called them 'Harijan'. Today, the majority of the scheduled castes address themselves as 'Dalits'. They argue that they still carry the stigma of names given by the caste system. However, the central government has not recognized this nomenclature. Christians, who come from Scheduled Castes, are called Dalit Christians. More details are given in the later part of the chapter.
2. The term Scheduled Tribes (ST) referto to tribal communities in India. They are known by different names. Like scheduled castes, they are also stigmatized by the caste system in the larger society.

3. It refers to the communities having inferior social status in the caste structure but socially, economically and educationally advanced than SCs and STs.
4. Malavika Prasad, 'From the Constituent Assembly to the Indra Sawhney caste, tracing the debate on economic reservation', *The Caravan,* 28 March 2019, https://caravanmagazine.in/law/economic-reservations-constituent-assembly-debates, accessed on 9 February 2023.
5. James Ponniah, 'Taking the Cross and Walking from Subalternity to Modernity', in *Constructing Indian Christianities: Culture, Conversion, and Caste,* ed. Chad M. Bauman and Richard Fox Young (New Delhi: Routledge, 2014), 149.
6. Felix Wilfred, *Asian Public Theology* (New Delhi: Indian Society for Promoting Christian Knowledge, 2010), 14-15.
7. Felix Wilfred, *Asian Dreams and Christian Hope: At the Dawn of the Millennium* (Delhi: Indian Society for Promoting Christian Knowledge, 2000), 137.
8. K.S. Chalam, *Caste-based Reservations and Human Development in India* (New Delhi: Sage, 2007), 17.
9. Ibid., 18.
10. Koride Mahesh, 'A lot of reservations about Muslim Quota', *The Times of India*, Hyderabad, 19 May 2022, https://timesofindia.indiatimes.com/city/hyderabad/a-lot-of-reservations-about-muslim-quota/articleshow/91656467.cms, accessed on 9 February 2023.
11. 'The EWS quota excludes beneficiaries of SC/ST/OBC reservations, and the annual income of the beneficiary's family must be less than eight lakhs', *The Indian Express,* Pune (8 November 2022), 12.
12. Anantha Krishnan G, 'Quota for General poor gets top court seal'. *The Indian Express,* Pune (8 November 2022), 2.
13. Editorial, 'Mandal Plus', *The Indian Express,* Pune (8 November 2022), 10.
14. 'How parties and politicos reacted to Supreme Court's EWS quota verdict', *The Times of India,* 7 November 2022, https://timesofindia.indiatimes.com/india/how-parties-and-politicos-reacted-to-scs-ews-verdict/articleshow/95355343.cms, accessed on 9 February 2023.
15. Guru Prakash Paswan, 'Extending Social Justice', *The Indian Express,* Pune (9 November 2022), 13.
16. K.S. Chauhan, 'Failing the Constitution', *The Indian Express,* Pune (10 November 2022), 13.
17. Manuraj Shunmugasundaram, 'Setback for Social Justice', *The Indian Express,* Pune (11 November 2022), 11.

18. P. Chidambaram, 'Blessed are the Poor (but not all)', *The Indian Express,* Pune (13 November 2022), 12.
19. Christophe Jaffrelot, ed., *Hindu Nationalism: A Reader* (Delhi: Permanent Black, 2007), 256-60.
20. Bhagwan Das, 'Moments in a History of Reservations', *Economic and Political Weekly* (28 October 2000): 31-4 at 34. The OBC reservation was implemented after the recommendation of the Mandal Commission.
21. The Parliament passed the Constitution (one hundred and twenty-fourth Amendment) Bill to provide 10 per cent to the EWS.
22. https://www.lawinsider.in/columns/what-is-the-current-structure-of-reservation-in-india, accessed on 8 February 2023 & *The Indian Express,* Pune (8 November 2022), 12 & *The Indian Express,* Pune (8 November 2022), 12.
23. https://www.lawinsider.in/columns/what-is-the-current-structure-of-reservation-in-india, accessed on 8 February 2023.
24. https://bcdd.kerala.gov.in/en/reservation/employment-reservation/, accessed on 8 February 2023.
25. *The Constitution of India* (Ministry of Law and Justice, Government of India, 1989), 1.
26. *The Constitution of India,* ibid., 7.
27. Ibid., 12.
28. S. Lourduswamy, *Towards Empowerment of Dalit Christians, Equal Rights to all Dalits* (New Delhi: Centre for Dalit/ Subaltern Studies, 2005), 106-7 & 109-110.
29. Satish Deshpande and Geetika Bapna, *Dalits in Muslim and Christian Communities* (New Delhi: Centre for Dalit Studies, Catholic, Bishops Conference of India and National Council of Churches in India and NCCI, 2010), 52.
30. Laura Dudley, 'Scheduled Castes, Christians and Muslims: The Politics of Macro-Majorities and Micro-Minorities', in *Minority Studies,* ed. Rowena Robinson (New Delhi: Oxford University Press, 2013), 98.
31. Satish Deshpande, 'A question of Intent', *The Indian Express* (Pune, 1 September 2022), 8.
32. 'Religious conversion does not change a person's caste, rules Madras High Court', *Financial Express,* 26 November 2021, https://www.financialexpress.com/india-news/religious-conversion-does-not-change-a-persons-caste-rules-madras-high-court/2376717/, accessed on 7 February, 2023.
33. *The Indian Express,* Pune (8 November 2022), 12.

34. Prannv Dhawan, Christophe Jaffrelot and Kalaiyarasan, 'Debate, don't dilute reservation', *The Indian Express,* Pune (18 November 2022), 11.
35. *Census of India 2011, Tables on Houses, Household Amenities and Assets for Scheduled Castes* (New Delhi: Registrar General and Census Commissioner, India, 2012), xliii-xlvi.
36. Felix Wilfred, 'Editorial', *Jeevadhara,* vol. XLI, no. 241 (January 2011): 3-5 at 3.
37. K.E. Rajpramukh, *Dalit Christians of Andhra* (New Delhi: Serials Publications, 2008), 80. It is argued that they might constitute 50-70 per cent of the Christian population. Cf. Satish Deshpande and Geetika Bapna, *Dalits in Muslim and Christian Communities,* 60 & 108 (reference no. 5.)
38. While engaging with other sources, the following sections depend heavily on *Christians of Scheduled Caste Origin in India: The Study of Their Socio-Economic, Cultural and Political Status,* a study jointly conducted by Centre for Dalit/ Subaltern Studies, New Delhi, Commission for SC/ST/BC of the Catholic Bishops Conference of India, New Delhi and Delhi School of Social Work Society, Delhi. It was carried out under the leadership of James Massey. This study has brought out the present standing of the Christians of Scheduled Caste origin in social, economic, political and educational realms of life. It was published as a book edited by James Massey and T.K. John S.J. (James Massey and T.K. John, eds., *Christians of Scheduled Caste Origin in India,* New Delhi: Centre for Dalit /Subaltern Studies, 2013.)
39. Massey and John, eds., *Christians of Scheduled Caste Origin in India,* op. cit., 149f; K. Jesurathnam, 'Yerraguntala Peraiah: An Honorable Dalit Christian Missionary', *Journal of Subaltern and Cultural Theology* (2013): 20-4 at 22-3; S. Lourduswamy, 'Catholic Church and Dalit-Tribal Movements in India', in *Rethinking Theology in India,* ed. James Massey and T.K. John (New Delhi: Manohar and Centre for Dalit/Subaltern Studies, 2013), 190.
40. S. Lourduswamy, 'Catholic Church and Dalit-Tribal Movements in India', 185 & idem, *Towards Empowerment of Dalit Christians,* 20-1.
41. Names of Dalit communities.
42. Satish Deshpande and Geetika Bapna, *Dalits in Muslim and Christian Communities,* 128.
43. Massey and John, eds., *Christians of Scheduled Caste Origin in India,* 16; Indukuri John Mohan Razu, 'Towards a Critical Theology of Risk Taking: The Changing Landscape and Discourse', in *Rethinking Theology in India,* ed. James Massey and T.K. John (New Delhi: Manohar and Centre for Dalit/Subaltern Studies, 2013), 362.

44. Massey and John, eds., *Christians of Scheduled Caste Origin in India*, op. cit., 75-82.
45. S. Lourduswamy, 'Catholic Church and Dalit-Tribal Movements in India', op. cit., 186.
46. Lourduswamy, 'Dalit Christians: Has Anything Changed?', *Jeevadhara*, vol. XLI, no. 241 (January 2011): 7-13 at 12-13; idem, *Towards Empowerment of Dalit Christians, Equal Rights to all Dalits*, op. cit., 26-7.
47. Camil Parkhe, *Dalit Christians: Right to Reservations* (Delhi: ISPCK, 2007), 4.
48. Wilfred, 'What Can 'Upper Caste' Christians Learn from Dalit Christians?' op. cit., 66-76 at 68.
49. Massey and John, eds., *Christians of Scheduled Caste Origin in India*, op. cit., 83-6.
50. Ibid., 87-90.
51. Ibid., 92-3 & 98-9 & Lourduswamy, *Towards Empowerment of Dalit Christians, Equal Rights to all Dalits*, op. cit., 29-30.
52. Deshpande and Bapna, *Dalits in Muslim and Christian Communities*, op. cit., 129.
53. Massey and John, eds., *Christians of Scheduled Caste Origin in India*, op. cit., 132-5.
54. This order is a continuation of the Government of India (Scheduled Castes) Order, 1936 that stipulated that 'no Indian Christian shall be deemed to be member of a scheduled caste'. https://socialjustice.gov.in/public/ckeditor/upload/82951673327147.PDF, accessed on 7 February 2023.
55. Camil Parkhe, *Dalit Christians: Right to Reservations*, op. cit., 31-4.
56. Massey and John, eds., *Christians of Scheduled Caste Origin in India*, op. cit., 163-70 & 224-6; Lourduswamy, *Towards Empowerment of Dalit Christians, Equal Rights to all Dalits*, op. cit., 21-2.
57. Rowena Robison, 'Introduction', in *Minority Studies*, edited by Rowena Robinson (New Delhi: Oxford University Press, 2013), 14.
58. Christophe Jaffrelot and Philip Varghese, 'A Continuing Exclusion', *The Indian Express* (Pune, 26 April 2022), 9 & Laura Dudley, 'Scheduled Castes, Christians and Muslims: The Politics of Macro-Majorities and Micro-Minorities', op. cit., 99.
59. Shyamlal Yadav, 'Express Explained', *The Indian Express* (Pune, 20 September 2022), 12.
60. Dudley, 'Scheduled Castes, Christians and Muslims: The Politics of Macro-Majorities and Micro-Minorities', op. cit., 96.
61. Ibid., 97 & 99.
62. Deshpande, 'A question of Intent', op. cit., 8.

63. *The Indian Express* (Pune, 8 October 2022), 1.
64. Ibid., 2.
65. Jaffrelot and Varghese, 'A Continuing Exclusion', op. cit., 9.
66. Robison, 'Introduction', in *Minority Studies*, op. cit., 13.
67. Parkhe, *Dalit Christians: Right to Reservations*, op. cit., 7; Deshpande and Bapna, *Dalits in Muslim and Christian Communities*, op. cit., 136.
68. *People's Reporter*, vol. 26, no. 24 (Mumbai, 25 December-10 January 2014), op. cit., 1 & 24; Lourduswamy, 'Catholic Church and Dalit-Tribal Movements in India', op. cit., 187-8 & 202-7.
69. Lourduswamy, 'Dalit Christians: Has Anything Changed?' op. cit., 7-13 at 11-12.

CHAPTER 9

Gender Justice*

Religions, ideologies, political systems, and democratic societies uphold values like justice, equality, freedom, fraternity, etc. to establish equal and humane societies. The Preamble of the Constitution of India also affirms 'to secure to all citizens'[1] these values to establish the nation as a 'sovereign, socialist, secular democratic, republic.' Before and after independence, 'justice' has been a subject of ideological and political discourses in India. They have placed justice in a socio-economic-political framework and advocated social/political/economic justice. But the feminist movements looked at justice through the lens of gender and argued for gender justice in different spheres of life. In light of women's experiences and feminist discourses, this chapter defines gender justice as 'equalizing the space.' The expression 'equalizing the space' stands for equal sharing of the space with 'her'[2] in all aspects of social life. This sharing is not 'his'[3] charity, but 'her' right. She deserves it. Justice demands 'him' to move away from the 'encroached' space, and share and celebrate life with her. It is not easy to evacuate the encroachers. He is strong in Indian society. He uses Scriptures, invokes traditions, and takes refuge in prejudiced sayings of philosophers and religious fathers to justify his encroachment that extends to social, political, economic, professional, religious and cultural, and cyberspace. She lives in limited space, if not spaceless. She has no control over the small space she occupies. 'She' needs to act and say that 'every common space is my space too.' Gender Justice becomes a reality when she enjoys the fruits grown in the space, where she also ought to have an equal share. This chapter provides a few reflections on gender justice (male-female gender relations) from a Christian perspective.

* This chapter is a revised version of an article that originally appeared in *USB Journal*, vol. 14, no. 1 (March 2021): 25-36.

'HER' REALITY IN 'HE' SOCIETY

Indian society is casteist and patriarchal. 'He' continues to be the 'norm' in society. His thinking, actions, decisions, perspective, etc. (forcibly) shape the social, economic, political, and religious life of the people. She is a historical victim of his hegemony. Therefore, she lives without adequate space. Every day, she struggles to make her voice heard in the common space, question unequal power relations, and resist gender devaluation. She continuously asks, 'Why is my space restricted?' 'Why am I monitored?' 'What blocks my upward and outward mobility?' Her inquiries lead her to put up resistance and self-assertion. Often, her boldness invites his derogatory comments, abusive behaviour, physical assaults, and iniquitous actions. Let's look at some realities of her space in 'he' society.

'He' society often boastfully talks about what it has done to enlarge the space of women. It will talk about the growing percentage of educated women, the financial independence that offers them a life of choice, and the growing trend of singletons (single women) in Indian society,[4] political empowerment, legal entitlements, and professional opportunities. This talk is a narrative of escapism. On the ground, what is happening is that 'he' can be 'liberal' in life and thinking but not 'she.' The moment she asserts her space or expresses her choice, she experiences the power of 'he' the liberal. Soma Bhowmik says, 'The day my boyfriend objected to my being 'liberal', I knew I could not allow someone to dictate my behaviour.'[5] Every day, with exceptions, this happens in different forms in the life of 'she', who aspires to be equal with him. She can enjoy her space under his strict supervision. He is expecting her not to think or act as he does.

She encounters him in every corner of society. When she walks through a street, she is 'welcomed' by the institutions, roads, chowks named after 'him'. She can't end her short walk without seeing the statues of 'him' who was a king, minister, poet, and social reformer. A street, mostly 'populated' by 'him', tells her the 'story of his power'.[6] It does not give her confidence to move forward but compels her to withdraw to the private space. She hardly finds 'her' statue or name on the streets that would give her energy for claiming space. Once again, 'public' space is assigned to him; private space to her! This is also the condition of religious communities. He is the public face of religion/Church and she is assigned inferior space and task with a few exceptions.

Her experience of the negation of space has intersectional nature. Gender, caste, class, community,[7] and religion equally contribute to her experiences of unequal sharing of space in society: family, workplace, faith community, democratic institutions, and other locations of expressing oneself. To create a space for her aspirations, she has to negotiate with social monitors of conventional practices and custodians of morality. He tells her where to go, what to do, and reminds her about her social value/standing, and disciplines her by mental torture, rape, molestation, and moral policing. With this, he wants to show her 'legitimate' space: below him! He admonishes her that 'Don't cross the boundaries!' Otherwise, it will invite further shrinking of her space! But he forgets the fact that 'public space is not public unless women (she) feel free'.[8] A religious 'he' tells her 'religious' restrictions, a caste 'he' marks boundaries for her social/familial/marital relations, a class 'he' looks at her through the eyes of capital, a patriarchal 'he' shouts at her and reminds her about her 'inferior' 'sub-ordinate' gender. This intersectionality gives her an unequal life.

However, she is not timid. She takes bold steps to respond to her unequal condition. If she attempts to equalize the space, he responds to it through his criminal behaviour. That is his immediate and last weapon. He acts as if he is licensed to do it, but not 'she'. It may take different forms. Rape is one of the most heinous among them. According to National Crime Records Bureau, rape cases have been steadily increasing over the years.[9] It was not long ago that the Thomas Reuters Foundation survey in 2018 identified India as 'the world's most dangerous country for women due to the high risk of sexual violence and being forced into slave labour.'[10] Though it is not 'literally' true for the entire nation, women are not fully safe in society. The increase in the number of crimes against her shows 'his' patriarchal indigestion of her bold visibility in 'he' space. Today, she boldly comes out and seeks education.

She attempts to make her presence felt in the job market. Her 'social' routine also gets changed.[11] She also questions his authority in religious communities and asserts her space. She has proved in traditionally 'his' areas. Yet, she is treated as if she has broken taboos. She is not intruding on 'his' space but instead attempts to claim her space for survival. He takes her mannerism as a threat to his beloved culture, revealed truth (religion), established tradition, centuries-old social structure, and brave 'man-ism'. He thinks that if she does not understand her 'given' space, then she must be taught. He believes that violence is the best weapon. However, her determination disproves his loving thesis. While her body carries the scars of his criminality, they are not deterrents for her to aim for equal space.

Her political space is another example of tokenism. The Parliament of India, fondly called the 'temple of democracy', tells you how her political space is restricted if not negated. In terms of members, she constitutes only 14.4 per cent of the 17th Lok Sabha (78 out of 543 MPs) and 10.7 per cent of Rajya Sabha (24 out of 224 MPs).[12] For her, this is 'he' Parliament. Its composition reflects the mindset of 'he' society. This space negation happens in a society where she constitutes a powerful voting bloc (almost half of the total voters). It does not matter for him because he controls most of 'her' votes. She is welcome to 'cast a vote' but not to 'share the space of power.' 'Temple of Democracy', controlled by him, can claim that she is considered in all forums and made strong legislations to protect her space. She still lives without complete justice. Complete injustice! Number matters in democracy, but not for her. 'He' in the family, political party and community controls her limited political power. But the recent legislation of the Constitution (One Hundred and Twenty-Eighth Amendment) Bill, 2023 gives hope for the political empowerment of women in India. It ensures 33 per cent reservation for women in Lok Sabha and State Assemblies.[13] With this affirmative action, women get 'rightful representation that has been hitherto denied'.[14] It is one step forward to equalize the political space in society.

Her hard labour is valued less than his labour. According to the World Economic Forum, she is equally talented and competent, but she is paid '63 per cent of what men earn'. In our country, she earns 19 per cent less than him (exceptions are applicable). She fights every day to prove her competency in the common economic space dominated by him. A female marketing professional in Delhi says that 'in her career of 13 years, she always has to walk that extra mile to show that she is as good, if not better than her male co-workers.'[15] For her, justice means allowing her to enjoy the space (economic empowerment and job career) at the same speed and level as him. Patriarchal 'he' does not allow her to be economically independent and equal with him in terms of work and wage.

The patriarchal caste continues to define woman 'honor' even today. Like her ancestors, she carries the burden of the community 'honor.' Caste teaches her that she ought to protect the honor of her family and caste by not marrying outside the caste or from an inferior caste. If she strictly observes caste rules, she is an epitome of honor. Her honor comes from obedience to the patriarchal caste. If she fails to maintain the honor, she is risking her life. In the case of marriage, her partner also faces the brunt of violation. The patriarchal caste inculcates her that she must be obedient, and should not raise her voice and question him. She should listen to him and obey him at the cost of her 'honor'. Caste gives power to him, not to her because she should live under his protection. In the caste framework, he controls her body, fertility, and mobility. By not allowing her to exercise her agency, not recognizing her potential, not respecting her choice, suppressing her voice, and keeping her away from power, the patriarchal caste takes her honor away and uses her as an 'object' to protect 'caste honor' in society. The postmodern world may claim the upward mobility and the 'honorable' position of women, still she continues to endure dishonor in society. The crimes like 'honor killing' points to the hold of caste 'honor' over 'her honor.' She has intrinsic honor. A new societal consciousness needs to be developed to counter patriarchal caste that kills her honor. An egalitarian human consciousness that honors women equal with men is needed to facilitate gender justice.

While experiencing these unequal realities, she takes a long sigh and realizes that her society is 'he' society where 'she' lives spaceless and powerless. She of lower caste origin is more 'spaceless' than she of high caste origin. 'He' controls everything, and 'she' is forced to dance according to 'his' tune in domestic and public space (acknowledging the exceptions). He controls not only social space but also religious space. She is not a priest but an 'unequal' participant in important ceremonies and rituals. She always constitutes more than half of the religious audience. In a way, she sustains religions through her 'spaceless' participation. For instance, the Church, part of a larger 'he' society, is also broadly 'he' community in sharing ministerial and administrative space with her. It is patriarchal in outlook, structure and theology. The majority of Indian Churches do not ordain her and elect/select her for leadership positions. She has subordinate roles in the Church. She is encouraged mostly to engage in the areas where she does not address him. The sacramental power rests with him. She is passive recipients of it. In power relations in ecclesial bodies: spiritual or temporal, she stands in the periphery. She can participate in worship but not leadership. She is taught that he should be her 'head'. Though there are theological and movement-based attempts to challenge the patriarchal mindset of the Indian Churches, her space is still limited in Christian communities. She encounters the same hurdles in other religious communities. Her realities in 'he' society demand an attitudinal change in 'him' to share equal space and power with her.

'HIS' INTROSPECTION AND PROGRESSIVE THINKING

She has the right to exist and celebrate her life. But she experiences discrimination in life. Why is she discriminated against? The answer is mainly 'his mindset' shaped by gender prejudices. He may not want to limit her space. Unfortunately, archaic thoughts/teachings about her feed his consciousness constantly, including Scriptural injunctions on he-she power equations. It does not mean that he is entirely an innocent 'he' who cannot initiate 'change' in himself. For him, she is emotional, not rational; therefore, she cannot handle common space of any kind. She is not only incompetent but also weak because of her gender. She is the 'devil's gateway' (Tertullian);

therefore, she should be kept away. Her primary duty is to 'help' him; so, she must occupy inferior space. She must consider 'him' as 'god' on earth. Her freedom is subject to the supervision of 'he'. *na stree svaatantryam arhati* (A woman does not deserve independence/freedom, Manu Smriti IX.3) sums up his argument! An ideal Indian 'she' is one who unquestionably assumes her subservient role as a submissive wife, self-sacrificing mother, and silent self-giving worker. This myth of the ideal 'she' facilitates her space restriction in sacred, domestic, and public locations.[16] In the past, in Travancore Kingdom society, people used to ask if someone sits sadly, 'Why do you sit as if a girl had been born at home?' The derogatory saying does not end there. The society welcomed a girl's birth with indifference: 'Through the midwife's incapacity, the infant is a female!'[17] Her education received disparaging comments such as 'To educate women is like putting a torch on the hand of a monkey'.[18] This 'historical' mindset continues to rule the conscience of 'he' society. His historically conditioned mind will be naturally disturbed if she endeavours to enlarge her space. There comes an urgent need for the introspection of an archaic mindset and cultivating a progressive thinking about her.

It's all about a radical change in the mindset of 'he' society. M. Venkaiah Naidu, former Vice-President of India, rightly said, 'We need to change the mindset of people. Bringing new laws will not help. . . . We brought a bill on Nirbhaya. . . . What happened? (in the context of recent rape incidents) Is the problem solved? A change in the mindset is the need of the hour'.[19] It means a radical change in 'his' thinking about 'her' body, dress, agency, competency, and potential is imperative. She is co-equal and competent to think and feel as he does. She is not '*paraya dhan*' (somebody else's property) but owns herself. Her identity derives not from him but from her very 'self'. She can express herself. Freedom does not have gender boundaries. Since she is born as a human being, she deserves it. He made her weak, submissive, and sacrificial. The ideal 'she' is a key to locking her in the patriarchal cage. There is no 'ideal' she or he, but only a human being. Only bold 'he' can initiate introspection and nurture progressive thinking.

It will be a moment of liberation for both. While he will be liberated from his archaic prejudiced thinking, she will be freed from the patriarchal cage. It will contribute to enlarging/equalizing her space in society. If he does not his mindset, she will not wait for his 'grace', but break the boundaries of 'given' space. She is capable of doing so.

HER AGENCY AND EQUAL HONOR

He thinks that she needs his guidance and help to make sound judgments in her life. She questions this myth and loudly proclaims that she has agency. Her agency refers to the capacity to act and remove the iniquities that disempowered her.[20] It is a transformative action she initiates to change her life situations and the lives of others in society.[21] Knowing her agency (knowing that she can act) is the first step towards equalizing the space. Through her agency, she questions the mindset that perpetuates her 'diminished humanity'.[22] Her agency and honor, according to Christian faith, comes from the realization that like him, she is also created in the image of God.

Christian faith affirms dignity and honor of every human being. Like him, she is also bestowed with same dignity and honor by God (Gen 1: 26-28). She is not 'something' but 'someone' with full humanity. She has selfhood, identity, freedom, and self-knowledge. Her dignity is integral to her birth and existence.[23] Since she is created in the image of God, she has the power of free choice. She can use her power of free choices and actions to transform her dishonored life.[24] In a society where the honor of a woman, particularly a subaltern, is defined by caste, negating her honor is synonymous with social death. If 'resurrection is an experience of liberation from death',[25] restoring her honor is an experience of resurrection from social death, her dishonored humanity. She should claim her honor not by becoming obedient to the patriarchal caste but by affirming the 'Image of God' in her. She exhibits the Image of God when she attempts to question those powers, beliefs, prejudices, ideologies, and structures which devalue her honor in society. Her honor does not come from caste but from her existence as an 'Image of God.' She shares the same honor with him through a shared Image of God. This thinking should facilitate the celebration of her honor in society. Jesus showed us how to honor her. In the patriarchal Jewish society, Jesus did not consider her an inferior being but a person with full humanhood.[26] He loved and honored her in a society where she was disrespected and considered an object.[27] He went against the traditions of Jewish-Greco-Roman society and maintained a more humane and liberal approach toward women.[28] His/her thinking patterns should be guided by the principle that she has equal honor with him.

She is not an object but an autonomous 'self' having the agency to discern marginalizing and domesticating realities and resist the powers that 'rule' her space. She can identify the patriarchal 'protective' mannerism that domesticates her. This internalization takes her to contest (exercising her agency) the powers, beliefs, prejudices, ideologies, and structures which restrict her space. She resists her experiences of space negation by exercising her 'informed and critical agency.' It involves freedom of action and freedom of thought.[29] She also knows that this is risky in a patriarchal society. Today, she is more conscious than her ancestors to exercise her agency. She knows how 'he' society practically restricts her space. Kavita Krishnan, a women's activist, says, 'We keep getting told that since sexual violence (*his problem*) in public spaces is a given, women can be kept 'safe' only if their freedom, autonomy, and mobility (space) is restricted. For your own *raksha* (safety), you must be kept in *bandhan* (bondage)'. For Kavita, this is an excuse to keep patriarchy and caste intact. The 'he' society knows the power of her agency. That is why she is kept in *bandhan* (bondage).[30] *Bandhan* is a patriarchal 'remedy.' It also shows his insecurity. He should come out of the *bandhan of* primitive thinking. But she, who knows her agency, breaks the bondage and finds her space.

She rejects the language of *bandhan* and strongly demands an equal right to public space. She wants to engage with the 'forbidden' space (his claimed space) and makes her presence felt. Today's 'she' is not simply satisfied with voting rights and job opportunities where she is 'traditionally fit'. She is not hesitant to chart her life journey in any unfamiliar location. Though it is challenging and not without taunts, it is a sign of her agency. Her presence in public space is therapeutic. According to Neha Singh, 'If people get used to seeing women on the road doing their own thing, wearing what they want, and being visible and vocal, then that is going to lead to change'. For instance, #MeetToSleep is one of the campaigns of Blank Noise, Bengaluru-based women's collective that encouraged its members to nap in public parks. These actions creatively respond to the concern of Kalpana Vishwanath, founder of Safetipin, 'how do we feminize public spaces, because if you have more women in public spaces, then they become safer'.[31] Feminizing the public spaces is another step towards equalizing the space. It also enables her to contribute to society positively. For that, she needs to actualize her agency. When she exercises her agency, she restores her honor equal with him as a human being.

INTENTIONAL ENGAGEMENT

Gender justice, equalizing the space, demands the unconditional and intentional engagement of both women and men. Though she has agency, she may not be able to enlarge her space without him (him without her also; often, she sacrifices her comfort). For me, she should take the initiative, and he should extend his solidarity with her. Both need the courage to walk the extra mile to equalize the space. While he stops living in the world of archaic thinking about her, she needs to be courageous to demand her space in society. Wo/man partnership is the need of the hour for equal space. It involves compromise, awareness, dialogue, confidence-building, and new expressions of boldness. 'Patriarchal' s/he cannot initiate the process of equalizing the space because patriarchy maintains unequal gender relations and hierarchical order. The following sections narrate his/her role in equalizing the space.

LIBERATING CAPITAL

The story of Queen Vashti in the Bible proves that a woman has liberating capital to assert her[32] honor. Vashti was the Queen of King Xerxes. In the third year of his rule, King Xerxes gave a banquet to his officials and ministers. During the feast, the King exhibited his wealth and grandeur. On the seventh day of the banquet, Queen Vashti was asked to appear and display her beauty before the King and nobles. But she refused to do so. Her refusal to obey King's command cost her status as queen in the country (Esther 1:1-2:4). In this story, Queen Vashti displayed her liberating capital by refusing to appear as King demanded. She did not allow herself to be reduced to an object of 'sex' or 'display'[33] or King's 'honor'. In her action, Vashti proved her competency in thinking about her 'selfhood.' By disobeying the King, Vashti questioned the oppressive patriarchal structure that objectified women and devalued their honor and conscience. Her open disobedience (display of liberating capital) was considered a threat to preserving the patriarchal norms that defined the honor of women. Therefore, she was disposed of her position. It is not uncommon that a woman, who opposes the oppressive structure/systems like caste through her speech or conduct, is punished or silenced so that the honor of caste (and male) can be protected. Vashti had to pay the price for exercising her liberating capital to affirm her honor and identity.[34] For her, human dignity and autonomy were more significant than royal position and token 'honor.' She did not allow 'the patriarchy' to decide her appearance before the King and nobles. Like Queen Vashti, women, particularly subaltern women, should resist the root cause of their dishonored position: the patriarchal casteist outlook. They should exhibit their liberating capital to counter the forces that kill their honor. They can think and act. This awareness should guide the thinking of a 'patriarchal' society to respect women's inherent value.

BE TAṈṮĒṬAKKĀRIKAL OR TAṈṮĒṬIKAL

To equalize the space, she must be *taṉṯēṭakkārikal* or *taṉṯēṭikal* (courageous women). The expression *taṉṯēṭakkārikal* or *taṉṯēṭikal* derives from a Malayalam word, *taṉṯēṭam* which primarily means 'courage'. 'Capacity', 'competency', 'arrogance', 'pride', etc. are other meanings of the word. A 'courageous/brave man' is called *tanṯēṭakkāran.* 'Courageous/brave woman' is referred to as *tanṯēṭakkāri* (singular)/ *tanṯēṭakkārikal* (plural). The term *tanṯēṭi* denotes one who is courageous, clever or arrogant.[35] However, the root word, *tanṯēṭam* (courage), is used in negative and positive senses. Its usage has gender prejudice. It is attributed to him with a positive sense and her with a negative connotation. This prejudice is in the 'DNA' of patriarchal society. If he does any courageous thing, he is called *tanṯēṭi* in a positive sense, and his action is considered as a result of his *tanṯēṭam.* However, she who is strong or courageous and takes any bold and positive step/initiative (attempts of equalizing the space) is *tanṯēṭi* with a negative connotation and portrayed as 'arrogant'.[36] If her action is not in terms of the existing norm or cultural/religious practices, she is defined as 'uncontrollable', 'disobedient', 'defiant', etc. In the feminist theological discourse, *tanṯēṭam* (courage) is understood positively. For her, *tanṯēṭam* is a 'power within'[37] facing the oppressive systems and standing against the negation of space. She must exercise her *tanṯēṭam* to get her share in the shared space. It means she must become *tanṯēṭakkārikal* or *tanṯēṭikal* who would exhibit her inherent power.

The term *tanṯēṭam* has 'space' implications also. Etymologically, *tanṯēṭam* has two words: *tanṯē* means one's/his/her and *ēṭam*, space/place/room.[38] The implied meaning is one's space/his space/ her space. 'Space' is 'a continuous area or expanse which is free, available, or unoccupied.' It also refers to 'the freedom to live, think and develop in a way that suits one'.[39] It is both a mental and physical zone, voluntarily and consciously created to obtain and enjoy certain benefits.[40] It facilitates the freedom and unrestricted mobility of a person and enables her/him to do what s/he plans to execute. There are different levels and forms of space: physical, mental, economic, religious, socio-cultural, and political.[41] However, her space is restricted in the larger space of Indian society. She can equalize her space (*tanṯēṭam*) with him only through *tanṯēṭam* (courage). It means her space in social, political, economic, and religious realms can be affirmed only by enabling her to become *tanṯēṭakkārikal* or *tanṯēṭikal* (courageous women) who will say 'no' to the patriarchal norms which define her space.[42] By catering quality education, facilitating critical thinking, equipping her with job and life skills, conscientizing her rights and equal space, and instilling her with self-esteem and competency, *tan̲ṯēṭam* can be developed in her. A *tan̲ṯēṭakkāri* or *tan̲ṯēṭi* (courageous woman) alone could step into equalizing *tan̲ṯēṭam* (one's space) in society.

Becoming *tan̲ṯēṭakkārikal* or *tan̲ṯēṭikal* (courageous women) is a Biblical virtue. The contemporary 'she' can get inspiration from the stories of *tan̲ṯēṭakkārikal* or *tan̲ṯēṭikal* in the Bible. Shiphrah and Puah (Ex. 1: 15 ff) became *tan̲ṯēṭakkārikal* or *tan̲ṯēṭikal* through their bold action. The *tan̲ṯēṭam* (courage) of midwives (disobeying the order of Pharoah to kill Hebrew boys) led to the expansion of the *tan̲ṯēṭam* (one's space) of the people of Israel (v20) and those midwives (v 21). It was the *tan̲ṯēṭam* (courage) of Ruth (The Book of Ruth) that helped her to take the initiative to go into the field of an Israelite despite her non-Israelite identity. She had *tan̲ṯēṭam* (courage) to assert her right as a widow of an Israelite man. She did not depend on others for her livelihood. She ventured out and claimed her right. Her courageous step gave her and her mother-in-law *tan̲ṯēṭam* (one's space) in the Israelite society. She who has *tan̲ṯēṭam* (courage) only can venture out and claim space in 'he' society. Mahlah, Noah, Hoglah, Milcah, and Tirzah, Zelophehad's daughters, demanded their right to inheritance and property (Num. 27: 1-8 and 36: 2-12). In the patriarchal Israelite society, their demand was a courageous step to challenge the age-old cultural practice. They showed their *tan̲ṯēṭam* (courage) to break the silence and demand their right and won it. In their daring attempt, they were trying to end cultural subordination.[43] They were claiming their *tan̲ṯēṭam* (one's space) within the community. The biblical *tan̲ṯēṭakkārikal* or *tan̲ṯēṭikal* were trying to equalize the space. She said she could say 'no' to patriarchal demands and question his social, cultural, and political power.

Tan̲ṯēṭakkārikal or *tan̲ṯēṭikal*, firstly, are resistant. With *tan̲ṯēṭam*, she resists the encroachment of space. Resistance protects and enlarges her *tan̲ṯēṭam* (one's space). Secondly, she is an empowered person. For that, she must continually nurture critical thinking, innate talents, and abilities to initiate the process of equipping her to have control over her life. Empowerment itself is the creation of *tanṯēṭam* (one's space) in 'he' society. Empowerment comes where *tanṯēṭam* (courage) is exercised. Thirdly, she is assertive. She asserts her right of any kind to secure her *tanṯēṭam* (one's space). Asserting rights corresponds to enlarging one's space. Fourthly, she is autonomous. Autonomy is a natural outcome of *tanṯēṭam* (courage). Independent thinking, decisions, and actions expand her *tanṯēṭam* (one's space).[44] In short, *Tanṯēṭakkārikal* or *tanṯēṭikal* resist the forces of space negation, assert her rights and privileges, act as autonomous beings and initiate the process of empowerment. Can she alone can create and celebrate *tanṯēṭam* (one's space) in the respective context? She also needs 'him' in her journey. What is 'his' role?

'HIS' SOLIDARITY FOR 'HER' SPACE

Many think she has to deal with her issues; he does not have a role. Of course, she must work for her space. However, she would say that he, who is conscious of gender discrimination/inequality and stands against it,[45] has some role to play in equalizing the space in favour of her. He can identify with her in her efforts to come out of patriarchal spacing. His solidarity would complement her *tanṯēṭam* (courage). Solidarity is a biblical virtue. Taking sides with those who strive to equalize space is a divine mandate.[46] In the Bible, we see God, who expressed liberating solidarity with humanity (different communities) and expanded their space in history. It does lay the theological foundation for 'his' solidarity for 'her' space in 'he' society. Genuine 'he' solidarity is a sign of divine solidarity in the world. It contributes to her liberation from patriarchal *bandhan* (bondage) and facilitates the celebration of 'her' life in its fullness. This solidarity contributes to her upward mobility in all spheres of life. The solidarity gives her confidence to resist oppressive forces and claim her space. As a margin, she comes to the centre (where he and she are supposed to share the space) when he sides with her. 'His' solidarity takes different forms: standing with her in her resistance against any form of exploitation or marginalization, raising his voice along with her against the attempts of devaluation, deconstructing his patriarchal mind, expressing moral support for her struggles of existence, sharing economic resources and opportunities with her for wholistic development, organizing programs for developing her liberative capital, influencing the government to design policies and programs for her empowerment, conscientizing the faith communities about her equal space, organizing civil societies, advocating her human rights, proclaiming the liberating values of religious traditions, and in Christian language living out the Gospel of Jesus Christ gender sensitively in personal and public life.

Jesus, the climax of Divine Solidarity with humanity, is the model for 'his' solidarity for 'her' space. For instance, in His dialogue with the Samaritan woman (John 4: 1-41), a marginal 'she' in the Indian context, Jesus Christ attacked the patriarchal social order, which prohibited a public conversation with a woman, particularly a Samaritan woman. Jesus stood for a social order where 'she' also gets equal space to interact and share her feelings and thoughts. He had liberating attitude toward women. For Him, both male and female have equal value and space (Galatians 3: 28). In the Old Testament understanding, 'salvation' is meant 'to be wide' or 'to be spacious.' God in Jesus met 'him' and 'her' equally and enabled 'him' and 'her' to enlarge their space. Jesus taught the values of love, equality, justice, peace, and freedom. The praxis of these values brings 'her' out of patriarchal *bandhan.* Jesus, 'the Word Became Flesh' (God's solidarity with Humans John 1: 14) tells 'him' that when 'he' takes side with her in equalizing the space 'the Word becomes Flesh' again through 'his' actions because Jesus came to this world to identify with 'her' and enlarge 'her' space also. The result is she becomes *taṉṯēṭakkārikal* or *taṉṯēṭikal* (courageous 'she' who has space) in 'he' society. 'He' society/Church/religious community becomes 'we' (s/he) community where 'he' is no more the norm.

She equalizes the space with him when her voice is heard, freedom respected, choice honoured, the opportunity given, selfhood dignified, mobility unrestricted, life celebrated in its fullness as a human being, labour valued, agency recognised, body not objectified, and leadership accepted. It is a moment of recognizing her gender as equal to his gender in social, political, economic, religious, and cultural realms. In that moment, she feels that she is not excluded because of her gender but adds beauty to human life. She proclaims that her energy, potentiality, beauty, and gender do not make common space unequal again but straighten the social curve created by patriarchy. It happens when she embodies *taṉṯēṭam* (courage), and he steps out of his patriarchal house and stands with her for the sake of justice. Both he and she should embody courage to have bold egalitarian vision to equalize space in Church and society.

NOTES

1. *The Constitution of India,* Ministry of Law and Justice, Government of India, 1989, 1.
2. 'She' or 'her' refers to the shared experiences of women irrespective of religious traditions.
3. 'He,' 'his,' or 'him' refers to men collectively.
4. Aroon Purie, 'Editorial', *India Today* (21 October 2019), 5. Many women consciously choose to remain single to be answerable to their 'self' alone.
5. Chinki Sinha and Romita Datta, 'Single Women', *India Today* (21 October 2019), 34 & Sagarika Ghose, 'With local roots, feminism in India is not a blind copy of the Western model', 2 January 2019, https://scroll.in/article/907485/with-local-roots-feminism-in-india-is-not-a-blind-copy-of-the-western-model-writes-sagarika-ghose, accessed on 20 May 2021.
6. *The Times of India,* Pune (Friday, 17 January 2020), 2.
7. Amartya Sen, *The Argumentative Indian* (London: Penguin Books, 2005), 207-8.
8. *The Times of India,* Pune (Friday, 17 January 2020), 2.
9. 'Horrendous Rape Cases in 2021 . . .,' *Outlook,* 9 March 2021, https://www.outlookindia.com/website/story/india-news-horrendous-rape-cases-in-2021-so-far-show-that-minors-are-biggest-victims-of-sexual-assaults/376609, accessed 20 May 2021 & 'India lodged average 86 rapes daily, 49 offences against women per hour in 2021: NCRB data', *The Hindu,* 31 August 2022, https://www.thehindu.com/news/national/india-lodged-average-86-rapes-daily-49-offences-against-women-per-hour-in-2021-government-data/article65833488.ece, accessed on 22 December 2022.

10. *The Times of India,* Pune (Wednesday, 4 December 2019), 13.
11. Arvind Verma and et al., 'How Real is the Crime Decline in India?' *Economic & Political Weekly,* vol. LIV/No. 45 (16 November 2019): 37-45 at 43.
12. https://www.mpa.gov.in/sites/default/files/Women%20in%20 Parliament_0.pdf, accessed on 21 September 2023.
13. *The Indian Express* (Pune, 21 September 2023), 1.
14. Aditi Narayani Paswan, 'A more welcoming House', *The Indian Express* (Pune, 21 September 2023), 11.
15. *Sunday Times of India,* Pune (1 December 2019), 15; 'Gender Pay Parity: 37 per cent Indian Working Women Get Paid Less than Men', *ABP News,* 2 March 2021, https://news.abplive.com/business/37-percent-working-women-in-india-get-paid-less-than-men-here-s-what-more-this-linkedin-report-reveals-1446666, accessed on 20 May 2021 & Basant Kumar Mohanty, 'Women are paid less than men. . . ,' *The Telegraph online,* 29 September 2022, New Delhi, https://www.telegraphindia.com/india/women-are-paid-less-than-men-finds-study/cid/1889306, accessed on 22 December 2022.
16. Kochurani Abraham, 'And She Was Made Straight: A Feminist Theological Engagement with the 'Bent' lives of Indian Women,' in *Margins in Conversation: Methodological Discourses in Theological Disciplines,* edited by Joseph Prabhakar Dayam and P. Mohan Larbeer (Bangalore: BTESSC, 2012), 126.
17. Samuel Mateer, *Native Life in Travancore* (London: W.H. Allen & Co, 1883), 208-9.
18. I.H. Hacker, *A Hundred Years in Travancore (1806-1906)* (London: H.R. Allenson Limited, 1908), 83.
19. *The Times of India,* Pune (Monday, 9 December 2019), 3.
20. Amartya Sen, *Development as Freedom* (Oxford: Oxford University Press, 1999), 190-1.
21. Meeta Deka, *Women's Agency and Social Change: Assam and Beyond* (New Delhi: Sage, 2013), xiii.
22. Shalini Mulackal, 'Living with Diminished Humanity: A Theological Critique,' *Oriens Journal for Contextual Theology,* vol. 4 (2013): 118-34 at 120.
23. Shalini Mulackal, 'Sexual Abuse and the Church: Some Moral Dilemmas,' in *Gender Relations in the Church: A Call to Wholeness and Equal Discipleship,* edited by Astrid Lobo Gajiwala, Varghese Theckanath S.G. and Raynah Braganza Passanha (Pune: Streevani & Hyderabad: Montfort Social Institute, 2012), 117.

24. Shalini Mulackal, 'Sexual Abuse and the Church: Some Moral Dilemmas,' 120; Prasanna Kumari, 'God's Image and Women', in *Feminist Theology: Perspectives and Praxis,* edited by Prasanna Kumari (Chennai: Gurukul, 1999), 382.
25. Raj Irudaya, *Dalit Bible Commentary, New Testament, vol. 4, The Gospel According to John* (New Delhi: CDS, 2009), 169.
26. Shalini Mulackal, 'Living with Diminished Humanity: A Theological Critique', 133.
27. Chung Hyun Kyung, *Struggle to be the Sun Again* (New York: Orbis Books, 1990), 54.
28. Evelyn Monteiro, 'Re-imaging Woman and Reshaping her Destiny, An Indian Feminist Reading of the Bent Body (Lk 13: 10-17)', in *Body and Sexuality: Theological-Pastoral Perspectives of Women in Asia,* edited by Agnes M. Brazal and Andrea Lizares (Manila: Ateneo De Manila University Press, 2007), 146.
29. Amartya Sen, *The Argumentative Indian,* 240.
30. Amulya Gopalakrishnan, Interview with Kavita Krishnan, *Sunday Times of India,* Pune (8 December 2019), 18.
31. Sonam Joshi, 'With Public Naps and Midnight Strolls. . .,' *Sunday Times of India,* Pune (8 December 2019), 15. *pothuçmam enteçmam* (public space, my space) was organised by the Women and Child Development Department, Kerala Government, to embolden women to engage in public space without fear. It was a night walk (11 p.m. to 1 a.m.) of women. It was intended to instil courage in the minds of women to walk at night. It is an attempt of feminising public spaces. 'Public Space is Mine too': Thousands of Kerala Women attend govt's Night Walk Initiative,' *The New Indian Express,* Thiruvananthapuram, 30 December 2019, https://www. newindianexpress.com/cities/thiruvananthapuram/2019/dec/30/public-space-is-mine-too-thousands-of-kerala-women-attend-govts-night-walk-initiative-2082795.html, accessed on 21 May 2021.
32. In this section, after this, she or her refers to Queen Vashti and he/his/him, the King.
33. Evangeline Anderson-Rajkumar, 'New Eyes, New Reading, New Woman. . .,' in *Feminist Hermeneutics.* Edited by Lalrinawmi Ralte and Evangeline Anderson-Rajkumar. Delhi: IWTI/ISPCK, 2002), 108.
34. Shalini Mulackal, *Dalit Bible Commentary, Old Testament, vol. 6, Ruth, Esther and Judith* (New Delhi: Centre for Dalit/Subaltern Studies, 2011), 54-5.
35. B.C. Balakrishnan, ed., *Malayalam Lexicon,* vol. VI (Trivandrum: The University of Kerala, 1988), 113.

36. Kochurani Abraham, 'And She Was Made Straight: A Feminist Theological Engagement with the "Bent" lives of Indian Women', 131; Theramma Prayikalam, *Manakaruth Spirituality of Fisherwomen: Inspiration and Challenge to Consecrated Women* (Delhi: Media House, 2011), 307.
37. Theramma Prayikalam, *Manakaruth Spirituality of Fisherwomen: Inspiration and Challenge to Consecrated Women*, 108, 152 & 165-6.
38. B.C. Balakrishnan, ed., *Malayalam Lexicon, vol. VI*, 112-113 & 250; Suranad Kunjan Pillai, ed., *Malayalam Lexicon Vol II* (Thiruvananthapuram: The University of Kerala, 2003), 272.
39. Catherine Soanes and Angus Stevenson, eds. *Concise Oxford English Dictionary, Indian Edition.* (New Delhi: Oxford University Press, 2007), 1694.
40. Fernando Franco, Jyotsna Macwan and Suguna Ramanathan, eds., *The Silken Swing* (Calcutta: Stree, 2000), 97.
41. Metti Amirtham, *Women in India: Negotiating Body, Reclaiming Agency* (Delhi: ISPCK, 2011), 162.
42. Kochurani Abraham, 'And She Was Made Straight: A Feminist Theological Engagement with the "Bent" lives of Indian Women', 131.
43. Prasanna Kumari, 'God's Image and Women', in *Feminist Theology: Perspectives and Praxis,* edited by Prasanna Kumari (Chennai: Gurukul, 1999), 383.
44. Viju Wilson, *The Upper Cloth Revolt in South Travancore: Theological Interpretation of a Subaltern Movement* (Delhi: Manohar Publishers, 2021), 230-2.
45. Kamla Bhasin and Nighat Said Khan, *Some Questions on Feminism and Its Relevance in South Asia* (New Delhi: Kali for Women, 1999), 3.
46. Viju Wilson, *Theology of Solidarity: A Study on the Theology of James Massey* (Delhi: ISPCK, 2019), 20-36.

Bibliography

Books

Abraham, K.C. *Transforming Vision.* Tiruvalla: Christava Sahitya Samithi, 2006.

Abraham, P.G. *Caste and Christianity: A Pentecostal Perspective.* Kumbazha: Crown Books, 2003.

Agur, C.M. *Church History of Travancore.* Madras: S.P.S. Press, 1903. New Delhi: Asian Educational Service, 1990.

A.H. *Day Dawn in Travancore: A Brief Account of the Manners and Customs of the People and the Efforts that are being Made for their Improvement.* Kottayam: C.M.S. Press, 1860.

Akkara, Anto. *Shining Faith in Kandhamal.* Revised Edition. Bangalore: ATC, 2010.

Amaladoss, Michael. *Becoming Indian: The Process of Inculturation.* Bangalore, Rome: CISS & DP, 1992.

Amaladoss, Michael. *Beyond Inculturation.* Delhi: ISPCK/Vidyajyoti, 1998.

——, *Life in Freedom: Liberation Theologies from Asia.* Oregon: WIPF and Stock Publishers, 2014.

Amirtham, Metti. *Women in India: Negotiating Body, Reclaiming Agency.* Delhi: ISPCK, 2011.

Andrews, C.F. *Handbook of English Church Expansion North India.* London: A.R. Mowbray & Co. Ltd, 1908.

Antony Raj, Y. *Social Impact of Conversion.* Delhi: ISPCK, 2001.

Arul Raja, A. Maria. *Dalit Bible Commentary, Old Testament*, vol. 1: *Genesis.* New Delhi: CDS, 2012.

Barnhill, Carla. *A Year with Dietrich Bonhoeffer.* New York: HarperCollins, 2005.

Bhasin, Kamla and Nighat Said Khan. *Some Questions on Feminism and its Relevance in South Asia.* New Delhi: Kali for Women, 1999.

Bonhoeffer, Dietrich. *Ethics.* New York: Mac Millan Company, 1962.

——, *No Rusty Swords.* New York: Harper & Row Publishers, 1965.

——, *The Cost of Discipleship.* Revised and Unabridged Edition. New York: The Macmillan Company, 1966.

——, *Christology.* London: Collins, 1966.

——, *Letters and Papers from Prison.* New York: Macmillan Publishing, 1972.

Boff, Leonardo. *Good News to the Poor*. New York: Orbis books, 1992.

Boyd, Robin. *An Introduction to Indian Christian Theology*. Revised Edition. Delhi: ISPCK, 2004 Reprint.

Brown, L.W. *The Indian Christians of St. Thomas*. Cambridge: Cambridge University Press, 1956.

Calvin, John. *Commentary on a Harmony of the Evangelists-Mathew, Mark and Luke*. Michigan: Baker Book House, 1989 Reprint.

Census of India 2011, Tables on Houses, Household Amenities and Assets for Scheduled Castes. New Delhi: Registrar General and Census Commissioner, India, 2012.

Centre for Study of Science and Secularism and Minority Rights Group International, *A Narrowing Space: Violence and Discrimination against India's Religious Minorities*. London: Minority Rights Group International, 2017.

Chandra, Bipin. *Essays on Contemporary India*. Revised Edition. Delhi: Har-Anand Publications, 1999.

Chandran, J. Russell. *Christian Ethics*. Delhi: ISPCK, 2002.

Chakkalakal, Pauline. *Discipleship: A Space for Women's Leadership*. Mumbai: Pauline Publications, 2004.

Chalam, K.S. *Caste-based Reservations and Human Development in India*. New Delhi: Sage Publications, 2007.

Chaudhuri, Nirad C. *The Continent of Circe*. London: Chatto & Windus, 1967.

Cheema, Iqtidar Karamat. *Constitutional and Legal Challenges Faced by Religious Minorities in India*. Washington, D.C.: United States Commission on International Religious Freedom, 2017.

Cherian, M.T. *Hindutva Agenda and Minority Rights: A Christian Response*. Bangalore: CFCC, 2007.

Deka, Meeta. *Women's Agency and Social Change: Assam and Beyond*. New Delhi: Sage, 2013.

Deshpande, Satish and Geetika Bapna. *Dalits in Muslim and Christian Communities*. New Delhi: CDS, CBCI and NCCI, 2010.

Dubois, Abbe J.A. *Hindu Manners, Customs and Ceremonies*. New Delhi: Rupa Publications (Reprint) 15th Impression 2018.

E. Mcgrath, Alister. *Christian Theology: An Introduction*. Third Edition. Oxford: Blackwell Publishing, 2001.

Ebeling, Gerhard. *Luther: An Introduction to His Thought*. Philadelphia: Fortress Press, 1980.

Evans, Robert A. and Alice Frazer Evans. *Human Rights: A Dialogue between the First and Third Worlds*. Maryknoll: Orbis Books, 1983.

Firth, Cyril Bruce. *An Introduction to Indian Church History*. Madras: CLS, 1983 Reprint.

Forrester, Duncan B. *Caste and Christianity*. London and Dublin: Curzon Press Ltd & NJ: Humanities Press Inc, 1979.

Franco, Fernando, Jyotsna Macwan and Suguna Ramanathan. eds. *The Silken Swing*. Calcutta: Stree, 2000.

Gangwal, Sunita. *Minorities in India: A Study in Communal Process and Individual Rights*. Jaipur: Arihant, 1995.

Gandhi, M.K. *An Autobiography or The Story of My Experiments with Truth*. Ahmedabad: Navajivan Publishing House, 1927, rpt. 1996.

Ghurye, G.S. *Caste and Race in India*. Reprint of Fifth Edition. Bombay: Popular Prakashan, 1994.

Gladstone, J.W. *Protestant Christianity and People's Movements in Kerala*. Trivandrum: The Seminary publications, KUTS, 1984.

Golwalkar, M.S. *We or Our Nationhood Defined*. Nagpur: Bharat Prakashan, 1947.

Golwalkar, M.S. *Bunch of Thoughts* Second Edition-Revised and Enlarged. Bangalore: Jagarana Prakashana, 1980.

Godsey, John D. *The Theology of Dietrich Bonhoeffer*. London: SCM Press Ltd, 1960.

Grant, John W. *God's People in India*. Madras: CLS, 1960.

Griffith, Ralph T.H. (tr. & cr.), *The Hymns of the Rigveda*. New Revised Edition. Delhi: Motilal Banarsidass, 1986 rpt.

Guha, Ramachandra. *India After Gandhi*. 10th Anniversary Edition. New Delhi: Picador India, 2017.

——, *Rebels Against the Raj: Western Fighters for India's Freedom*. Gurugram: Penguin Random House India, 2022.

Hacker, I.H. *A Hundred Years in Travancore (1806-1906)*. London: H.R. Allenson Limited, 1908.

Hall, Christopher A. *Reading Scripture with the Church Fathers*. Downers Grove, Illinois: IVP Academic, 1998.

Hebden, Keith. *Dalit Theology and Christian Anarchism*. Farnham, Surrey, England: Ashgate, 2011.

Hekman, Susan J. *Moral Voices, Moral Selves: Carol Gilligan and Feminist Moral* Theology. Pennsylvania: The Pennsylvania State University Press, 1995.

Irudaya, Raj. *Dalit Bible Commentary, New Testament*, vol. 4: *The Gospel According to John*. New Delhi: CDS, 2009.

Jaffrelot, Christophe. ed. *Hindu Nationalism A Reader*. Delhi: Permanent Black, 2007.

James, Woba. *Revisiting Ecumenical Theological Education in India.* New Delhi: CWI, 2016.

Jeffrey, Robin. *The Decline of Nair Dominance.* New Delhi: Manohar Publishers, 1994.

Jeyakumar, D. Arthur. *History of Christianity in India: Selected Themes* Revised and Enlarged Edition. Chennai: The Author, 2014 rpt.

John, Binu. *Christian Contribution to Nation Building.* Delhi: ISPCK, 2004.

John, Mary. *Indian Catholic Christians and Nationalism: A Study Based on the Official Catholic Journals of the Period* (1857-1947). Delhi: ISPCK, 2011.

Joshi, G.N. *The Constitution of India.* Fifth Edition. Calcutta: Macmillan & Co. Limited, 1966.

Joseph, M.P. *Legitimately Divided: Towards a Counter Narrative of the Ethnographic History of Kerala Christianity.* Tiruvalla: CSS, 2004.

Juergensmeyer, Mark. *Religious Nationalism Confronts the Secular State.* Delhi: Oxford University Press, 1994.

Kalland, Earl S. 'Deuteronomy'. *The Expositor's Bible Commentary.* vol. 3. Grand Rapids, Michigan: Zondervan Publishing House, 1992.

Kaye, John William. *Christianity in India: A Historical Narrative.* London: Smith, Elder and Co., 1859.

Keay, F.E. *A History of the Syrian Church in India.* Madras: SPCK, 1951.

Koshy, Ninan. *Caste in the Kerala Churches.* Bangalore: CISRS, 1968.

Kumari, Meera. *Religious Freedom.* New Delhi: Capital Publishing House, 1990.

Kuriakose, M.K. *History of Christianity in India: Source Materials.* Madras: CLS, 1982.

Kyung, Chung Hyun. *Struggle to be the Sun Again.* New York: Orbis Books, 1990.

Letter from Rev. E. Lewis to the Resident, 21 January 1859, Bundle No. 29, Cover File No. 2115 of 1858, *Shanar Disturbances in South Travancore.* Trivandrum: Archives Directorate.

Logan, William. *Malabar,* vol. I. Madras: Government Press, 1887. Trivandrum: Charithram Publications, 1981 Reprint.

Lourduswamy, S. *Towards Empowerment of Dalit Christians, Equal Rights to all Dalits.* New Delhi: Centre for Dalit/ Subaltern Studies, 2005.

Madan, T.N. *Modern Myths, Locked Minds: Secularism and Fundamentalism in* India. Second Edition. New Delhi: Oxford University Press, 2009.

Malhotra, Rajiv and Aravindan Neelakandan. *Breaking India: Western Interventions in Dravidian and Dalit Faultlines.* New Delhi: Amaryllis, 2011.

Mangalwadi, Vishal and Ruth. *The Legacy of William Carey.* Illinois: Crossway Books, 1999 rpt.

Mar Gregorios, Paulose. *The Secular Ideology: An Impotent Remedy for India's Communal Problem.* Delhi: ISPCK/ Mar Gregorios Foundation, 1998.

Mar Paulose, Paulose. *Swathanthryamanu Daivam* (Malayalam) [*God is Freedom*]. Ariyannur: Patabhedam, 1996.

——, *Nisabdharayirikkan Ningalkkenthadhikaram?* (Malayalam) [*What Right you have to be Silent?*]. Noorannad: Fabian Books, 1998.

——, *Spirituality for Struggle.* Thiruvalla: CSS, 1999.

——, *Vithakyappetta Vithukal* (Malayalam) [*Sowed Seeds*]. Collection by K.J. Thomas. Trissur: Paulose Mar Paulose Foundation for Socio-Cultural Development, 2005.

——, *Church's Mission.* Bombay: BUILD, n.d.

Mar Osthathios, Geevarghese. *Sharing God and a Sharing World.* Delhi: ISPCK & CSS, 1995.

——, *Theology of Classless Society.* Second Impression. Thiruvalla: CSS, 2004.

——, *God of Agape Leads Us to Justice and Peace.* Thiruvalla: CSS, 2013.

Marshman, John Clark. *The Life and Times of Carey, Marshman and Ward: Embracing the History of the Serampore Mission.* vols. 1& 2. London: Longmans & Roberts, 1859.

Massey, James. *Dalits in India: Religion as a Source of Bondage or Liberation with Special Reference to Christians.* New Delhi: Manohar Publishers, 1995.

——, *Minorities and Religious Freedom in a Democracy.* New Delhi: Manohar Publishers & CDS, 2003.

——, *Introducing Dalit Theology.* New Delhi: Centre for Dalit Studies, 2004.

——, *Caste-Class Victims and their Assertion for Justice.* New Delhi: CDS, 2013.

Massey, James and T.K. John. eds. *Christians of Scheduled Caste Origin in India.* New Delhi: Centre for Dalit /Subaltern Studies, 2013.

Mateer, Samuel. *Land of Charity.* London: John Snow & Co, 1871.

——, *Native Life in Travancore.* London: W.H. Allen & Co, 1883.

Mathew, C.P. and M.M. Thomas. *The Indian Churches of Saint Thomas.* Delhi: DJVP/ISPCK, 2005.

Menon, P. Shungoonny. *A History of Travancore from the Earliest Times.* Madras: Higginbotham and Co., 1878.

Menon, K.P. Padmanabha. *History of Kerala*, vol. II. Ernakulam: Cochin Govt. Press, 1929.

Menon, A. Sreedhara. *Social and Cultural History of Kerala.* New Delhi: Sterling Publishers, 1979.

——, *A Survey of Kerala History.* Revised Edition. Madras: S. Viswanathan Pvt. Ltd., 1998 Reprint.

Moon, Vasant. Comp. *Dr. Babasaheb Ambedkar: Writings and Speeches,* vols. 1 & 5. Bombay: Education Department, Government of Maharashtra, 1989.

Mulackal, Shalini. *Dalit Bible Commentary, Old Testament,* vol. 6: *Ruth, Esther and Judith.* New Delhi: Centre for Dalit/Subaltern Studies, 2011.

Nehru, Jawaharlal. *The Discovery of India.* London: Meridian Books Limited, 3rd Edition, 1951.

Nigam, Aditya. *The Insurrection of Little Selves: The Crisis of Secular-Nationalism in India.* New Delhi: Oxford University Press, 2006.

Novak, Michael. *The Spirit of Democratic Capitalism.* New York: Simon and Schuster, 1982.

Pandey, Gyanendra. *The Construction of Communalism in Colonial North India.* Delhi: Oxford University Press, 1990.

Panicker, P.L. John. *Gandhi on Pluralism and Communalism.* Delhi: ISPCK, 2006.

Parkhe, Camil. *Dalit Christians: Right to Reservations.* Delhi: ISPCK, 2007.

Peter, D. and Ivy Peter. *Liberation of the Oppressed: A Continuous Struggle.* Nagarcoil: Kanyakumari Institute of Development Studies, 2009.

Prayikalam, Theramma. *Manakaruth Spirituality of Fisherwomen: Inspiration and Challenge to Consecrated Women.* Delhi: Media House, 2011.

Puniyani, Ram. *Communal Politics.* Mumbai: J. & P. Publishers, 2003.

Rajpramukh, K.E. *Dalit Christians of Andhra.* New Delhi: Serials Publications, 2008.

Reservations for Backward Classes, Mandal Commission Report of the Backward Classes Commission, 1980. Delhi: Akalank Publications, 1990.

Robertson, S. *Freedom of Religion: A Human Rights Issue.* Bangalore: BTESSC/SATHRI, 2007.

Sahajananda, John Martin. *Mission without Conversion.* Delhi: ISPCK, 2013.

Sahayadhas, R. *Hindu Nationalism and the Indian Church: Towards an Ecclesiology in Conversation with Martin Luther.* New Delhi: Christian World Imprints, 2013.

Savarkar, V.D. *Hindutva.* Bombay: Veer Savarkar Prakashan, Fifth Edition, 1969.

Selvanayagam, Israel. *Samuel Amirtham's Living Theology.* Bangalore: BTESSC/SATHRI, 2007.

Selected Proclamations by the Sovereign from 1811-1939 AD. Trivandrum: Government Press, 1937.

Sen, Amartya. *The Argumentative Indian.* London: Penguin Books, 2005.

——, *Identity and Violence.* New Delhi: Penguin Books, 2006.

——, *Development as Freedom.* Oxford: Oxford University Press, 1999.

Shilling, Chris. *The Body and Social Theory.* London: Sage, 2003.

Shorter, Aylward. *Toward a Theology of Inculturation.* New York: Orbis Books, 1997.

Shourie, Arun, *Missionaries in India Continuities, Changes, Dilemmas.* New Delhi: ASA Publications, 1994.

Shourie, Arun. *Harvesting Our Souls.* New Delhi: ASA Publications, 2000.

Sproul, R.C. *Essential Truths of the Christian Faith.* Illinois: Tyndale House Publishers, 1992.

Stark, Rodney. *One True God: Historical Consequences of Monotheism.* Princeton, N.J.: Princeton University Press, 2001.

Stephen, M. *Human Rights: Concepts and Perspectives.* New Delhi: Concept Publishing Company, 2002.

Thapar, Romila. *The Past as Present: Forging Contemporary Identities Through History.* New Delhi: Aleph, 2014.

Tharoor, Shashi. *Why I am a Hindu.* New Delhi: Aleph Book Company, 2018.

The Constitution of India. New Delhi: Ministry of Law and Justice, Government of India, 2011.

The Constitution of India. Delhi: Ministry of Law and Justice, Government of India, 1989.

Thomas, M.A. *The Struggle for Human Rights.* Bangalore: ATC, 1992.

Thomas, M.M. Comp. *Christian Participation in Nation-Building.* Bangalore: NCCI and CISRS, 1960.

——, *Salvation and Humanization.* Madras: The C.L.S., 1971.

——, *New Creation in Christ.* Delhi: ISPCK, 1976.

——, *Man and the Universe of Faiths.* Madras: The CLS, 1975.

——, *Some Theological Dialogues.* Madras: The CLS, 1977.

——, *Towards a Theology of Contemporary Ecumenism.* Madras: The CLS, 1978.

——, *Bharathathil Christava Sabhayude Samuhika Dharmam* (Malayalam) [Social Responsibility of Indian Church]. Thiruvalla: The TLC, 1981.

——, *Religion and the Revolt of the Oppressed.* Delhi: ISPCK, 1981.

——, *Parivarthanathinte Daivasasthram* (Malayalam) [*Theology of Transformation*]. Thiruvalla: The TLC, 1982.

——, *Ideological Quest within Christian Commitment.* Madras: The CLS for CISRS, Bangalore, 1983.

——, *Church and Human Community.* Delhi: ISPCK, 1985.

——, *Risking Christ for Christ's Sake: Towards an Ecumenical Theology of Pluralism.* Geneva: WCC Publications, 1987.

——, *The Gospel of Forgiveness and Koinonia.* Delhi: ISPCK and Thiruvalla: CSS, 1994.

——, *The Church's Mission and Post-Modern Humanism.* Delhi: ISPCK and Thiruvalla: CSS, 1996.

Thomas, V.V. *Dalit Pentecostalism: Spirituality of the Empowered Poor.* Bangalore: ATC, 2008.

Vinaya Raj, Y. T. *Re-imagining Dalit Theology, Post Modern Readings.* Thiruvalla: CSS, 2008.

Vogel, Arthur. *Body Theology: God's Presence in Man's World.* New York: Harper & Row, 1973.

Walker, F. Deaville. *William Carey: Missionary Pioneer and Statesman.* London: SCM, 1926.

Webster, John C.B. *The Dalit Christians: A History.* Revised and Enlarged Version. New Delhi: ISPCK, 2009.

Wilfred, Felix. *Asian Public Theology.* New Delhi: ISPCK, 2010.

——, *Asian Dreams and Christian Hope: At the Dawn of the Millennium.* Delhi: ISPCK, 2000.

Wilson, Viju. *The Upper Cloth Revolt in South Travancore: Theological Interpretation of a Subaltern Movement.* Delhi: Manohar, 2021.

——, *Theology of Solidarity: A Study on the Theology of James Massey.* Delhi: ISPCK, 2019.

Yesudian, Prakash. *Fishers of Men.* Chennai: RZIM Life Focus Society, 2001.

Chapters, Introduction and Preface in Books

Abraham, Kochurani. 'Women and Violence: A Feminist Socio-Theological Enquiry.' In *Violence in Today's Context.* Edited by Shalini Mulackal and Roy Lazar A. Bangalore: Indian Theological Association & Asian Trading Corporation, 2012.

Abraham, Kochurani. 'And She Was Made Straight: A Feminist Theological Engagement with the 'Bent' lives of Indian Women.' In *Margins in Conversation: Methodological Discourses in Theological Disciplines.* Edited by Joseph Prabhakar Dayam and P. Mohan Larbeer. Bangalore: BTESSC, 2012.

Alangaram, A. 'Self-Understanding of the Indian Church as a Minority and its Theological Implications'. In *Towards a Theology of Christian Minorities in the Indian Scenario Today.* Edited by Roy Lazar and Shalini Mulackal. Bengaluru: ITA & ATC, 2017.

Anderson-Rajkumar, Evangeline. 'New Eyes, New Reading, New Woman…' In *Feminist Hermeneutics.* Edited by Lalrinawmi Ralte and Evangeline Anderson-Rajkumar. Delhi: IWTI/ISPCK, 2002.

Banerjee, Prathama. 'Caste and History Writing'. In *Dalit Assertion in Society, Literature and History.* Edited by Imtiaz Ahmad and Shashi Bhushan Upadhyay. New Delhi: Orient Black Swan, 2010.

Bauman, Chad M. and Richard F. Young. 'Minorities and the Politics of Conversion with Special Attention to Indian Christianity'. In *Minority Studies.* Edited by Rowena Robinson. New Delhi: Oxford University Press, 2013.

Bauman, Chad M. 'The Interreligious Riot as a Cultural System'. In *Constructing Indian Christianities.* Edited by Chad M Bauman and Richard Fox Young. New Delhi: Routledge, 2014.

Bhargava, Rajeev. 'Indian Secularism: An Alternate, Trans-cultural Ideal'. In *History of Science, Philosophy and Culture in Indian Civilization,* Vol. X, Part 7. Edited by V.R. Mehta and Thomas Pantham. New Delhi: SAGE Publications, 2006.

Bilgrami, Akeel. 'Secularism, Nationalism and Modernity'. In *Secularism and Its Critics.* Edited by Rajeev Bhargava. New Delhi: Oxford University Press, 1988.

Devanandan, P.D., Korula Jacob and M.M. Thomas. 'Preface'. In M.M. Thomas. Comp. *Christian Participation in Nation-Building.* Bangalore: NCCI and CISRS, 1960.

Devasahayam, V. 'Doing Dalit Theology: Basic Assumptions'. In *Frontiers of Dalit Theology.* Edited by V. Devashayam. Delhi: ISPCK/Gurukul, 1997.

Dube, Leela. 'Caste and Women'. In *Caste: Its Twentieth Century Avatar.* Edited by M.N. Srinivas. New Delhi: Penguin Books, 1996.

Dudley, Laura. 'Scheduled Castes, Christians and Muslims: The Politics of Macro-Majorities and Micro-Minorities'. In *Minority Studies.* Edited by Rowena Robinson. New Delhi: Oxford University Press, 2013.

Gonsalves, Francis 'Body Symbols and Symbolic Bodies: Reaffirming Womanhood in the Church and Society.' In *In Search of Spae. . .* New Delhi: Commission for Women, Catholic Bishops' Conference of India, 2008.

Gudorf, Christine E. 'Body, Self and Sexual Identity: Reflections on the Current Evidence'. In *Body and Sexuality: Theological-Pastoral Perspectives of Women in Asia.* Edited by Agnes M. Brazal and Andrea Lizares. Manila: Ateneo De Manila University Press, 2007.

Illickamury, Cyprian. 'Judaeo-Christian Tradition and Communalism'. In *Communalism in India: A Challenge to Theologizing.* Edited by S. Arulsamy. Bangalore: Claretian Publications, 1988.

Jayasingh, Herbert. 'The Christian Community in a Secular State'. In *Secularism: Collection of Articles.* Compiled by Vincent Rajkumar. Bangalore: CISRS, 2018.

Jogdand, P.G. 'Caste System in India: Dr. Ambedkar's Perspective'. In *Dalit Assertion in Society, Literature and History.* Edited by Imtiaz Ahmad and Shashi Bhushan Upadhyay. New Delhi: Orient Black Swan, 2010.

John, V.J. 'Jesus and Nationalism: Some Insights from the Synoptic Gospels'. in *Nationalism and Hindutva: A Christian Response.* Edited by Mark T.B. Laing. Pune, Delhi: CMS/UBS/ISPCK, 2005.

Kujur, Joseph Marianus. 'Christian and Tribal: The Dynamics of Scheduled Tribe Status in the Field'. In *Minority Studies.* Edited by Rowena Robinson. New Delhi: Oxford University Press, 2013.

Kumari, Prasanna. 'God's Image and Women.' In *Feminist Theology: Perspectives and Praxis.* Edited by Prasanna Kumari. Chennai: Gurukul, 1999.

Lourduswamy, S. 'Catholic Church and Dalit-Tribal Movements in India'. In *Rethinking Theology in India.* Edited by James Massey and T.K. John. New Delhi: Manohar and Centre for Dalit/Subaltern Studies, 2013.

M. Athyal, Jesudas. 'The Return of the Sacred: An Indian Christian Perspective on Religion and Politics.' In *Nationalism and Hindutva: A Christian Response.* Edited by Mark T.B. Laing. Pune, Delhi: CMS/UBS/ISPCK, 2005.

Mathew, E.V. 'Secular State in India'. In *Secularism: Collection of Articles.* Compiled by Vincent Rajkumar. Bangalore: CISRS, 2018.

Massey, James. 'Inter-Play of Religion, Politics, and Communalism in India'. In *From Truth to Truth, A Journey through Faiths: A Selection of Representative Essays by Dr. James Massey.* Edited by Deepak Seth. New Delhi: CDS and NOIDA: Academy Press, 2008.

Massey, James. 'On Being a New Community and Ecclesia of Justice and Peace'. In *On Being a New Community and Ecclesia of Justice and Peace.* Edited by James Massey and NOH Jong Sun. Bangalore: BTESSC/SATHRI, 2010.

Massey, James. 'Christianity to be Renewed? Rethink Theology'. In *Rethinking Theology in India.* Edited by James Massey and T.K. John. New Delhi: Manohar and Centre for Dalit/Subaltern Studies, 2013.

Mies, Maria. 'Class Struggles and Women's Struggles in Rural India'. In *Women: The Last Colony.* Edited by Maria Mies, et al. New Delhi: Kali for Women, 1988.

Mohan Razu, Indukuri John. 'Towards a Critical Theology of Risk Taking: The Changing Landscape and Discourse'. In *Rethinking Theology in India.* Edited by James Massey and T.K. John. New Delhi: Manohar and Centre for Dalit/Subaltern Studies, 2013.

Monteiro, Evelyn. 'Re-imaging Woman and Reshaping her Destiny, An Indian Feminist Reading of the Bent Body (Lk 13:10-17)'. In *Body and Sexuality: Theological-Pastoral Perspectives of Women in Asia.* Edited by Agnes M. Brazal and Andrea Lizares. Manila: Ateneo De Manila University Press, 2007.

Mulackal, Shalini. 'Sexual Abuse and the Church: Some Moral Dilemmas'. In *Gender Relations in the Church: A Call to Wholeness and Equal Discipleship.* Edited by Astrid Lobo Gajiwala, Varghese Theckanath S.G. and Raynah Braganza Passanha. Pune: Streevani & Hyderabad: Montfort Social Institute, 2012.

Oommen, T.K. 'Religious Nationalisms and Democratic Polity in India: Impossibility of Reconciliation'. In *Nationalism and Hindutva: A Christian Response.* Edited by Mark T.B. Laing. Pune, Delhi: CMS/UBS/ISPCK, 2005.

Pachuau, Lalsangkima. 'Nationhood in Conflict: Ethnonationalism and (Indian) Political Nationalism in North East India'. In *Nationalism and Hindutva: A Christian Response.* Edited by Mark T.B. Laing. Pune, Delhi: CMS/UBS/ISPCK, 2005.

Pearl, Drego. 'Communal Politics and Violence: Towards a Theological Response'. In *Indian Secularism: A Theological Response.* Edited by Antony Kalliath and Raj Irudaya. Bangalore: Indian Theological Association, 2011.

Ponniah, James. 'Taking the Cross and Walking from Subalternity to Modernity'. In *Constructing Indian Christianities: Culture, Conversion, and Caste.* Edited by Chad M. Bauman and Richard Fox Young. New Delhi: Routledge, 2014.

Prabhakar, M.E. 'Introduction'. In *Towards a Dalit Theology.* Edited by M.E. Prabhakar. Delhi: ISPCK, 1989.

——, 'Christology in Dalit Perspective.' In *Frontiers in Dalit Theology.* Edited by V. Devasahayam. Madras: Gurukul, 1997.

——, 'The Search for a Dalit Theology'. In *A Reader in Dalit Theology.* Edited by Arvind P. Nirmal. Chennai: Gurukul, 2007 rpt.

Pushparajan, A. 'Mission of the Christian Community in the Present-Day Indian Context'. In *Towards a Theology of Christian Minorities in the Indian Scenario Today.* Edited by Roy Lazar and Shalini Mulackal. Bengaluru: ITA & ATC, 2017.

Puthur, Bosco. 'Mission of the Church in the Context of Communalism'. In *Communalism in India: A Challenge to Theologizing.* Edited by S. Arulsamy. Bangalore: Claretian Publications, 1988.

Puthanangady, Paul. 'Communalism: A Theological Reflection'. In *Communalism in India: A Challenge to Theologizing.* Edited by S. Arulsamy. Bangalore: Claretian Publications, 1988.

Puthiadam, Ignatius. 'Communalism: An Analysis and a Christian Answer'. In *Responding to Communalism.* Edited by S. Arokiasamy. Anand: Gujarat Sahitya Prakash, 1991.

Raja, R.J. 'Communal Conflicts in the Nascent Church'. In *Responding to Communalism.* Edited by S. Arokiasamy. Anand: Gujarat Sahitya Prakash, 1991.

Rayan, Samuel. 'The Other and the Theologian'. In *Responding to Communalism.* Edited by S. Arokiasamy. Anand: Gujarat Sahitya Prakash, 1991.

Robinson, Rowena. 'Afterword'. In *Constructing Indian Christianities.* Edited by Chad M. Bauman and Richard Fox Young. New Delhi: Routledge, 2014.

Robinson, Rowena. 'Introduction'. In *Minority Studies.* Edited by Rowena Robinson. New Delhi: Oxford University Press, 2013.

Sebastian, V. 'Cultural Constructions of Indian Christian Theology'. In *Indian Theologies: In Search of Methods and Models for Theologizing.* Edited by Mathew Jayanth. New Delhi: CWI and Pune: JDV, 2017.

Shimray, Shimreingam. 'Tribal Theology and Human Rights'. In *Tribal Theology: A Reader.* Edited by Shimreingam Shimray. Jorhat: ETC, 2003.

Singh, Herbert Jaya. 'The Christian Community in a Secular State'. *Secularism: Collection of Articles.* Compiled by Vincent Rajkumar. Bangalore: CISRS, 2018.

Smith, D.E. 'India as Secular State'. In *Secularism and Its Critics.* Edited by Rajeev Bhargava. New Delhi: Oxford University Press, 1988.

Soares-Prabhu, George M. 'Religion and Communalism: The Christian Dilemma'. In *Responding to Communalism.* Edited by S. Arokiasamy. Anand: Gujarat Sahitya Prakash, 1991.

Stanislas, S. 'Biblical Understanding of the Identity, Role and Rights of Minorities'. In *Towards a Theology of Christian Minorities in the Indian Scenario Today.* Edited by Roy Lazar and Shalini Mulackal. Bengaluru: ITA & ATC, 2017.

Thomas, M.M. 'Indian Nationalism: A Christian Interpretation'. In *Secularism: Collection of Articles.* Compiled by Vincent Rajkumar. Bangalore: CISRS, 2018.

Vivekananda, Swami. 'Speech of Mr. Vivekananda', In *The World's Parliament of Religions: An Illustrated and Popular Story of the World's First Parliament of Religions, Held in Chicago in Connection with the Columbian Exposition of 1893.* Edited by John Henry Barrows. Chicago, Ill.: Parliament Publishing Co., 1893.

Articles, Editorials and Interviews in Journals and Magazines

Amalorpavadass, D.S. 'Efforts Made in the Roman Catholic Church towards Indigenization.' *Bangalore Theological Forum,* vol. V/1 (January-June, 1973): 4-21.

Anderson-Rajkumar, Evangeline. 'Significance of the 'Body' in Feminist Theological Discourse.' *Bangalore Theological Forum* vol. xxxiii no. 2 (December, 2001): 80-98.

Bama. 'Dalit Christian Women Today: Their Struggles and Prospects for Future.' *Jeevadhara,* vol. XLI/No. 241 (January, 2011): 35-44.

Chandi, P.T. 'Christian Colleges in India and Their Role in National Development'. *International Journal of Christianity and Education,* vol. 14/ No. 3 (December, 1971): 126-31.

Das, Bhagwan. 'Moments in a History of Reservations'. *Economic and Political Weekly* (28 October 2000): 31-4.

Delotavo, Alan J. 'Images of Christ in Filipino Culture and Atonement Experiences'. *Asia Journal of Theology,* vol. 15/No. 1 (April, 2001): 143-4.

Dhote, Yashwant. 'Streak of Violence'. *Outlook* (28 July 2014): 14.

Donald, Nidhin. 'The "Brahmin" in Syrian Christian Family Histories'. *Indian Church History Review,* vol. 56/No. 2 (July, 2022): 63-81.

Doniger, Wendy. 'The Hindu Code in Vanishing Ink'. *Outlook* (24 February, 2014): 16-18.

Editorial Board. 'Editorial: Christians and Politics'. *Vidyajyoti Journal of Theological Reflection,* vol. 77/no. 8 (August, 2013): 1-8.

E. Hedlund, Roger and Lisa R. Roberts. 'Tracing Indigenous Christianity in South Asia'. *ICHR,* vol. 52/No. 1 (January, 2018): 8-26.

Grinsell, Scott. 'Caste and the Problem of Social Reform in Indian Equity Law'. *Yale Journal of International Law* 35, no. 1 (2010): 199-236.

Indian Currents, vol. XXVII/No. 36 (7-13 September 2015): 26-8.

Islam, Shamsul. 'Suitable Heroes!.' *Indian Currents,* vol. xxviii/No. 41 (10-16 October 2016): 20-22.

Joseph, Tony. 'A Religion That Lost The Race'. *Outlook* (13 April 2015): 30.

Lourduswamy, S. 'Dalit Christians: Has Anything Changed?' *Jeevadhara,* vol. XLI/No. 241 (January 2011): 7-13.

Mahajan, Anilesh S. and Sunil Menon. 'The Pastors of Punjab'. *India Today,* vol. 47/No. 46 (14 November 2022): 46-59.

Maheshwari, S.R. 'Reservation Policy in India: Theory and Practice'. *Indian Journal of Public Administration,* vol. 43/No. 3 (July, 1997): 662-79.

Mangai, Poulose. 'Editorial: Stand for Stan'. *VJTR,* vol. 84/No. 11 (November, 2020): 3-6.

Massey, James. 'Minority Rights'. *NCC Review* CXXI/2 (February-March, 2001): 119-44.

——, 'Dalits and Human Rights'. *Religion and Society*, vol. 49/No. 2-3 (June-September, 2004): 1-9.

Mitra, N.B. 'Bishops Condemn Government Assault on Minority Rights'. *People's Reporter*, vol. 20/No. 3 (10-25 February 2007): 3.

Mulackal, Shalini. 'Living with Diminished Humanity: A Theological Critique'. *Oriens Journal for Contextual Theology*, vol. 4 (2013): 118-34.

Nariculam, Anthony. 'Incarnation and Inculturation'. *The Living Word*, vol.100/6 (November-December 1994): 420-32.

Noorani, A.G. 'Conversion to Hindu Raj'. *Frontline* (9 January 2015): 123.

People's Reporter, vol. 26/No. 24 (Mumbai, 25 December -10 January 2014): 1 & 24.

Pradhan, Kunal. 'Riot for Vote'. *India Today* (23 September 2013): 26.

Pramanik, Probir. 'Bugles Before Round Two'. *Outlook* (17 June 2019): 20.

Purie, Aroon. 'Editorial', *India Today* (21 October 2019): 5.

——, 'From the Editor-in-Chief'. *India Today* (23 September 2013): 1.

Radha Krishnan, M.G. 'Ire of the Minorities'. *India Today*, vol. XXXIII/No. 1 (1-7 January, 2008): 20-21.

Rajkumar, Vincent. 'Editorial'. *Religion and Society*, vol. 64 /No. 3 (July, 2019): iii-vi.

Raman, Anuradha. 'Can Christians and Muslims say all religions are one? A Hindu can say that'. Interview with Yellapragada Sudershan Rao. Chairman. Indian Council of Historical Research. *Outlook* (21 July 2014): 15.

Salam, Ziya Us. 'Unfazed by Attack'. *Frontline*, vol. 33/No. 18 (16 September, 2016): 123-5.

——, 'Christians as Target'. *Frontline* (28 August 2020): 58-9.

——, 'Interview with Aakar Patel, former director of Amnesty International India.' *Frontline*, vol. 38/No. 6 (26 March 2021): 95-7.

——, 'Christians at Receiving End'. *Frontline*, vol. 39/No.1 (1-14 January, 2022): 56-8.

Sinha, Chinki and Romita Datta. 'Single Women'. *India Today* (21 October, 2019): 34.

Stephen, Cynthia. 'The Theory of Reservations in India from the 1800s to the 1950s.' *Integral Liberation*, vol. 10/No. 2 (June, 2006): 17-25.

Thomas, K.T. 'Not an Article of Special Privilege but Only a Provision for Protection.' Reported by R.C. Thomas, *People's Reporter*, vol. 19/No.14 (25 July -10 August 2006): 1 & 7.

Thomas, M.M. 'The Churches and the Future of Indian Democracy'. *NCCR* vol. XCVII / No. 6-7 (June-July, 1977): 341-4.

Thomas, Shibu. 'Persecution and Relief.' *Voice of the Christians,* vol. 1/No. 12 (October, 2018): 7-23.

Varughese, George. 'The Caste Identity of the Indian Orthodox Church: An Appraisal from Christian Ministry Perspective'. *UBS Journal,* vol. 12/No. 2 (September, 2018): 91-110.

Verma, Arvind and et al. 'How Real is the Crime Decline in India?' *Economic & Political Weekly,* vol. LIV/No. 45 (16 November 2019): 37-45.

Weil, Shalva. 'Symmetry between Christian and Jews in India: The Cnanite Christians and the Cochin Jews of Kerala'. *Contributions to Indian Sociology,* vol. 16/No. 2 (1982): 175-96.

Wilfred, Felix. 'Editorial'. *Jeevadhara,* vol. XLI/No. 241 (January, 2011): 3-5.

Wilfred, Felix. 'What Can 'Upper Caste' Christians Learn from Dalit Christians', *Jeevadhara,* vol. XLI/no. 241 (January, 2011): 67-76.

Zachariah, George. 'The Grand Inquisitor and the Syrian Christian Primates in Kerala: Musings on the Pastoral Letter'. *Gurukul Journal of Theological Studies,* vol. XVIII/ No.1 (January, 2007): 40-8.

Dictionary/Lexicon

Soanes, Catherine and Angus Stevenson, eds. *Concise Oxford English Dictionary, Indian Edition.* New Delhi: Oxford University Press, 2007.

Balakrishnan, B.C., ed. *Malayalam Lexicon,* vol. VI. Thiruvananthapuram: The University of Kerala, 1988.

Kunjan Pillai, Suranad., ed. *Malayalam Lexicon,* vol. II. Thiruvananthapuram: The University of Kerala, 2003.

Articles, Editorial and Reports in Newspapers

Chauhan, K.S. 'Failing the Constitution'. *The Indian Express* (Pune, 10 November 2022): 13.

Chidambaram, P. 'Blessed are the Poor (but not all)'. *The Indian Express* (Pune, 13 November 2022): 12.

Chowdhury, Neerja. 'Taking Fight to BJP'. *The Indian Express* (Pune, 29 October 2022): 15.

Dhawan, Prannv Christophe Jaffrelot and Kalaiyarasan. 'Debate, don't dilute reservation'. *The Indian Express* (Pune, 18 November 2022): 11.

Editorial. 'Mandal Plus'. *The Indian Express* (Pune, 8 November 2022): 10.

G, Ananthakrishnan. 'Minority Tag for Hindus: Govt seeks time. . .' *The Indian Express* (Pune, 2 November 2022): 1 & 2.

——, 'Quota for General poor gets top court seal'. *The Indian Express* (Pune, 8 November 2022): 2.

Gopalakrishnan, Amulya. 'Interview with Kavita Krishnan'. *Sunday Times of India (*Pune, 8 December 2019): 18.

Jaffrelot, Christophe and Philip Varghese. 'A Continuing Exclusion'. *The Indian Express* (Pune, 26 April 2022): 9.

Joshi, Sonam. 'With Public Naps and Midnight Strolls. . .' *Sunday Times of India (*Pune, 8 December 2019): 15.

Karat, Brinda. 'Chhattisgarh's area of darkness'. *The Indian Express* (Pune, 11 February 2023): 11.

Khaliq, Abdul. 'Crisis of Fraternity'. *The Indian Express* (Pune, 24 February 2022): 11.

Mustafa, Faizan. 'Who's afraid of conversion?' *The Indian Express* (Pune, 18 November 2022): 11.

Nair, Avinash. 'Rioters given lesson in 2002. . .' *The Indian Express* (Pune, 26 November 2022): 1 & 2.

Narayan, Badri. 'Winning Gujrat'. *The Indian Express* (Pune, 26 November 2022): 12.

Paswan, Guru Prakash. 'Extending Social Justice'. *The Indian Express* (Pune, 9 November 2022): 13.

Paswan, Aditi Narayani. 'A more welcoming House'. *The Indian Express* (Pune, 21 September 2023): 11.

Pattanaik, Devdutt. 'Hinduism isn't a Country Club one can Waltz in and out of'. *Sunday Times* (New Delhi, 4 January 2015): 12.

Shunmugasundaram, Manuraj. 'Setback for Social Justice'. *The Indian Express* (Pune 11 November 2022): 11.

Siddique, Iram. 'HC: MP Law requirement on declaration before conversion is illegal'. *The Indian Express* (Pune, 19 November 2022): 3 & 4.

Singh, Priyadarshini. 'Ideas of Indian-ness.' *The Indian Express* (Pune, 1 February 2022): 11.

Sunday Times of India (New Delhi, 23 February 2014): 26.

Sunday Times of India (Pune, 1 December 2019): 15

The Times of India (Mumbai, 21 March 2014): 6.

The Times of India (Pune, 4 December 2019): 13.

The Times of India (Pune, 9 December 2019): 3.

The Times of India (Pune, 17 January 2020): 2.

The Indian Express (Pune, 8 November 2022): 12

The Indian Express (Pune, 8 October 2022): 1 & 2.

The Indian Express (Pune, 1 September 2022): 2

The Indian Express (Pune, 8 November 2022): 12.

The Indian Express (Pune, 21 September 2023): 1.

Varadarajan, Siddharth. 'Why can't Mr. Zaveri live where he wants?' *Sunday Times of India* (New Delhi, 12 April 2015): 12.

Yadav, Shyamlal. 'Express Explained'. *The Indian Express* (Pune, 20 September 2022): 12.

Waghmore, Suryakant. 'Whose Hinduism'. *The Indian Express* (Pune, 14 February 2023): 15.

ONLINE SOURCES

Ahmad, Tariq. 'State anti-Conversion Laws in India.' Library of Congress, October 2018. https://www.loc.gov/law/help/anti-conversion-laws/india.php#:~:text=Summary,Pradesh%2C%20Jharkhand%2C%20and%20Uttarakhand (accessed on 5 April 2021).

Ajayan. 'It Is Church vs. State in Kerala over Education.' *LiveMint* (New Delhi). 30 July, 2007. https://www.livemint.com/Politics/AxI5EYbaYrgup67rb2WphK/ It-is-church-vs-state-in-Kerala-over-education.html (accessed on 14 January 2019).

Ameerudheen, T.A. 'Under Pressure from Christian Community, Kerala Government decides not to back Church reform bill.' *Scroll.in.* 7 March, 2019. https://scroll.in/article/915654/under-pressure-from-christian-community-kerala-government-decides-not-to-back-church-reform-bill (accessed on 8 November 2022).

Bhattacharya, Abhik. 'Forced Gharwapsi, Molestation and Series of Attacks: Hundreds of Christian Adivasis Leave Their Villages in Chhattisgarh.' *Outlook.* 21 December 2022. https://www.outlookindia.com/national/forced-gharwapsi-molestation-and-series-of-attacks-hundreds-of-christian-adivasis-leave-their-villages-in-chhattisgarh-news-246858 (accessed on 5 February 2023).

Bhattacharya, Abhik. 'Hindutva in Indian Hindu Diaspora. . .' *Outlook.* 31 October 2022. https://www.outlookindia.com/national/hindutva-in-indian-hindu-diaspora-where-the-far-rights-back-home-meet-their-global-cousins—news-233586 (accessed on 19 January 2023).

Chaudhuri, Dibyendu and Parijat Ghosh. 'Why Inequality is India's Worst Enemy'. *Down To Earth.* 5 March, 2021. https://www.downtoearth.org.in/blog/economy/why-inequality-is-india-s-worst-enemy-75778 (accessed 6 April 2021).

Constitution of India. Article 26. http://legislative.gov.in/sites/default/files/ coi-4March2016.pdf (accessed 14 January 2019).

Deshmane, Akshay. 'Demand for Minority Status'. https://frontline.thehindu.com/cover-story/article24200995.ece (Accessed on 11 October 2022).

Ghose, Sagarika. 'With local roots, feminism in India is not a blind copy of the Western model.' 2 January, 2019. https://scroll.in/article/907485/with-local-roots-feminism-in-india-is-not-a-blind-copy-of-the-western-model-writes-sagarika-ghose (accessed on 20 May 2021).

Henry, Nikhila. 'Church Properties Face Encroachment in TS, AP.' *The Hindu.* 14 July, 2015. https://www.thehindu.com/news/national/andhra-pradesh/church-properties-face-encroachment-in-ts-ap/article 7419019.ece (accessed on 7 April, 2021).

Hussain, Wasbir. 'The Church: Tackling Politics'. *Outlook.* 3 February 2022. https://www.outlookindia.com/website/story/the-church-tackling-politics/218361 (accessed on 8 November 2022).

Kakvi, Kashif. 'Madhya Pradesh: Is Anti-Conversion Law being used to Target Muslim, Christian Youth?' *News Click.* 20 March 2021. https://www.newsclick.in/madhya-pradesh-anti-conversion-law-being-used-target-muslim-christian-youth (accessed on 6 April 2021).

Kulkarni, Pavan. 'Deendayal Upadhyaya, Bigoted "Guiding Force" of a Hindu Rashtra'. *The Wire.* 30 October 2017 https://thewire.in/history/deendayal-upadhyaya-guiding-force-hindu-rashtra (accessed on 31 March 2021).

Kumar, Raksha. 'Religious Conversion in Punjab: Not All Churchgoers are Christian and That Makes Majority Sikhs Nervous'. *article 14.com.* 6 September 2022. https://article-14.com/post/religious-conversion-in-punjab-not-all-churchgoers-are-christian-that-makes-majority-sikhs-nervous-6316b7212f2d7 (accessed on 19 November 2022).

Mahesh, Koride. 'A lot of reservations about Muslim Quota'. *The Times of India.* Hyderabad. 19 May 2022. https://timesofindia.indiatimes.com/city/hyderabad/a-lot-of-reservations-about-muslim-quota/articleshow/91656467.cms (accessed on 9 February 2023).

Mishra, Ishita. 'Population Imbalance due to Infiltration and Conversion: RSS.' *The Hindu* (New Delhi). 20 October, 2022. https://www.thehindu. com/news/national/population-policy-should-be-made-applicable-to-all-in-the-country-rss/article66031659.ece (accessed on 6 November 2022).

Mohanty, Basant Kumar. 'Women are paid less than men. . .' *The Telegraph Online* 29 September 2022. New Delhi, https://www.telegraphindia.com/india/women-are-paid-less-than-men-finds-study/cid/1889306 (accessed on 22 December, 2022).

Mukherjee, Mita. 'Missionary Schools Seek Exit from Panel'. *Telegraph* (Kolkata). 28 December, 2017. https://www.telegraphindia.com/states/west-bengal/missionary-schools-seek-exit-from-panel/cid/1396723 (accessed on 14 January 2019).

Naik, Raqib Hameed and Divya Trivedi. 'Sangh Parivar's US Funds Trails'. *Frontline.* 4 July 2021.https://frontline.thehindu.com/the-nation/sangh-parivars-us-funds-trail/article35117629.ece (accessed on 19 January 2023).

National Commission for Minorities Act of 1992, III.9.a, b, http://www.minorityaffairs.gov.in/sites/default/files/ncm_act1992.pdf (accessed on 16 January 2019).

Prasad, Malavika. 'From the Constituent Assembly to the Indra Sawhney caste, tracing the debate on economic reservation'. *The Caravan.* 28 March 2019. https://caravanmagazine.in/law/economic-reservations-constituent-assembly-debates (accessed on 9 February 2023).

Sharma, Ashutosh. 'Spectre of Mob Lynchings Continues. . .' *Outlook.* 28 April 2022. https://www.outlookindia.com/national/spectre-of-mob-lynchings-continues-to-haunt-india-amid-lacklustre-laws-news-193743 (accessed on 10 August 2022).

Thomas, Franklin Caesar. 'Why SC status for Dalit Christians, Muslims should not be linked to religion'. *The Federal* (15 August 2020). https://thefederal.com/opinion/why-sc-status-for-dalit-christians-muslims-should-not-be-linked-to-religion/ (accessed on 5 April 2021).

Thomas, Saji. 'Hindu Hardliners Try to Damage Mission Schools' Image'. *UCA News.* 3 October 2017. https://www.ucanews.com/news/hindu-hardlinerstry-to-damage-mission-schools-image/80407 (accessed on 14 January 2019).

Vishwanath, Apurva. '3 states, 3 anti-conversion laws: What's similar, what's different'. *The Indian Express* (New Delhi). 3 January 2021. https://indianexpress.com/article/explained/religion-conversion-bill-bjp-7129285/ (accessed on 6 April 2021).

Wilken, Robert Louis. *Liberty in the Things of God: The Christian Origins of Religious Freedom.* New Haven and London: Yale University Press, 2019. 1. https://books.google.co.in/books/about/Liberty_in_the_ Things_of_God.html?id=2ik_vAEACAAJ&redir_esc=y (accessed on 5 April, 2021.

'BJP Terms Mamata's decision to construct dining halls for Muslim majority schools as 'minority appeasement'. 28 January, 2019. https://www.timesnownews.com/india/article/bjp-terms-mamatas-decision-to-construct-dining-halls-for-muslim-majority-schools-as-minority-appeasement/444990 (accessed on 7 April 2021).

'Brawl breaks out over Khalistan referendum in Australia. . .' *The Economic Times,* 30 January 2023. https://economictimes.indiatimes.com/news/india/brawl-breaks-out-over-khalistan-referendum-in-australia-india-raises-concerns-with-authorities/articleshow/97439452.cms (accessed on 31 January 2023).

'Centre Stops Maulana Azad Scholarship for Research Scholars from Minority Communities'. *The Hindu.* New Delhi. 9 December 2022. https://www.thehindu.com/news/national/centre-stops-maulana-azad-scholarship-for-research-scholars-from-minority-communities/article66238681.ece (accessed on 9 December 2022).

'Christian Community dismayed over passing of anti-conversion bill in Karnataka.' *Hindustan Times.* Bengaluru. 17 September 2022. https://www.hindustantimes.com/cities/bengaluru-news/christian-community-dismayed-over-passing-of-anti-conversion-bill-in-karnataka-101663382749928.html (accessed on 8 November 2022).

'Church denies involvement in Mizoram elections.' *Business Standard.* 22 November, 2018. https://www.business-standard.com/article/news-ani/church-denies-involvement-in-mizoram-elections-118112201290_1.html (accessed on 8 November 2022).

'Encroachments on Gurdaspur Cemeteries Christians Livid'. *The Tribune.* 14 February 2017. https://www.tribuneindia.com/news/archive/features/encroachments-on-gurdaspur-cemeteries-christians-livid-363838 (accessed on 7 April 2021).

'Gender Pay Parity: 37% Indian Working Women Get Paid Less than Men.' *ABP News.* 2 March 2021. https://news.abplive.com/business/37-percent-working-women-in-india-get-paid-less-than-men-here-s-what-more-this-linkedin-report-reveals-1446666 (accessed on 20 May 2021).

'Government Targets Delhi's Biggest Christian School'. *Asia News.* 17 December 2018. http://www.asianews.it/news-en/Government-targetsDelhi%E2%80%99s-biggest-Christian-school-45760.html (accessed on 14 January 2019).

'Horrendous Rape Cases in 2021. . .' *Outlook.* 9 March 2021. https://www.outlookindia.com/website/story/india-news-horrendous-rape-cases-in-2021-so-far-show-that-minors-are-biggest-victims-of-sexual-assaults/376609 (accessed on 20 May 2021.

'How parties and politicos reacted to Supreme Court's EWS quota verdict'. *The Times of India.* 7 November 2022. https://timesofindia.indiatimes.com/india/how-parties-and-politicos-reacted-to-scs-ews-verdict/articleshow/95355343.cms (accessed on 9 February 2023).

'India lodged average 86 rapes daily, 49 offences against women per hour in 2021: NCRB data'. *The Hindu.* 31 August 2022. https://www.thehindu.com/news/national/india-lodged-average-86-rapes-daily-49-

offences-against-women-per-hour-in-2021-government-data/article65833488.ece (accessed on 22 December 2022).

'Indian Hindus, Muslims share same ancestry: RSS Chief Mohan Bhagwat'. *Hindustan Times.* 7 September 2021. https://www.hindustantimes.com/india-news/indian-hindus-muslims-share-same-ancestry-rss-chief-mohan-bhagwat-101630952385870.html (accessed on 21 October 2022).

'Lynching: Christian Body Fumes over RSS Chief's Remark'. *Outlook.* 13 October 2019. https://www.outlookindia.com/newsscroll/lynching-christian-body-fumes-over-rss-chiefs-remark/1639492 (accessed on 31 March 2021.

'MP: Pastor among seven held for pressuring tribal man to change religion'. *The Print.* 25 January 2023. https://theprint.in/india/mp-pastor-among-seven-held-for-pressuring-tribal-man-to-change-religion/1335283/ (accessed on 5 February 2023).

'Nuns accused of conversion, forced to get off train Jhansi'. *The Hindu* (Lucknow). 24 March 2021. https://www.thehindu.com/news/national/other-states/nuns-accused-of-conversion-forced-to-get-off-train-in-jhansi/article34153286.ece (accessed on 29 March 2021).

'Religious Liberty Commission Yearly Report 2021'. https://efionline.org/2022/02/15/religious-liberty-commission-yearly-report-2021/ (accessed on 10 August 2022).

'Religious conversion does not change a person's caste, rules Madras High Court'. *Financial Express.* 26 November, 2021. https://www.financialexpress.com/india-news/religious-conversion-does-not-change-a-persons-caste-rules-madras-high-court/2376717/ (accessed on 7 February 2023).

'Term Mob Lynching Comes from Bible, says Mohan Bhagwat'. *India Today.* 8 October, 2019. https://www.indiatoday.in/india/story/lynchings-being-used-to-defame-india-hindus-rss-chief-mohan-bhagwat-1607257-2019-10-08 (accessed on 30 March 2021).

The New Indian Express. Thiruvananthapuram. 30 December 2019. https://www.newindianexpress.com/cities/thiruvananthapuram/2019/dec/30/public-space-is-mine-too-thousands-of-kerala-women-attend-govts-night-walk-initiative-2082795.html (accessed on 21 May 2021).

'UP and Tamil Nadu top attacks on Christians. . .' *National Herald.* 31 October 2019. https://www.nationalheraldindia.com/india/up-and-tamil-nadu-top-attacks-on-christians-247-attacks-reported-up-to-september (accessed on 29 March 2021).

'Why are Christians attacked, accused of conversion. . .' *The Indian Express.* Kolkata. 21 January 2023. https://indianexpress.com/article/political-pulse/christians-attacked-accused-of-conversion-modi-advice-union-minister-john-barla-8396398/ (accessed on 22 January 2023).

http://www.censusindia.gov.in/2011census/c-01.html (accessed on 24 November 2020).

http://www.dnaindia.com/india/report-want-to-make-gujarat -a-vegetarian-state-cm-rupani-after-making-cow-slaughter-a-life-term-offence-2377704, *DNA*. 1 April 2017 (accessed on 20 January 2021).

http://socialjustice.nic.in/writereaddata/UploadFile/arpcr08.pdf (accessed on 6 April 2021).

http://socialjustice.nic.in/writereaddata/UploadFile/The%20Scheduled%20Castes%20and%20Scheduled%20Tribes.pdf (accessed on 6 April 2021).

https://www.lausanne.org/content/covenant/lausanne-covenant (accessed on 5 May 2018).

http://w2.vatican.va/content/paul-vi/en/apost_exhortations/documents/hf_p-vi_exh_19751208_evangelii-nuntiandi.html (accessed on 8 May 2018).

http://archive.indianexpress.com/news/credit-for-minorities-govt-s-priority-no.1/31705/ (accessed on 7 April 2021).

https://www.hindustantimes.com/analysis/muzaffarnagar-riots-judicial-commission-fails-to-hold-up-the-light-to-the-truth/story-L58wKP4Ln9gTTr0c9myHIJ.html (accessed on 7 April 2021).

https://zeenews.india.com/news/nation/cong-appeasing-muslims-to-retain-lost-glory-advani_234101.html (accessed on 29 October 2022).

http://ncm.nic.in/homepage/homepage.php (accessed on 30 October 2022).

http://www.nmdfc.org/index1.aspx?lsid=59&lev=2&lid=32&langid=1 (accessed on 30 October 2022).

https://www.minorityaffairs.gov.in/en/schemesperformance (accessed on 30 October 2022).

http://www.minoritywelfare.kerala.gov.in/schemes-implemented.php?token= (accessed on 30 October 2022).

https://www.newindianexpress.com/nation/2021/mar/29/congress-used-minorities-as-commodity-exploited-their-sentiments-for-vote-bank-politics-jitendra-2283188.html (accessed on 5 April 2021).

https://sabrangindia.in/article/muslims-and-christians-will-be-wiped-out-india-december-31-2021-bjp-leader-rajeshwar-singh (accessed on 31 March 2021.

https://www.mangalorean.com/bjp-leader-eshwarappas-remarks-christians-are-not-loyal-honest-citizens-of-india-fumes-christians/ (accessed on 31 March 2021).

https://www.lawinsider.in/columns/what-is-the-current-structure-of-reservation-in-india (accessed on 8 February 2023).

https://www.lawinsider.in/columns/what-is-the-current-structure-of-reservation-in-india (accessed on 8 February 2023).

https://bcdd.kerala.gov.in/en/reservation/employment-reservation/ (accessed on 8 February 2023.

https://socialjustice.gov.in/public/ckeditor/upload/82951673327147.PDF (accessed on 7 February 2023).

https://www.orfonline.org/research/womens-representation-in-indias-parliament/ (accessed on 22 December 2022).

Index